Dominus Mortis

Dominus Mortis

Martin Luther on the Incorruptibility of God in Christ

David J. Luy

Fortress Press
Minneapolis

DOMINUS MORTIS

Martin Luther on the Incorruptibility of God in Christ

Cover image: Christ on the Cross, 1552-55 (oil on panel), Cranach, Lucas, the Elder (1472-1553) / Stadtkirche St. Peter und Paul, Weimar, Germany / Bridgeman Images

Cover design: Laurie Ingram

Library of Congress Cataloging-in-Publication Data

Print ISBN: 978-1-4514-8270-6

eBook ISBN: 978-1-4514-8959-0

The paper used in this publication meets the minimum requirements of American National Standard for Information Sciences — Permanence of Paper for Printed Library Materials, ANSI Z329.48-1984.

Manufactured in the U.S.A.

This book was produced using PressBooks.com, and PDF rendering was done by PrinceXML.

"I will deliver this people from the power of the grave;

I will redeem them from death.

Where, O death, are your plagues?

Where, O grave, is your destruction?"

—Hosea 13:14 (NIV)

"Since the children have flesh and blood, he too shared in their humanity so that by his death he might break the power of him who holds the power of death—that is, the devil."

—Hebrews 2:14 (NIV)

"Sceleratum est, cum noveris, pium et sanum esse alicuius sensum, ex verbis incommode dictis statuere errorem."

—Martin Luther, WA 39/II:95

Contents

Acknowledgements

I have relied upon the support, wisdom, and patience of many people during the composition of this work. I am especially indebted to Stephen Long and Mickey Mattox for their advice and encouragement. They have been stimulating conversation partners, and have both forced me to think more deeply about the questions in this study than would otherwise have been the case. I would also like to thank Risto Saarinen, Doug Sweeney, Thomas McCall, Fr. Philip Rossi, S.J., and Wanda Zemler-Cizewski for their willingness to provide additional constructive feedback. Several graduate students at Trinity Evangelical Divinity School were kind enough to lend their assistance. Isuwa Atsen, David Moser, and Alexander Pierce furnished help on matters pertaining both to content and formatting. I am similarly indebted to the many members of the Fortress Press team who have labored to bring this work to publication. In particular, I would like to thank Michael Gibson, Lisa Gruenisen, David B. Lott, Christopher Wogaman and Amy Sleper for their help in this undertaking.

I am deeply grateful to Robert Jamison for his willingness to volunteer assistance for sundry translation questions along the way. He is surely among the most generous people I have ever met. It goes without saying, as acknowledgment sections are wont to clarify, that the mistakes within the following manuscript remain solely the fault of its author. The reader may be assured, however, that such mistakes would surely have multiplied had it not been for the labors of these exemplary scholars.

I could not have written this book without the abiding support of friends and family. I am grateful especially for my dear wife, Pam, and our daughter, Kara, for the unspeakable joy they are to me on a daily basis. Additional thanks are due to Phillip Anderas and Chris Ganski for their ongoing encouragement and Christian fellowship. It is my honor to dedicate the following study to my father Lawrence Luy, with whom I have enjoyed many engaging theological conversations, and eagerly anticipate many more in the future. *Soli Deo Gloria!*

Introduction

Contemporary appraisals routinely allege that Luther's theology marks a watershed moment in the history of dogma, specifically as it pertains to the doctrine of God. Luther is supposed by many to espouse a conception of the divine being that departs in fundamental and portentous respects from his theological forebears. The contents of the alleged departure are variously elaborated. As a general point of consensus, however, the shift is taken to signal nothing less than the inception of an alternative dogmatic trajectory within Christian thought. At its root, the cusp of the departure consists in a single, positive affirmation, which Luther leverages against the prevailing currents of antecedent theological tradition: God suffers, and does so in God's very nature. Luther's endorsement of this material claim is the determinative presupposition and touchstone for many modern receptions of his thought.

Constructive appropriations of the alleged shift are variegated. The suffering of God in Luther's theology has been construed, for instance, as emblematic of a reconfigured theological epistemology. Here, Luther assumes the form of a strident dialectician, intent upon the repudiation of every attempt to know or identify God by way of conceptual abstraction. To know the divine being is, rather, to embrace the scandalous self-presentation of God without philosophical qualification. The God of Christianity is the God who suffers in the person of Christ—a stumbling block to the imaginings of metaphysical projection.[1] In a similar vein, Luther's "passionate" doctrine of God has also been identified as a station within the *Vorgeschichte* (prehistory) of Hegelian philosophy, with its characteristic insistence upon a divine being actualizing itself in and through dialectical engagement with history and finitude.[2] These diverse episodes of Luther's theological reception represent a prevailing tendency within contemporary appraisals of the reformer's significance. Beneath differences in emphasis or constructive extension, it is broadly assumed that an unprecedented doctrine of God emerges within Luther's theological corpus. The reformer is significant, to a large extent, because he represents a monumental fork in the weaving path of dogmatic development.

The source of this appraisal is an influential interpretation of Luther's Christology, which has accrued considerable momentum within Luther scholarship during the past fifty years. Unlike previous models of christological description, this interpretation urges, Luther insists that the incarnate Christ suffers, not just according to his human nature, but according to his divine nature as well. Luther's patristic and medieval forebears labored diligently to bypass such an implication. Classical accounts of the "communication of attributes" constrict the ascription of suffering to God via qualification. The

1. For an iconic instance of this creative reception, see Jürgen Moltmann, *The Crucified God: The Cross of Christ as the Foundation and Criticism of Christian Theology*, trans. R. A. Wilson and John Bowden (Minneapolis: Fortress Press, 1993 [1974/German ed. 1973), 65–75. Not all contemporary appropriations of Luther's theology of the cross presuppose the ontological claim that Moltmann goes on to defend, namely, that God suffers. For a helpful introduction to how this aspect of Luther's theology has been interpreted, see Hubertus Blaumeiser, *Martin Luthers Kreuzestheologie: Schlüssel zu seiner Deutung von Mensch und Wirklichkeit: eine Untersuchung anhand der Operationes in Psalmos, 1519–1521* (Paderborn: Bonifatius, 1995).
2. See, for instance, Peter Hünermann, "Geschichte der Christologie: Geschichte Jesu Christi mit den Menschen?" *Theologische Quartalschrift* 164 (1984): 102–120. These two strands of reception are not mutually exclusive. See, for instance, Michael Welker, *God the Revealed: Christology* (Grand Rapids: Eerdmans, 2013), 144–69.

divine *Logos* suffers as the single subject of the incarnation, but does so according to the humanity that he has assumed. The divine nature subsists in this same, single subject (the person of Christ), but this does not entail ontological conditioning. The divinity of Christ per se does not share in the sufferings sourced in Christ's humanity.

Luther allegedly repudiates these delicate qualifications. On the prevailing account, the hypostatic union effects an ontological change in God's very being. Jesus' human sufferings do not fail to affect his divinity. On the contrary, the divine nature participates deeply in the defects and frailties of Christ's humanity. Luther's modern interpreters are right to assume that such an adjustment would cast a long shadow. To insist that divinity can and does suffer strikes a blow at the presuppositional core of antique theological tradition. Once the embedded implications of Luther's christological claim are traced outward, a (de)constructive conclusion ineluctably materializes. A wide gamut of traditional, philosophical assumptions about the being of God must be destabilized or altogether banished. In this way, Luther's christological divergence appears momentous, indeed. It precipitates nothing less than a massive reconceptualization of the doctrine of God.[3]

The account just summarized has enhanced perceptions of Luther's importance for contemporary inquiry, with its characteristic preoccupation with doctrines of divine immanence. Discursive exchanges on this topic usually have at their center the sharply contested doctrine of divine impassibility. The emergence of a widespread modern rejection of this doctrine is well chronicled in

3. The logical relationship expressed in this sentence stands at the center of the present work. It will assume that the prominent reception of Luther as a decisive turning point in the history of dogmatic reflection upon God more or less stands and falls depending upon the legitimacy of Luther's widely alleged christological adjustment. If the latter interpretation accurately describes Luther's treatment of Christ, then the former appropriation of his theology must be accepted as well.

recent theological literature.[4] A growing number of theologians regard divine impassibility as a conceptual obstruction, which bars the way to an adequate and biblically faithful rendering of God's intimate involvement with God's creation. Those who appreciate Luther's christological "adjustment" typically align with such an appraisal. Luther's passibilist description of God in Christ is esteemed for its willingness to take the reality of divine immanence with a greater degree of seriousness than prior formulations of doctrine could entertain.[5] In this way, Luther's Christology is leveraged constructively against perceived inadequacies of the tradition—conceptual abnormalities that are latent within articulations of ancient dogma. The reformer is appropriated as a catalyst for outlining new structures of thought, which are more transparent to God's passionate involvement in the person and work of Christ.

Luther's alleged course correction is adjudicated favorably, so long as his modern appraisers regard the doctrine of impassibility as theologically problematic. Those who defend divine impassibility within contemporary debates about divine immanence

4. A sampling of the myriad, recent publications that address this debate include Thomas G. Weinandy, *Does God Suffer?* (Notre Dame, IN: University of Notre Dame, 2000); D. Stephen Long, *Speaking of God: Theology, Language, and Truth* (Grand Rapids: Eerdmans, 2009); David Bentley Hart, *The Beauty of the Infinite: The Aesthetics of Christian Truth* (Grand Rapids: Eerdmans, 2003); idem, "No Shadow of Turning: On Divine Impassibility," *Pro Ecclesia* 11, no. 2 (March 1, 2002): 184–206; James Keating and Thomas Joseph White, *Divine Impassibility and the Mystery of Human Suffering* (Grand Rapids: Eerdmans, 2009); Daniel Castelo, *The Apathetic God: Exploring the Contemporary Relevance of Divine Impassibility* (Milton Keynes, UK: Paternoster, 2009); Richard E. Creel, *Divine Impassibility: An Essay in Philosophical Theology* (Cambridge: Cambridge University Press, 1986); Kevin J. Vanhoozer, *Remythologizing Theology: Divine Action, Passion, and Authorship* (Cambridge: Cambridge University Press, 2010); Paul L. Gavrilyuk, *The Suffering of the Impassible God: The Dialectics of Patristic Thought*, Oxford Early Christian Studies (New York: Oxford University Press, 2004); and Robert W. Jenson, *Systematic Theology* (New York: Oxford University Press, 1997).
5. This is not to say that Luther gets things exactly right in the appraisal of many contemporary divine passibilists. Many who purport to follow in Luther's legacy understand themselves to extend the trajectories in his thought to a more satisfying degree of internal consistency.

understandably advance an alternative evaluation. These "defenders" regard the claim that God can suffer less as dogmatic progress and more as pagan regress. Criticisms of divine passibility, like the arguments of those who defend it, are far from homogenous. Some theologians worry that a rejection of divine impassibility signals a forfeiture of God's transcendence. Others lament the apparent repaganization of God, which such a claim seems to connote.[6] Many insist that an ontological entanglement of God within the mélange of finitude formulates a "tragic" description of God's being, which undermines the reality of redemption.[7] Perhaps most seriously, a number of recent theologians have suggested that a god thus "entangled" seems implicitly to require suffering in order to achieve his own self-constitution—an entailment that portends chilling implications for questions of theodicy.[8] Evaluated within these adjudicatory prisms, Luther's widely alleged dogmatic novelty appears far less friend than foe.

The fact that Luther is praised by some and chastised by others should not be allowed to obscure the underlying agreement shared on both sides of the debate when it comes to specifying the nature of Luther's theological significance. Luther's christological contribution remains more or less the same, regardless of whether the central "adjustment" is regarded to be a swerve into heterodoxy, or an urgently needed course correction away from nonbiblical conceptualities. Despite the starkly opposed evaluative options now on offer, the specification of Luther's relation to modern debates is a relatively fixed constant. Whether lauded as a Moses leading theology out from its Hellenist captivity, or decried as an Ahaz offering up idolatrous sacrifices to proto-Hegelian Baals, Luther is

6. In other words, the celebration of a god characterized by ontological limitations and potentially volatile passions.
7. That is, a God who *cares*, but can't really *help*.
8. See, for instance, Hart, "No Shadow of Turning."

deemed significant on all sides because his Christology is supposed to pioneer a fundamentally new doctrine of God. His is a legacy of punctuated divergence.

It is the burden of the present work to demonstrate that this point of historical consensus, to which I will refer as the "divergence thesis," is mistaken.[9] Contrary to widely held opinion, Luther nowhere rejects the doctrine of divine impassibility. Careful examination of key texts reveals an abiding commitment to the invulnerability of Christ's divinity as a criterion of christological description. Luther's doctrine of Christ should not be regarded as the seminal hinge point in the emergence of an alternative doctrine of God. By demonstrating all this to be true, the present study will create the conditions necessary for an alternative appropriation of Luther's significance within contemporary theology.

As this last statement indicates, the intent of this work is not entirely deconstructive in nature. Its purpose is not merely to expose the divergence thesis's exegetical weaknesses and leave the matter there to rest. It is surely true, as the prevailing account assumes, that Luther lays particular emphasis upon the radical immanence of God in Christ. This observation qualifies the reformer as a significant conversation partner for ongoing constructive endeavors to forge adequate doctrinal conceptualizations of divine nearness. So, although its focus rests primarily upon the more basic matter of historical accuracy, the present study will intentionally address questions of constructive theological import. The question that will ultimately emerge is whether Luther's rendering of divine immanence can still possess ongoing significance once he is shown no longer to reject the doctrine of divine impassibility. The central goal of what follows, then, is to create the conditions necessary for an alternative appropriation of Luther's Christology, and to outline

9. For a thicker description of all that is included within this neologism, see ch. 1.

a few programmatic gestures of what such an appropriation might entail.

The execution of this task unfolds in three stages of argument, which are subdivided into five major chapters. The first stage includes only one chapter (chapter 1), and provides a careful specification of the divergence thesis, as expressed in major historical and theological literature composed during the past half-century. This preparatory identification is necessary (if also a bit tedious), because it excavates and outlines the essential exegetical and conceptual claims upon which the self-purported descriptive legitimacy of the divergence thesis rests. The second stage of the argument (chapters 2–4) is by far the most detailed in its approach. Having identified the divergence thesis's constitutive claims, each of those claims is exposed to critical scrutiny over the course of these three chapters.

The product of this sequential assessment is the decisive refutation of the divergence thesis as a viable interpretation of Luther's Christology.[10] Chapters 2 through 4 will also provide an alternative specification of Luther's theology as it pertains to each element of the displaced interpretation. The third stage of the argument (chapter 5) is constructive in nature. It focuses upon the task of redirecting contemporary appropriations of Luther's theological significance. The space necessary for this "redirection" is established on the basis of the alternative specification of Luther's christological views provided in chapters 2 through 4. As the result of the three stages of argument, the present study will demonstrate the inadequacy of the prominent divergence reception and provide the outline for a historically responsible alternative.

10. This refutation also intrinsically destabilizes the appraisals of Luther, whether positive or negative, which the underlying "divergence interpretation" has mediated.

1

The Road Oft-Taken

A Thematic Anatomy of the Divergence Thesis

This chapter sketches a thematic anatomy of the divergence thesis; that is, it organizes and bibliographically documents the governing interpretive claims that reside within this thesis. The literature survey provided in the pursuit of this task does not purport to provide a comprehensive treatment of modern scholarship on Luther's Christology. It seeks, far more modestly, to call the reader's attention to the various interpretive claims, which collectively account for the presumption of plausibility that passibilist appropriations of Luther now enjoy in contemporary theology. These isolated claims are significant because they furnish the core basis for the divergence thesis's self-avowed legitimacy. The success of this study's attempt to engage critically these appropriations will depend upon isolating the constitutive interpretive claims, which lend the divergence receptions of Luther's theology their apparent force. To neglect this task would effectively preclude not only the success, but also the very possibility, of the refutation that is embedded in this study's governing thesis.

The aim of this chapter is therefore descriptive and diagnostic. It will paint a clear picture of the divergence thesis by identifying the crucial interpretive elements necessary for defending its claim to historical legitimacy. Taken together, these elements form an implicit, conceptual, and sequential logic, which places Luther's Christology on a trajectory beyond the rigid supervisory qualifications of classical dogma and onward to a thoroughly historicized ontology of the divine life.[1] It is this general logical sequence that comprises what we are calling, for the sake of brevity, the "divergence thesis."[2] A robust description of this logical sequencing serves a diagnostic function in this book's argument. By identifying the essential interpretive elements needed to reinforce such a trajectory, this chapter excavates specific historical claims that later chapters will scrutinize. This diagnosis is crucial, for all divergence appropriations of Luther's theology presuppose some version of this "sequential logic" to be accurate.

This chapter may therefore be understood as a conceptually organized literature review, the contents of which are designed to furnish particular objects of critique and counterargument for later chapters. This preparatory analysis will enable subsequent assessment to focus upon demonstrably refutable (and thus, also potentially

1. In the appraisal of most of the Luther scholars surveyed in this chapter, notions of divine immutability, simplicity, and impassibility serve only to mitigate, if not entirely obscure, the radicality of God's immanent involvement with the full situation of human beings in the fallen world. To the extent that Luther rejects this inheritance, he seems to anticipate the work of G. W. F. Hegel. For more on Hegel's conception of the relation between God and history, see Peter C. Hodgson, *Hegel and Christian Theology: A Reading of the Lectures on the Philosophy of Religion* (New York: Oxford University Press, 2005); Quentin Lauer, *Hegel's Concept of God*, SUNY Series in Hegelian Studies (Albany: State University of New York Press, 1982); and Cyril O'Regan, *The Heterodox Hegel*, SUNY Series in Hegelian Studies (Albany: State University of New York Press, 1994).
2. By the same token, we will refer to appropriations of Luther's theology, which assume this basic sequencing, as "divergence receptions."

verifiable) aspects of interpretation, and thereby avoid the hazards of generalized or vague counterassertion.[3] The tangible product of this chapter consists in a final series of concrete questions that will determine the focus of each subsequent chapter. Before turning to the literature survey, it will be helpful, first of all, to provide a preliminary specification of the divergence thesis's central orienting claims. The logical organization of these claims lends this book its macrostructure.

A Preliminary Survey of the Operative Logic

Stripped to its simplest form of argumentation, the divergence thesis operates on three planes or "tiers" of analysis, which are mutually reinforcing. They relate to one another within a fairly straightforward linear sequence of argument. Organized according to this logic, the central tiers of the divergence thesis include the following: (1) a reconceptualization of the metaphysics of the hypostatic union; (2) a soterio-logic, which not only assumes but depends upon the suffering of Christ's divine nature; and (3) a resultant modification of God's relation to the world, which blurs (or at least reinterprets) the mode of divine involvement within history. Each tier of this logical progression will now be expounded with a bit more specificity.

The first tier of analysis contains two subsidiary claims. In the first place, it contends that Luther rejects the late medieval means of conceptualizing the hypostatic union through use of the quasi-Aristotelian concept of "suppositional carrying."[4] As to the specific

3. I am aware that the argument of this study is "iconoclastic" in the sense that it calls into question a widely celebrated account of Luther's theological significance. Such a project owes its reader a nuanced and sympathetic presentation of the narrative being displaced.
4. This model of explanation is an application of the Aristotelian-inspired distinction between a thing's essential "what-ness" and the individuated existent thought to sustain or "carry" (hence

contents of Luther's alternative conceptualization, there remains considerable difference of opinion among scholars. Some interpreters favor a composition model in which the personhood of Christ is somehow ontologically constituted by the union of humanity and divinity. For others, Luther clearly has in mind a dialectical union of opposites on the order of conjunctive aggregation. Still others insist that Luther instrumentalizes Jesus' human flesh, regarding it as a *Werkzeug* ("instrument" or "medium") of divine operations. These proposals are not necessarily mutually exclusive. What matters, for now, is that all agree upon the basic assumption that Luther discards "suppositional carrying" and moves on to a unitary, explanatory mechanism, which seeks to deliver a more intimate rendering of the relation between divinity and humanity.[5]

The second, subsidiary claim of the first tier specifies the inner relations of this more intimate union. Above all, Luther is alleged to endorse a sympathetic co-suffering of Christ's divine nature. This particular claim constitutes the descriptive axis of the divergence thesis. The core element, which is necessary to the progression of

suppositio) that "what-ness" into discrete ontic expression. In the case of the incarnation, such a framework suggests that the subsistence of the human nature of Christ cuts against the general tendency elsewhere for specific natures to attain individual expression through their own *self*-supposition (i.e., individual "rockness" subsists through self-individuating "rock-supposits," etc.), a pattern that, in the instance of Christ having both a human *and* divine nature, would entail a Nestorian doctrine of *two* persons. So, in order to sidestep this heretical entailment, the schoolmen of the late medieval period insisted upon the subsistence of the human nature of Christ through an extraordinary instance of "alien" suppositional carrying; that is, that the human nature comes to subsist individually *exclusively* in and through the divine supposit of the Word which assumes it into union with itself, and thus effectively takes the place of the human self-supposition that would ordinarily be the metaphysical ground for its individual existence. For more on the expansion of Aristotelian philosophy to make sense of the hypostatic union, see Marilyn McCord Adams, "What's Metaphysically Special about Supposits? Some Medieval Variations on Aristotelian Substance," *Aristotelian Society Supplementary Volume* 79 (2005): 15–52. See also her essay "Relations, Inherence, and Subsistence; or, Was Ockham a Nestorian in Christology?" *Nous* 16 (1982): 62–75. See also the fuller discussion of medieval metaphysics of the incarnation in ch. 2, below.

5. I insert the word *seeks* because not all of the interpreters surveyed within this chapter believe that Luther is successful in achieving this higher unity.

the logical sequence, is the assertion that Luther endorses a mutual exchange of predicates between the humanity and divinity of Christ. On this basis, he is able to insist that it is not only Christ's human nature, which is affected by suffering and death, but the divine nature as well.

This account departs rather markedly from traditional renderings of the communication of idioms. Even the most unitive Christologies of the ancient church (e.g., Cyril of Alexandria) were careful to qualify the sense in which suffering may be applied to God. For much of the tradition, God suffers in Christ only in the sense that the divine *Logos* is the single subject of the incarnation. The second person of the Trinity is therefore the proper referent for all christological predicates, but the divine nature (per se) does not and, indeed, cannot suffer.[6] Christ suffers, according to this view, but only on account of the human nature, which he assumes. Luther's account of the *communicatio idiomatum* is markedly different on a divergence reading. He affirms precisely what the tradition labors so carefully to deny. In Christ, the divine nature shares in the sufferings of the frail humanity with which it is hypostatically united.

Luther's alleged deviation from the dogmatic and philosophical constraints of his theological forebears is set in motion by an underlying rationale. The second tier of the divergence thesis posits this rationale as soteriological in nature. According to this appraisal of Luther's theology, God can only redeem insofar as God truly

6. Cyril makes this point abundantly clear in his "Second Letter to Nestorius." The following excerpt is copied from Richard A. Norris, ed. and trans., with Robert C. Saler, *The Christological Controversy*, Sources of Early Christian Thought (Minneapolis: Fortress Press, 2012), 103. "It is not that the Logos of God suffered in his own nature, being overcome by stripes or nail-piercing or any of the other injuries; for the divine, since it is incorporeal, is impassible. . . . God's Logos is by nature immortal and incorruptible and Life and Life-giver, but since, as Paul says, 'by the grace of God' his very own body 'tasted death on behalf of every person' [Heb. 2:9], he himself is said to have suffered this death which came about on our account. It is not that he actually experienced death as far as anything which touches his [divine] nature is concerned; to think that would be insanity. Rather it is that, as I said earlier, his flesh tasted death."

enters into the human situation and genuinely suffers the defects of sin, corruption, and death in genuine solidarity with God's covenant creatures. The salient feature of this claim is not the theme of solidarity itself, something many theologians of antiquity also emphasize.[7] It is, rather, the narrower allegation that Luther affirms a form of solidarity, which entails the actual passibility of divinity per se, as the condition of possibility for redemption itself. In short, God must suffer because the efficacy of Christ's salvific work hinges upon it.

The final tier of the divergence thesis draws each of the preceding threads together. It deduces on the basis of tiers one and two that Luther introduces (or at least tacitly assumes) an alternative framework for making sense of God's relation to the world. Instead of the putatively static metaphysics of his forebears, Luther is said to embrace the intrinsic, ontological relationality between God and the created order. Luther's Christology and soteriology are taken as tangible indication of the fact that the perceived incongruities of classical philosophy (infinity and finitude, eternity and history, and so forth) no longer function as a procrustean bed of theological inquiry. Instead, Luther points the way forward to a historicized metaphysics, a point of view, that recognizes the self-actualization of God within the unfolding process of historical development, the apex of which is the Christ event itself, wherein divinity and humanity are taken up into previously unforeseeable synthesis with one another.[8]

7. Again, Cyril of Alexandria provides a useful point of contrast. Like Luther, Cyril will continually insist upon the fact that Christ's death is *God's* death; that his blood is *God's* blood. The impetus for Cyril, as for Luther, is largely soteriological. The question, however, is whether Luther's emphasis upon this solidarity motif maintains the qualifications specified so clearly in Cyril's soteriology, which stipulate the abiding impassibility of the divine nature in the midst of God's solidarity with corruptible humanity. See, for instance, St. Cyril of Alexandria, *On the Unity of Christ*, ed. John Anthony McGuckin, Popular Patristics (Crestwood, NY: St. Vladimir's Seminary Press, 2000), 125–33.

8. Here again, there exists considerable diversity of opinion on what all of this means exactly for how to appropriate Luther's theological insights into the present. I do not mean in this overview

The logical sequence of interpretation, which animates divergence receptions of Luther's Christology, may therefore be recapitulated as follows.

> A twofold christological adjustment (rejection of suppositional carrying along with insistence upon the predication of human attributes to the divinity of Christ) is oriented toward a soteriology of suffering solidarity, of which the intrinsic passibility of God is a requisite constitutive part. The far-sweeping implications of these doctrinal adjustments represent the inauguration of a historicized metaphysics that does away with a classical account of God's being as existing wholly and immutably intact in isolation from the events of salvation history.

The internal relationships that unite the three elements of this sequence are important to the shape of this book's argument as it will unfold in subsequent chapters. As a preliminary methodological consideration, it may be observed that the various elements comprising the argument's anatomy stand or fall, to some extent, together. It is feasible, for instance, that an interpreter of Luther could argue for the third tier (a renovated understanding of the God–world relation) in the absence of tiers one and two, but such a claim would be rendered rather tenuous by its tacit admission that Luther still operates effectively within traditional doctrinal parameters, which grate intrinsically against the notion of a reciprocally conditioning overlap between God's being and the events of history. In a similar manner, it would be strange to claim that Luther endorses a soteriology of divine passibility, while conceding that he retains a traditional christological restriction of "suffering" to Christ's human

to over-determine the theological uses to which this general notion of Luther's "historicizing metaphysics" has been or could be put. The reception of Hegel is itself an infinitely complex enterprise, and not one that this study will seek artificially to simplify. The main point here is that the interpretation of Luther's Christology and soteriology outlined in tiers one and two has made his thought appear congenial, in the eyes of a number of scholars and theologians, to a rejection of classical metaphysics (also not a homogenous concept!) in favor of an understanding of God and history in which there is more openness to a relationship of mutual conditioning between them.

nature. Such a point of view could be rationally defended only if a rather egregious conceptual inconsistency were shown to afflict Luther's thought, a thesis that, speaking from a historical vantage point, can count only as a proposal of exegetical last resort.

So, although it would be an overstatement to insist that the three tiers of the analysis just described are reciprocally entailing, it may reasonably be observed that the disparate components of the divergence thesis garner a cumulative rhetorical strength that is, in many ways, greater than the logical sum of its parts. It is upon the strength of these claims, not just separately, but especially cumulatively, that the legitimacy of the divergence reception stands or falls. To devalidate one element of this logical sequence is to weaken each of the subsequent claims that build upon that element's momentum. Moreover, the extent to which the claims of each tier are shown to be misleading is the extent to which the divergence reception as a whole is deprived of its fundamental warrant. It will be the task of subsequent chapters to pursue precisely this sort of refutation, thus calling into question a widespread appraisal of Luther's theological significance. In this chapter, the sole remaining task consists in documentation. It must demonstrate the widespread acceptance of these various interpretive claims within scholarship and highlight the way in which versions of the logical anatomy sketched in this preliminary overview have, in fact, served to commend the plausibility of a divergence reception.[9]

A Sequentially Organized Review of the Literature

Each of the subject headings within this section corresponds with a specific "tier" of the divergence thesis's analysis of Luther's

9. Those uninterested in the particularities of Luther scholarship compassed within the following survey may advance to ch. 2.

Christology. Because the organization is topical in nature, the claims of individual scholars will sometimes appear in several subsections, rather than merely in one. The advantage of this presentation format is that it focuses on the interpretive elements themselves, and thus highlights what is logically and historically most important to the divergence thesis's descriptive viability. The intended product of this survey will be an extracted set of very specific claims and questions, which will provide determinate grist for critical adjudication in subsequent chapters.

Twofold Christological Divergence

The first tier of the logical anatomy includes two separate, but closely interrelated, claims. In the first instance, it suggests that Luther decisively rejects the late medieval nominalist account of the hypostatic union in terms of "suppositional carrying." It also argues that Luther insists upon a *mutual* communication of attributes between the two natures of Christ. At the heart of this second claim is the insistence that, for Luther, the divine nature participates directly in all that pertains to the Son's humanity, including its capacity for and experience of suffering. These two claims are often oriented toward one another in major works on Luther's Christology. The second (divine suffering) may be viewed either as the practical outcome of the first (a more intimate account of union), or the first may be understood simply as a necessary preparatory dogmatic adjustment for securing the second.[10] Despite this close interconnectivity, clarity demands that each subdivision of this "tier" be presented in distinct successive phases.

10. These options are not mutually exclusive. They differ only in the perception of which "aspect" is the determinative one for Luther. In either case, the two are interpreted as mutually entailing.

Subdivision 1: Redefining Personhood

In his highly influential 1966 essay "Gott ist Mensch: Zur Lehre von der Person Christi bei den Ockhamisten und bei Luther," Reinhard Schwarz begins with a reiteration of Karl Holl's pronouncement that, though Luther *thought* he was simply repeating classical dogma, he actually interprets its major doctrines in an idiosyncratic and, by the standards of the early church, nearly heretical manner.[11] Schwarz endorses a version of Holl's insight, and suggests that the inadvertent idiosyncrasy of Luther's position most visibly manifests itself in a highly critical appraisal of Ockhamist Christology, which he derides at one point as crude (*geschmacklos*) and outrageous (*ungeheuerlich*).[12] The five sections that comprise Schwarz's essay seek to document the nature of Luther's criticism of late medieval Christology and identify what it is that Luther evidently found so offensive about it.

At the heart of Luther's harsh criticism is his decidedly negative appraisal of "suppositional carrying," the explanatory model through which late medieval Scholastics interpret the hypostatic union. According to Schwarz, Luther reacts against the ostensibly extrinsic or remote relationship that this descriptive model creates between the divine person of the *Logos* and Christ's human nature. The originating factor behind this distant association is a philosophical principle, which Schwarz characterizes as the "neuralgic point" of

11. "In seiner Christologie hat Luther das altkirchliche Dogma nicht unbedacht nachgesprochen, sondern nach seinem Verständnis der Sache interpretiert," from Reinhard Schwarz, "Gott ist Mensch: zur Lehre von der Person Christi bei den Ockhamisten und bei Luther," *Zeitschrift für Theologie und Kirche* 63 (1966): 289. Schwarz goes on to quote Karl Holl's verdict: "Denn in Wahrheit hat Luther das alte Dogma nicht nur aufgenommen, sondern fortgebildet, und zwar in einer Weise, die, wenn man den Standpunkt der alten Konzilien einnimmt, überall nahe an das Ketzerische anstreifte," from Holl, *Gesammelte Aufsätze zur Kirchengeschichte*, I (Tübingen: J. C. B. Mohr [Paul Siebeck], 1928), 71.

12. Schwarz, "Gott ist Mensch," 292. Schwarz is echoing here a line from a christological disputation from 1540. This text, very important in his interpretation, will be discussed at some length in ch. 2.

Ockhamist Christology: the axiom that uncreated Being must be kept strictly separate from created being. This principle is laconically enunciated, for Schwarz, in the dictum "*nulla proportio est finiti ad infinitum*" ("there is no proportion between the finite and the infinite").[13] The problems with Ockhamist Christology, to which Luther reacts, are primarily a function of its attempt to affirm christological teaching within the restrictive boundaries erected by this philosophical rule. For Schwarz, the late medieval rendering of suppositional carrying is the regrettable conceptual byproduct of this ill-fated enterprise.

How is it exactly that Luther criticizes and rectifies the philosophical extrinsicism of late medieval Christology? Schwarz addresses this question in the second major section of his essay, by drawing especially from a christological disputation Luther composed in 1540.[14] The main object of Luther's discontent, as expressed in this disputation, is the customary Scholastic expression that the divine person merely "carries" the human nature. Luther objects to this way of speaking, according to Schwarz, because the term *carrying* connotes a relationship between God and man that is far too distant.[15] The formulation practically denies the human nature any share in the personal existence of Christ, thus implicitly rendering the incarnate Son something less than fully God *and* fully man.[16] Such a view is able, in Luther's view, to affirm the phrase "Christ is a human person" only on the basis of a fundamental equivocation of terms.

The statement is true, in other words, *only* if the term *person* is stripped of all durable content. The resultant fissure of meaning can

13. Ibid., 300–301: "Dieses Axiom ist der neuralgische Punkt der ockhamistichen Christologie."

14. That is, Luther's "Disputation on the Divinity and Humanity of Christ," located in WA 39/II:95, 34ff.

15. Schwarz, "Gott ist Mensch," 301–302.

16. Ibid., 302. In light of this criticism, Schwarz surmises: "Es ist praktisch der Vorwurf des Doketismus, den Luther gegen die ockhamistische Christologie erhebt."

be explicated by the juxtaposition (and analysis) of two christological statements: (1) "Christ is a divine person"; and (2) "Christ is a human person." According to the rules of late medieval description, the first statement means that Christ *is* a divine *suppositum*. On the other hand, the second statement really only means that Christ is a divine *suppositum*, which "carries" a human nature along with it.[17] This rather sophisticated sleight of hand is necessary, on Schwarz's account, in order to maintain the semantic affirmation of christological teaching within a philosophical context (*nulla proportio est finiti ad infinitum*) intrinsically hostile to its original contents. The result, from Luther's alleged point of view, is nothing less than a functional denial of the incarnation beneath a thin veil of superficial assent.

On first glance, it appears that Luther is content simply to reiterate the substance of traditional Christology and eschew the tensions created by late medieval nominalist philosophy. According to Schwarz, however, Luther's incredulous reaction to suppositional carrying betrays a deeper reformulation of church teaching than the initial façade of Luther's traditionalism might indicate.[18] The crucial shift that takes place has to do with Luther's reinterpretation of Christ's personhood. For him, Christ is constituted in and through the joining of divinity and humanity, thus making the incarnate person a kind of dynamic mixture or composite.[19] Although Schwarz

17. Ibid., 302–303. Schwarz advances this interpretation on the basis of a disputation on John 1:14 from 1539.
18. Ibid., 304: "Auf den ersten Blick scheinen Luthers christologische Äußerungen nicht mehr zu sein als seine Bekräftigung des altkirchlichen Bekenntnisses. . . . Luthers nachdrückliches Festhalten am alten Bekenntnis ist aber getragen von einem spezifischen Verständnis der 'Sache'." In this way, Schwarz basically corroborates Holl's programmatic statement cited at the outset of his essay. The "first glance traditionalism," which Schwarz and Holl acknowledge, is likely an allusion to Luther's regular assent to creedal orthodoxy.
19. Ibid., 304–305. This is the critical claim that will prove to be so influential in later studies of Luther's Christology. The point is not that Christ is now a *tertium quid*, but that divinity and humanity play an equally constitutive role in the personal existence of his incarnate personhood. A composite view flattens the asymmetry of traditional, christological dogma.

admits that Luther continues to invoke semantic formulations that are reminiscent of the late medieval view, he insists that such instances are always superficial. The apparent endorsement of suppositional carrying is disrupted by Luther's ardent insistence that the event of the incarnation brings about a constitutive change in "what" the person of Christ is, a view that shatters the fundamental trajectory of late medieval Christology.[20]

The real source of the disagreement between Luther and the Ockhamists resides at the level of conceptual presuppositions. Whereas the latter begin with an abstractly derived postulate (the philosophical assumption that an infinite distinction must always separate divinity and humanity from one another), Luther begins with the identity of God and man in the person of Christ. He ignores a priori questions of "whether" such unity is philosophically possible and contents himself with the biblical affirmation of its actuality.[21] On the basis of this fundamental difference, Luther's Christology departs not only from the view of his immediate predecessors, but also redirects the meaning of Chalcedonian Christology.[22] What

The late medieval notion of suppositional carrying expresses this asymmetry well by according clear pride of place to the identity of Christ as *divine*. In this view, the humanity is merely a contingently appropriated identity, and not one that ontologically alters the divine Son. By rejecting this asymmetry, Luther implicitly overturns patristic christological norms, even though his proximate "target" is late medieval Christology.

20. Ibid., 305: "Die Annahme der menschlichen Natur bedeutet indessen nicht eine Aufnahme in suppositale Abhängigkeit, sondern ein Geschehen im Sein der Person . . ." Thus, although Schwarz concedes that Luther's proximate target is the Ockhamists, the substance of his criticism extends beyond the late medieval context. Many of the same presuppositions that Luther apparently detests occupy a supervisory role throughout the development of patristic Christology as well. See ibid., 306.

21. See ibid., 306–308. This distinction is a hallmark of modern Luther research as a device for distinguishing the reformer from his Scholastic context. In my opinion, such a sharp procedural bifurcation represents an artificial polarization of *both* groups by underestimating the extent to which medieval theologians sought to reason out from the biblical witness on the one hand, and the extent of Luther's employment of reason in theology on the other—the latter's well-known diatribes against philosophy notwithstanding. This pattern of interpretation will be discussed in greater detail in ch. 4.

22. Note that Schwarz's essay does not view this inadvertent deviation (inadvertent because, as Holl notes, Luther *thought* he was simply Chalcedonian) to be a failure or defect of Luther's

Schwarz characterizes as an unsatisfactorily "extrinsic" relation between Christ's natures must be dissembled in favor of a new relation capable of securing a real communication of attributes between humanity and divinity.

Theobald Beer's magisterial study, *Der fröhliche Wechsel und Streit: Grundzüge der Theologie Luthers*, is strangely congenial to the arguments Schwarz advances, although Beer directs his interpretation to a very different evaluative end.[23] Like Schwarz, Beer thinks that Luther decisively rejects the late medieval doctrine of suppositional carrying. In Beer's interpretation, however, the result of the shift is not an increased emphasis upon the unity of divinity and humanity (even if this may have been Luther's intent), but a conceptual fissure between Christ's two natures of unresolvable, diametric antithesis.[24]

For Beer, Luther's doctrine of Christ creates an insidious dualism because it advances a functional definition of "divinity" and

Christology. To be sure, there will be scholars later (most notably Theobald Beer and Axel Schmidt) who would use this interpretation as the basis of a trenchant criticism of Luther's theology. Schwarz, though, seems to fall in the larger group of those who view main ingredients of traditional Christology (at the very least, its antiquated conceptual scaffolding) to be problematic, and therefore are rather congenial to Luther's alleged modifications.

23. Theobald Beer, *Der fröhliche Wechsel und Streit: Grundzüge der Theologie Luthers* (Leipzig: St. Benno-Verlag, 1974).

24. Beer provides a multitiered investigation of Luther's treatment of the "wonderful exchange," a soteriological motif he claims occupies so central a position in his theology that it conditions all other salient aspects of the reformer's thought. In the course of his book, Beer argues that Luther's unique rendering of this motif depends upon the doctrine of divine monergism as expressed, most prominently in Beer's presentation, in the motif of the devil (or Leviathan) being "tricked" by the apparently helpless humanity of Christ. At the root of this image for Beer is a fundamental bifurcation between divine activity and human passivity, and Beer suggests that this programmatic dualism is reflected at every level of Luther's theology. The result of this bifurcation manifests itself in Luther's alleged tendency to separate all the various aspects of his theology into two fundamentally unrelated and often diametrically opposed domains. So, for instance, there is a radical division between imputed righteousness (the grace of God) and actual righteousness (the gift of God). Or, there is the radical demarcation of gospel over against law that characterizes Luther's theology as a whole. See ibid., 13–33, 360–61. For one example of Beer's emphasis upon the pure passivity of the humanity in Luther's theology, see ibid., 328; also 344. An important goal of Beer's study is to interpret Luther in his own context and vocabulary, and thus shed light on whether the alleged points of convergence between modern-day ecumenical conversation partners are real or only illusory.

"humanity" within the economy of salvation: an antimetaphysical reduction that creates an oppositional relation between natures. Luther's functionalist Christology ironically precludes the possibility of any real affirmation of the hypostatic union.[25] Luther does not identify Christ as a "person" in the traditional sense, but invents his own description.[26] The incarnate "person," for Luther, is theologically interchangeable with a "combative unity of *functions*," on Beer's account.[27] Because he continues to use the ordinary theological vocabulary, Luther initially seems to build his theology on the basis of traditional conceptualities. In reality, he subverts this traditional vocabulary by inserting a foreign element. The contaminating assumption (which works its way through Luther's theology like yeast through a batch of dough) is Luther's view that divinity and humanity are always engaged with one another in a relation of antithesis, which can only intersect in a functional concursus of otherwise immiscible operations. In order to explicate the underlying transformation of meaning effected by Luther's appropriation of traditional terms, Beer seeks to demonstrate the way in which the reformer co-opts classical vocabulary and enlists it for his own idiosyncratic purposes.

25. Because the only Christ that matters for Luther is the Christ *for us*, Beer perceives him to reject any reflection upon the metaphysical realities necessary for securing the union of divinity and humanity in a way that goes beyond sheer juxtaposition. For an example of Beer's suggestion of Luther's indifference or hostility toward abstract questions concerning "what" Christ is, see ibid., 329–31. For Beer's claim that Luther "functionalizes" the doctrine of two natures and thus creates potential problems for his attempt to affirm the hypostatic union in any traditional sense, see ibid., 382–83.
26. That is, he does not regard the "person" of Christ as a *suppositum*—an entity ontologically distinct from the two natures individually subsisting through it.
27. Ibid., 398: "Die christliche Metaphysik definiert dieses 'Wer' [that is, the question of "who" Christ is] nicht-hellenistisch als Suppositum der Person, Luther dagegen als kämpferische Einheit von Funktionen." For confirmation of this claim, Beer turns to the 1540 disputation and interprets it in a way remarkably similar to the afore-described essay by Schwarz. See ibid., 404–406.

Beer admits, for instance, that Luther continues to enlist the language of "suppositional carrying." Like Schwarz, however, he insists that the reformer makes use of this vocabulary in a manner rather different from his late medieval teachers. For Luther, all of the terms traditionally intended to express the source of union take on a merely linguistic function. Suppositional carrying is no longer used as a descriptive analogy through which to make conceptual sense of Christ's two natures subsisting together within a higher order of union. Instead, it is used to express a chronologically sequential distinction. It distinguishes between a nonconnotative description of divinity and humanity on the one hand, and a connotative treatment of the two on the other; that is, it provides only a functional analysis of the incarnation. Christ's natures may be analyzed as they "act" separately (abstractly), or within the dynamic coordination of their antithetical functions, which coincide in the work of Christ (concretely).[28] The result is not, in either case, a robust account of genuine union. Ironically, Luther's rejection of suppositional carrying ends up, for Beer, emphasizing the separation of humanity and divinity.[29]

Because he banishes the nuanced sophistication of metaphysical analysis, Luther can only situate humanity and divinity beside one another as sheer juxtaposition. The hypostatic union deteriorates into a dynamic union of opposites whose respective, immiscible functions happen to coincide for a single redemptive goal.[30] Because there is no higher conceptual plane retained for a classical explanation of the

28. Ibid., 406. This interpretation of the abstract/concrete is rather common in the interpretation of Luther's Christology. Its adequacy will be addressed in ch. 2.

29. Ibid., 412. Here Beer points out that major images enlisted in Luther's vocabulary (for example, the theme of "covering") point more to the separation then the unification of divinity and humanity. This claim cuts against the insistence among other Luther scholars that Luther's Christology lays primary emphasis upon the *union* of divinity and humanity in Christ. See, for instance, Ian D. Kingston Siggins, *Martin Luther's Doctrine of Christ,* Yale Publications in Religion 14 (New Haven: Yale University Press, 1970), 227.

real union between natures, Beer chastises Luther's Christology as crypto-Nestorian. This is because Luther does not base the union of divinity and humanity in the internal continuity of the preexistent Son as the abiding single subject, but in a concept of "composition" in which divinity and humanity come together in standing tension.[31] So, although many of Luther's statements make him appear Chalcedonian (an ostensible source of ecumenical *ressourcement*), the reality beneath Luther's traditional vocabulary is a Christology that departs rather dramatically from the tradition.[32]

Marc Lienhard's influential book *Luther: Witness to Jesus Christ* is more optimistic than Beer in affirming the extent of Luther's christological traditionalism. Despite this alternative evaluation, Lienhard acknowledges many of the same, alleged "deviations" in Luther's Christology that cause a scholar like Beer to doubt his orthodoxy.[33] Their analyses differ, so far as the present topic is

30. Thus, according to Beer, the *communicatio idiomatum* expresses for Luther not the unity of God and humanity, but the struggle between divinity and its contrary form. See Beer, *Der fröhliche Wechsel*, 380.

31. Ibid., 380–81: "Im fröhlichen Wechsel ist nicht der Gottmensch in der Einheit mit dem Präexistenten, wie im Christushymnus des Philipperbriefs, der Handelnde. Die Vereinigung von Gottheit und Menschheit wird nur als ein Kompositum bezeichnet . . ."

32. Beer's controversial interpretation of Luther's theology has been the object of serious criticism from a number of fronts. A thorough evaluation of his views lies outside the scope of this study. However, it is interesting to note the fact that, although Beer's *conclusions* have often been received with trenchant disapproval, the interpretation of Luther's Christology upon which these conclusions are based is not terribly idiosyncratic when compared objectively (that is, denuded of the intrinsically evaluative trajectory that conditions Beer's argument) with the other points of view articulated in the last fifty years. Like many others, he asserts that Luther redefines humanity and divinity in "functional" or "dynamic" categories in a way that is intentionally oriented toward soteriological considerations. Along with many others, he concludes that this point of view carries with it a "composite" doctrine of Christ's person that rejects the late medieval nominalist notion of suppositional carrying. While Beer carries these insights to evaluative ends that differ rather dramatically from the majority of other authors in this survey, this fact should not obscure the extent to which his interpretation is reinforced by standard interpretations advanced elsewhere. Thus, Ulrich Asendorf is perhaps a bit hasty when he argues that the books by Marc Lienhard, Kjell Ove Nilsson, and Dorothea Vorländer all refute Beer's interpretation of Luther's Christology. See Ulrich Asendorf, *Die Theologie Martin Luthers nach seinen Predigten* (Göttingen: Vandenhoeck & Ruprecht, 1988), 199n.303.

33. Marc Lienhard, *Luther: Witness to Jesus Christ: Stages and Themes of the Reformer's Christology* (Minneapolis: Augsburg, 1982 [1973]). The origin of Lienhard's diachronic study of Luther's

concerned, not so much in the interpretation they assign to Luther's apparent rejection of late medieval Christology, but in the varying assessment of the implications each author detects in this rejection for Luther's subsequent ability to remain within the parameters of Chalcedonian orthodoxy.[34] Like Beer, Lienhard claims that Luther defines the "person" of Christ as the concrete product of two natures coming together, although he admits that it is sometimes difficult to discern exactly what Luther has in mind.[35] What is clear, in Lienhard's interpretation, is that Luther redefines personhood, contrary to the tradition, for the sake of enabling a mutual sharing of attributes between the two natures of Christ.[36] Unlike Beer, then, Lienhard does not understand Luther's reconfiguration of this doctrine to leave the two natures standing in irresolvable antithesis with one another. If anything, Luther's emphasis upon the radical

Christology is an attempt to confront Yves Congar's verdict that Luther's soteriology reflects a heterodox Christology in which the humanity is entirely passive. See ibid., 13–14. For an affirmation of Luther's (premedieval) orthodoxy, see 18–26. Lienhard does not understand these "deviations" as swerves into heterodoxy, but as a resolution of inadequate conceptualities in the tradition.

34. Stated more specifically, I mean here to suggest that on the specific question of Luther's acceptance of suppositional carrying, both agree that Luther rejects it and embraces a point of view entailing a "composite" understanding of the person of Christ.

35. For the former claim, see ibid., 231. For the latter admission, see ibid., 230–31, 330. The difficulty stems from Luther's continued use of "assumption" language whose traditional intent was to locate personal continuity in the unchanged life of the divine Son—a perspective that, indirectly at least, serves to retain the doctrine of divine impassibility that Lienhard elsewhere argues Luther to reject. Lienhard's solution to this tension is to suggest that Luther espouses an exaggerated doctrine of the anhypostasis/enhypostasis distinction in which the assuming divine person itself enters a new reality through the full communicative participation of humanity with divinity and vice versa. See ibid., 230–35, 328–34.

36. So, Lienhard's synthetic summary on Luther's account of personhood: "the person of the Son unites in itself the two natures, but in this hypostatic union a history begins, an intimate communion which Luther calls personal, in which the divine nature participates in the human suffering, and reciprocally the human nature participates in the divine ubiquity. The divine *hypostasis* thus truly descends into the history of human beings. It does not remain beyond them as an unchanging concept, but participates entirely in the history of Jesus of Nazareth. This is why Luther uses the term *person* in a double sense: on the one hand, to designate the eternal author of the act of redemption founded on the *enhypostasis*, namely the *Logos*; on the other hand, to designate the *concretum* in which, on the basis of the *enhypostasis*, the Logos and humanity are intimately united for our salvation." Ibid., 235.

union of the two natures together is so acute that it occasionally borders upon Eutychianism or Monophysitism.[37] Both scholars conclude that Luther defines the personhood of Christ with a theory of "composition," which cuts against the late medieval doctrine of suppositional carrying. So far as Lienhard's importance in the outline of this chapter is concerned it must primarily be observed that the alleged reconfiguration of the doctrine of Christ's person he finds in Luther is oriented entirely in service of an alleged reciprocal exchange of the predicates of divinity and humanity in which the divine nature of Christ is said equally to share in the sufferings of the human nature.[38] This orientation of the first christological divergence in Lienhard's work provides additional corroboration for the sequential organization through which this literature review has been arranged.

Die Christologie in Martin Luthers späten Disputationen by Axel Schmidt reiterates and extends many aspects of Beer's interpretation of Luther's Christology. Unlike Beer, Schmidt limits his study to Luther's late disputations, which he regards as faithful and concise recapitulations of the reformer's theology as a whole.[39] Like previous Roman Catholic critics of Luther's Christology, Schmidt presupposes

37. Lienhard expresses this concern in ibid., 317, 344, 387. Another way of articulating the relation between Lienhard and Beer on this question would be to say that both agree Luther rejects the metaphysical strategy of locating the union of divinity and humanity in a supposit or individual substance that is somehow ontologically prior to and unchanged by the assumption of humanity. They disagree, however, on what Luther proposes as a replacement for this point of view. For Beer, the clear alternative is sheer juxtaposition, whereas for Lienhard the secondary vehicle of union remains (a concept of person) but is reconfigured in such a way that its ontology is at least partially constituted in and through the event of the natures coming together. This parting of ways is important because it reflects both the reason why thinkers like Beer belong within the logical anatomy of the divergence reception, *and* why and how their particular understanding of Luther's divergence takes them in a direction that differs from the broader reception treated in this study.

38. See ibid., 233. This orientation provides additional confirmation for the logical arrangement through which the literature covered in this chapter has been organized.

39. Axel Schmidt, *Die Christologie in Martin Luthers späten Disputationen* (St. Ottilien: EOS Verlag, 1990), 2.

a mutually determinative relation between Luther's soteriology and his Christology, and argues on its basis that, although Luther often enlists traditional christological vocabulary, the quasi-dualist antinomies that fracture his understanding of salvation preclude any meaningful affirmation of the personal unity of divinity and humanity in Christ.[40] Schmidt seeks to document the fissure's existence on the basis of Luther's late christological disputations.[41]

At the root of Luther's christological problems, for Schmidt, is an irresolvable antithesis between theology and philosophy that casts its shadow over the reformer's thought as a whole.[42] Luther's inability to maintain an orthodox doctrine of either the Trinity or Christ is but one byproduct of a deeper problem in the DNA of his theology itself. According to Schmidt, Luther's rejection of the late nominalist view of suppositional union catches the reformer on the horns of a rather ironic dilemma. On the one hand, Luther's rejection is animated by a concern for a deeper mode of union. Yet, the very distinction he denies provides the only conceptual vehicle capable of securing union without sheer antithesis.[43] Without the conceptual framework of suppositional carrying, Luther's Christology must terminate, inevitably, either in a relation of standing dialectical opposition (as Beer argues), or distinction-erasing, synthetic fusion. Schmidt concedes that Luther tries to affirm the Chalcedonian definition as normative. In the absence of a philosophically dense distinction between "persons" and "natures," however, Schmidt concludes that Luther inadvertently espouses a form of monophysitism with paradoxically Nestorian resonances to it.[44] Like Schwarz and Beer,

40. On the alleged mutual determinacy of these loci, see ibid., 14–15, w 178–80. Beer pursues a similar line of argument in *Der fröhliche Wechsel*. Among the first to advance a version of this opinion was Yves Congar.

41. In doing so, he leans rather heavily upon Schwarz's work.

42. See Schmidt, *Die Christologie*, 220–33.

43. That is, a unity without mixture or separation.

Schmidt argues that although Luther sometimes sounds as if he retains the late medieval mechanism of suppositional carrying (and with it a traditional rendering of the distinction between persons and natures), he actually rejects it in favor of an alternative proposal.[45]

Another important book recently arguing for a dramatic departure on Luther's part from the explanatory mechanism of suppositional carrying is *Christus Praedicatus et Creditus: Die reformatorische Christologie Luthers in den Operationes in Psalmos (1519–1521)* by Florian Schneider.[46] Schneider suggests that Luther develops a decidedly "reformational Christology," which emerges in his second commentary on the Psalms. His is a doctrine of Christ carefully calibrated to sync with the new doctrine of justification that gradually materializes in his theology during the second decade of the sixteenth century.[47] As the result of this shift, Luther no longer concerns himself with an "abstract" or "formal" presentation of Christ. His

44. Ibid., 247. That is, Luther holds the union together only on the basis of a dialectical fusion of opposites. Without a second conceptual tier in place to hold these two things together (i.e., a *suppositum*), Luther is left with either a monophysite account of their union, or a Nestorian account of their distinction. The dialectical character of Luther's thought tends in both directions, and hence Schmidt's invention of an unprecedented (and apparently self-contradictory) heresy to describe the contents of Luther's thought. The reason that Luther is deemed primarily to be a monophysite is because he clearly lays emphasis upon "union," but does so without a doctrine of Christ's "person" as distinct from the natures. See also ibid., 199–200. For Schmidt's interpretation of Luther's view of the hypostatic union, see 234–50. Also note that Schmidt appeals explicitly to Lienhard's interpretation of Luther on the "person" of Christ to support his understanding. See ibid., 246n.73. Schmidt finally locates the root of this dialectical Christology and its alleged rejection of "person" as a "subsisting supposit" in Luther's defective soteriology, which is the driving force of his theology (ibid., 250).

45. Schmidt concedes Luther's *apparent* traditionalism in ibid., 241, 246–47. Schmidt draws support for his interpretation of a fundamental departure from both Schwarz and Lienhard. For Schmidt's interaction with Schwarz, see ibid., 234f. For his citation of Lienhard, see 246. Schmidt is critical of Schwarz's pessimistic interpretation of Ockhamist Christology, preferring instead to see it as a particular vocabulary for affirming a traditional distinction. However, despite his criticism of Schwarz on the nominalists, he accepts his view that Luther criticizes their Christology and diverges decisively from it. Here, we see an example of a common analysis with internally divergent evaluations.

46. Florian Schneider, *Christus praedicatus et creditus: die reformatorische Christologie Luthers in den "Operationes in Psalmos" (1519–1521), dargestellt mit beständigem Bezug zu seiner Frühzeitchristologie* (Neukirchen-Vluyn: Neukirchener, 2004).

47. See ibid., 2–3, 10, 61, 100.

interest is limited to reflection upon Christ only as conjoined with the believer's subjective appropriation of salvation. This new dogmatic orientation carries with it, for Schneider, a fundamental shift away from classical christological reflection.[48] One of its more prominent consequences is the fact that Luther no longer conceives of "natures" as static but, rather, as dynamic or functional realities.[49] Luther's Christology is no longer bound to abstract Scholastic conceptualities, but refers instead to the subjective consciousness of the man Christ.[50] Interpreted in this manner, Schneider suggests that Luther's doctrine of a radical simultaneity between Jesus' divinity and humanity demolishes Aristotelian philosophy with its restrictive prohibition against a "coincidence of opposites."[51]

So, Schneider alleges that Luther moves beyond not just the late medieval understanding of "suppositional carrying" but beyond the formulation of two-nature Christology itself, since there is no longer a simultaneity of two distinct substantial-ontological natures. Instead, the person of Christ is constituted through the dynamic and subjective coming together of contrary predicates within the concrete consciousness of Jesus.[52] For Schneider, it is enough in Luther's mind simply to assert paradoxical statements of the being

48. Ibid., 81. So, for instance, Schneider here insists that Luther no longer entertains the notion of a Christ in himself, but knows only of the Christ *pro nobis*. The ontological implications of this view are made clear in the following statement: "Christus mag auch Person für sich selbst sein, aber erst im Sich-selbst-Ausschenken hat er seine eigentliche Identität. Luthers These lautet, daß Christus gerade in seinem Für-uns-Sein sein An-sich-Sein realisiert."

49. Ibid., 115–16.

50. Ibid., 117: "Im Zentrum stehen nicht die der Zweinaturenlehre verpflichteten scholastischen physischen und hyperphysischen Kategorien (persona, natura, substantia, suppositum, pars inferior et superior etc.), sondern die von Christus gemachte und insofern subjektbezogene Gewissenserfahrung." Also important is Schneider's explanation on 177: " Die Einheit zwischen Menschlichem und Göttlichem wird nicht mehr mit Hilfe von Naturkategorien beschreiben, sondern durch konkrete Bewußtseinsgehalte Christi. Es geht Luther nicht um die Simultaneität zweier substanzontologisch verstandener Naturen. Vielmehr werden dynamische und affektuale Begriffe zur Beschreibung des polaren Seins Christi in Anschlag gebracht."

51. Ibid., 176. Here, there is a latent similarity with Schwarz, who also argues that the *actuality* of divine-human union overcomes all discourse, which questions its philosophical possibility.

52. Ibid., 198–99.

of Christ within an acutely sharpened, discursive polarity. Luther redefines the personhood of Christ as the "concrete speaking together of opposites" in which such polarities collide. The personal union of divinity and humanity is termed a *Sprachereignis* ("a speech act or event").[53] Luther overcomes the Ockhamist notion of a suppositional union by understanding the person of Christ to be the result of a speech event that takes place in the prayer of Christ.[54]

In this subsection's brief documentation, it has become clear that a common thread unites a number of recent, major works on Luther's understanding of the hypostatic union. According to this view, Luther clearly rejects the late medieval doctrine of Christ's personhood and supplants it with something radically different.[55] In most cases, this radically different alternative is characterized as advocating a "composite" understanding of the hypostatic union, although what exactly is meant by this varies from author to author. In order to explore a commonly identified product (and impetus) of this reconfiguration, we now turn to the second aspect of the divergence thesis's first tier of analysis: the allegation that Luther's doctrine of the *communicatio idiomatum* espouses a two-way communication between natures in which the divine nature suffers. This survey will require tracing additional claims made by authors already cited and introducing others who build upon their work.

53. See ibid., 181, 190. See also 209–10, 351–55.

54. Ibid., 190.

55. We may also note that Schneider understands an important result of this reconfiguration to be the attribution of suffering to the divine nature over against the lingering docetism of the tradition. This again demonstrates the logical interconnectivity between various tiers expressed in the sequential arrangement of this chapter. See ibid., 135, 148, 355. Another book that reproduces the main themes of Schwarz's seminal essay, as far as Luther's relation to suppositional carrying is concerned, is Stefan Streiff, *"Novis linguis loqui": Martin Luthers Disputation über Joh 1,14 "verbum caro factum est" aus dem Jahr 1539* (Göttingen: Vandenhoeck & Ruprecht, 1993).

Subdivision 2:
The Divine Nature of Christ Also Suffers

The focus of Schwarz's essay rests primarily upon Luther's rejection of the late medieval nominalist mechanism for conceptualizing the hypostatic union. In addition to this main emphasis, however, Schwarz also makes it clear that the primary intended result of Luther's christological adjustment is an altered understanding of the relationship that exists between Christ's natures. According to Schwarz, Luther measures the success or viability of any doctrine of the hypostatic union against its capacity to support a robust account of the communication of idioms.[56] Such an account includes, for Schwarz, the mostly unprecedented assertion that the divine nature shares also in the attributes of the human nature.[57] Luther's doctrine of the *communicatio idiomatum* makes clear that the divine nature of Christ truly suffers along with the humanity.[58] To be sure, Schwarz admits that Luther continues to enlist qualificatory addenda such

56. Schwarz, "Gott ist Mensch," 309. It is fairly common, within recent scholarship on Luther's Christology, to insist that Luther lays a previously unprecedented degree of emphasis upon the communication of idioms. See, for instance, Oswald Bayer, "Das Wort ward Fleisch: Luthers Christologie als Lehre von der Idiomenkommunikation," in idem, *Creator est creatura* (Berlin: Walter de Gruyter, 2007), 23; and Johann Anselm Steiger and Carolyn Schneider, "The *Communicatio Idiomatum* as the Axle and Motor of Luther's Theology," *Lutheran Quarterly* 14, no. 2 (June 1, 2000): 125. I regard claims of this kind to be overstatements. Luther's late medieval predecessors were *highly* concerned with the *communicatio idiomatum*, and discussed it at considerable length. So far as patristic precedent is concerned, it hardly seems fair to suggest that this doctrine is uniquely central for Luther, when John Anthony McGuckin can summarize of Cyril of Alexandria that "the communicatio is shorthand for his whole doctrine of the incarnation as a transforming transaction whereby human nature is appropriated by God and deified in the process." John Anthony McGuckin, *St. Cyril of Alexandria: The Christological Controversy: Its History, Theology, and Texts* (Crestwood, NY: St. Vladimir's Seminary Press, 2004), 192.
57. Schwarz, "Gott ist Mensch," 311–12: "Es soll nur unterstrichen werden, daß Luther ebenso die andere Seite der communicatio idiomatum ganz erst nimmt. Die göttliche Natur hat teil an allen Eigentümlichkeiten der menschlichen Natur, also an allem, was zum irdischen Dasein des Menschen gehört."
58. Ibid., 311–13. So, Schwarz argues, although it is clear to most that Luther thinks the humanity can and does share in the attributes of divinity (as the eucharistic debates demonstrate), he stresses the fact that he insists upon the reverse of this relationship just as seriously.

as *secundum humanitatem* ("according to the humanity"), which are traditionally intended specifically to protect the abiding impassibility of divinity. Such addenda do not, however, indicate that Luther fails to embrace a real, two-way communication between natures. Their function, in Schwarz's interpretation, is simply to identify the proper nature from which equally shared attributes like suffering derive their origin within the concretion of Christ's person.[59] The central affirmation remains the same. Luther's christological course correction includes the suffering of divinity.

Kjell Ove Nilsson's book *Simul: Das Miteinander von Göttlichem und Menschlichem in Luthers Theologie* first appeared in 1966, more or less at the same time as Schwarz's influential essay.[60] Nilsson is more narrowly preoccupied with the *communicatio idiomatum* than Schwarz. And yet, Nilsson shares many of Schwarz's claims, and represents an important and oft-cited author in our survey. Despite an obvious terminological continuity between Luther and the theologians of medieval Scholasticism when it comes to a shared christological vocabulary, Nilsson argues that this formal similarity masks a vast, material difference. For instance, whereas the Scholastics identify persons and natures as static metaphysical substances possessing certain predetermined properties, Luther regards them as dynamic concepts.[61] This means, for Nilsson, that humanity and

59. Ibid., 312–13. In other words, the qualification is sequential in nature. For more on Luther's qualificatory discourse, see ch. 3.

60. Kjell Ove Nilsson, *Simul: Das Miteinander von Göttlichem und Menschlichem in Luthers Theologie*, Forschungen zur Kirchen- und Dogmengeschichte, Bd. 17 (Göttingen: Vandenhoeck & Ruprecht, 1966).

61. Ibid., 186–87: "Man darf Luther zufolge den Naturen keinen naturalistischen und metaphysischen Inhalt beilegen, sondern muß sie in einer dynamischen, beweglichen und lebendigen Weise definieren, so daß der Begriff Natur eigentlich die Bedeutung Werk erhält, menschliches Werk und göttliches Werk." "Divinitas und humanitas sind keine quantitative Größen oder metaphysichen Kontraste, sondern diese Worte sind auf eine *neue Weise* zu verstehen, und nicht nur, als bezeichneten sie ein Verhältnis zwischen Unendlichem und Endlichem, Volkommenem und Unvollkommenem, Unveränderlichkeit und Wechsel." Nilsson does not think, though, that this means that Luther wanted to eliminate completely

divinity are defined primarily in light of their respective "roles" in the salvation event.[62] Nilsson is less clear in his book than Schwarz is in his essay on how exactly this new content pushes Luther's definition of "personhood" away from the views of late medieval nominalism.[63] The functionalizing (nonspeculative) impetus of his interpretation could certainly be taken to imply that the personal union ought simply to be understood in terms of an inseparable, dynamic co-activity between divinity and humanity. In this case, the personhood of Christ would be seen as constituted by a pair of coordinated operations. Nilsson stops short of this view, however. His treatment is more attentive to the ongoing role of traditional concepts within Luther's vocabulary, which proscribe such a position. Nevertheless, he is willing to insist that Luther's Christology fundamentally transforms traditional vocabulary from the inside out.[64]

Nilsson's primary focus rests upon Luther's doctrine of the *communicatio idiomatum*, which he takes to be the organizing center of the reformer's entire theology.[65] His book seeks, on the basis

the concept of nature from his theology. At the very least, the conservative tendencies of his theology show up in his preservation of the term even if, as Nilsson suggests, he attaches to it his own peculiar meaning.

62. Ibid., 232–33. Nilsson admits that Luther also assigns certain "metaphysical" predicates to the natures, but claims that this aspect of his thought is secondary to his dynamic emphasis. Nilsson makes a similar point when he claims: "Hier finden wir also wieder, daß Luthers Auffassung von den Naturen Christi nicht durch abstrakte und spekulative Erwägungen bestimmt ist. Entscheidend ist vielmehr die Darstellung von Leben und Versöhnungswerk Christi, sein Kampf und Sieg, seine Entblößung und Verherrlichung. Dies drückt Luthers Beschreibung dessen, was Göttlich und Menschlich ist, seinen Stempel auf" (209). These sorts of claims bear a striking resemblance to Beer's claim that Luther "functionalizes" the two natures of Christ, though Nilsson would certainly not share Beer's appraisal of the shift.
63. Nilsson's characterization of "Scholastic Christology" is mostly content to comment that it is "speculative," "abstract," and "metaphysical," and does not, for the most part, get in to the finer points of which explanatory mechanisms are enlisted to make sense of the hypostatic union.
64. Ibid., 179–81. Note, for instance, Nilsson's affirmation here that the divine person assumes to itself a human nature, thus avoiding the implication that the person of Christ is constituted by the coming together of dynamic natures. Lienhard will also affirm something like this, though he still suggests that the divine person enters a new mode of existence in the incarnation, thus rendering Christ's person a composite. On Lienhard, see above.
65. Ibid., 228: "Hier können wir nun folgende These aufstellen: weil für Luther alles darauf ankommt, daß Christus wirklich das einheitliche, gottmenschliche Erlösungswerk pro nobis

of this conviction, to interpret Luther's doctrine of Christ (along with other major aspects of his theology) entirely in its light.[66] So, what is the communication of attributes in Nilsson's interpretation of Luther, and what sort of exchange between divinity and humanity does it inaugurate? As a starting point, Nilsson insists that Luther's treatment of the *communicatio idiomatum* is motivated entirely by soteriological concerns.[67] He shares Schwarz's view that the medieval period makes use of *secundum quid* qualifiers in order to protect the integrity of a preconceived philosophical polarity between divinity and humanity. Despite the shared formal vocabulary, Luther simply does not share these philosophical commitments.[68] The reformer's focus is soteriologically determined, and this entails a fundamental redefinition of what one means by "nature," "person," "God," "humanity," and so forth. Luther's doctrine of the *communicatio idiomatum* appears in some cases to dissolve the distinction between natures altogether, and thus tends toward a species of monophysitism. Nilsson insists, however, that such an accusation falls well short of Luther's intentions.[69] The main point is simply that divinity and humanity are united in a single act of God, which is carried out by Christ, an act in which the distinct soteriological functions pertaining to each nature remain distinguishable from one another.[70]

ausgeführt hat, und weil die Einheitlichkeit dieser Handlung ihrerseits mit der unitas der Person zusammenhängt, wobei die communicatio-Lehre das Zentrum bildet, deswegen macht die communicatio idiomatum das Herzstück der Theologie Luthers aus."

66. In this respect, Nilsson is an interesting precursor to the work of later scholars like Johann Anselm Steiger, who will later claim Luther's unique doctrine of the *communicatio idiomatum* to be the center and animating principle of his entire theology.
67. Ibid., 227.
68. Ibid., 237. This, despite the fact that Nilsson is clearly aware that Luther continues to make use of such qualifiers. See, for instance, his citation of similar phrases in Luther on 181. The question of how these qualifiers are employed in Luther's theology will be a major point of focus in ch. 2.
69. Ibid., 237–38.
70. Ibid., 244–45.

Luther will often speak of the lingering distinction between natures in rather traditional ways, by Nilsson's own admission. This may make it appear that Luther accepts the classical proscriptive boundaries, which deny any sharing of Christ's divine nature in the sufferings of the human nature. Nilsson argues, however, that Luther pushes beyond these restrictive borders, even though later Lutheran theology re-erects them.[71] The traditionalist language is confusing to some extent, but Nilsson is adamant that Luther embraces the *genus tapeinoticum* ("the communication of human attributes to the divine nature") as the symmetrical correlate of the *genus maiestaticum* ("the communication of divine attributes to the human nature").[72]

Naturally, the greatest obstacle to this reading of Luther's Christology resides in the fact that Luther occasionally insists, in very traditional form, that divinity does *not* suffer. Like Schwarz, Nilsson responds to this challenge by clarifying the sort of qualification Luther has in mind. On his account, Luther intends merely to differentiate the source of various predicates. Some predicates belong to the divine nature "prior to" or "outside" of its union with humanity in the incarnate Christ (abstract predicates). Others apply to the divinity of Christ only because it shares now in all predicates of the humanity (concrete predicates).[73] So, while "divinity-considered-on-

71. Ibid., 237–38nn.37–38.
72. Ibid., 249–50. The fact that Nilsson admits an unevenness in the evidence for this interpretation is to his credit. Not all proponents of the divergence interpretation are so forthcoming about the fact that Luther at least *sounds* in many places like he reproduces the traditional view, which denies any suffering of the divine nature. How such apparently heterogeneous evidence ought to be interpreted will be another key focus of ch. 2. The *genuses* mentioned here reflect the later language that emerged in the intra-Protestant and intra-Lutheran debates of the mid- to late-sixteenth century. Very briefly, the *genus maiestaticum* refers in this literature to the real sharing of the human nature in the predicates of divinity (most famously, the possibility or actuality of the human nature being present in more than one place as would be necessary for its real presence in the Lord's Supper). The *genus tapeinaticum* refers to the sharing of the divine nature in the predicates of the human nature. The Christology of the Lutheran confessions rejects this genus, although the Confessions do not name it as such.

its-own" does not suffer, the divine nature does suffer within the hypostatic union.[74]

Marc Lienhard acknowledges an apparent endorsement of divine impassibility in several of Luther's writings. He argues, however, that his affirmation of the traditional restriction progressively attenuates over time. Lienhard points to an implicit departure from the doctrine of divine impassibility already in some of Luther's very early works, but suggests that it took some years for this seminal insight to develop and consistently integrate with the more technical aspects of Luther's theological vocabulary.[75] In other words, there is a revisionist trajectory of development within Luther's corpus itself. It is a trajectory, however, that Luther never walked consistently. Lienhard acknowledges vestiges of the classical view (that is, that the divine nature does not suffer), which linger even in the later years of Luther's life.[76] Despite these mitigating factors, however, Lienhard is convinced that Luther clearly espouses a mutual communication of attributes between natures, a communication that includes the sharing of Christ's divinity in the sufferings of his humanity.[77] The break with traditional conceptualities may not be as tidy as one could hope, but the implicit shift is undeniable.

73. Ibid., 255–57. This seems to be the explanatory mechanism through which Nilsson also makes sense of *secundum quid* qualifiers in Luther's christological vocabulary. Here we observe yet another "sequential" interpretation of Luther's qualificatory discourse.
74. Nilsson summarizes his interpretation in the following closing statement: "Göttliches und Menschliches haben beide ihre speziellen Eigenarten und können niemals gegenseitig identifiziert werden; sie sind im Gegenteil die äußersten Gegensätze ihrer selbst, aber durch die communicatio idiomatum ist Gott mit dabei, offenbart er sich und handelt er mit dem Menschlichen zusammen, und dadurch sind Gott und Mensch in Christus zu einer Einheit verbunden, sodaß alles, was in Hinsicht auf Person und Werk Christi über die Gottheit gesagt werden kann, auch der Menschlichkeit gilt—und umgekehrt, jedoch ohne alle Verwandlung oder Vermengung." Ibid., 260.
75. Lienhard, *Luther*, 25, 53. For Lienhard, the Alexandrian notion of a one-way communication from divinity to humanity risks docetism, a verdict that reveals some of the presuppositions that animate his views of Christology in general. See ibid., 336.
76. Thus, there is an unresolved fracture in Luther's thought, as Lienhard explains in ibid., 379.
77. Ibid., 31, 138, 339–42.

To be sure, Luther makes use of qualifying distinctions traditionally enlisted to proscribe this implication. He will argue, for instance, that Christ suffers "on account of his humanity" (*secundum quid* qualifiers), or stipulate that divinity cannot suffer "in the abstract." Like Schwarz and Nilsson before him, Lienhard insists that the formal similarity masks a material difference. Luther does not intend these qualifications to express what they did within their original context. They certainly do not carry with them any implicit endorsement of divine impassibility. In the final evaluation, Lienhard suggests that the content of Luther's new Christology fits rather awkwardly within traditional vocabularies of theological expression. Luther does not enlist this vocabulary by conviction, but as a matter of habit or cultural inertia. In order to articulate Luther's views with a greater degree of consistency, one would need to do away with the conceptual categories Luther takes for granted by virtue of his late medieval context. The new wine of Luther's Christology bursts the old wineskins of medieval Scholasticism.[78]

Important works by Johann Anselm Steiger and Dennis Ngien likewise detect in Luther's treatment of the *communicatio idiomatum* a semirevolutionary endorsement of divine passibility.[79] Like Nilsson, Ngien acknowledges the obstacles that confront such an interpretation. He admits that Luther's insistence upon divine suffering emerges only occasionally within the reformer's late writings. Earlier works preserve traditional qualifications, which

78. Ibid., 345, 374.

79. See Dennis Ngien, *The Suffering of God According to Martin Luther's 'Theologia Crucis'* (Vancouver: Regent College Publishing, 2005); idem, "Chalcedonian Christology and Beyond: Luther's Understanding of the Communicatio Idiomatum," *Heythrop Journal* 45 (2004): 54–68; Johann Anselm Steiger, "Die communicatio idiomatum als Achse und Motor der Theologie Luthers: Der 'fröhliche Wechsel' als hermeneutischer Schlüssel zu Abendmahlslehre, Anthropologie, Seelsorge, Naturtheologie, Rhetorik und Humor," *Neue Zeitschrift für systematische Theologie und Religionsphilosophie* 38, no. 1 (January 1, 1996): 1–28. See also Steiger's later articulation of this same argument in his *Fünf Zentralthemen der Theologie Luthers und seiner Erben: Communicatio, Figura, Imago, Maria, Exempla* (Leiden: Brill, 2002).

specifically rule out the suffering of Christ's divinity. In this respect, Ngien shares Lienhard's view that Luther's work is internally inconsistent. What matters, though, is that the overall trajectory of development tilts toward an explicit affirmation of divine passibility.[80] Schneider postulates a similar commitment to the suffering of the divine nature in Luther's presentation of the communication of idioms. He argues that Luther's reconfigured Christology as a whole overcomes the latent docetism of the patristic and medieval traditions.[81] A wide assortment of contemporary, theological literature echoes this judgment. Luther's christological legacy is one of constructive divergence.[82]

Before transitioning to the second tier of the divergence thesis, it is worth pausing briefly to reflect upon the inner coherence of the first tier. Luther's alleged rejection of divine impassibility depends upon an underlying premise that he reconfigures medieval Christology

80. This account of development is significant for the present study. The texts that must attract our attention are the relatively few instances where Luther is alleged to break from tradition. There is little disagreement among scholars that he speaks more or less as a traditionalist for most of his life. The question is, Does the latter set of texts reflect an undeniable divergence from this earlier tendency? Chs. 2 and 3 are preoccupied with this issue.

81. Schneider, *Christus Praedicatus*, 117–19, 135, 148: "Die kreuzes- und leidenstheologischen Aussagen Luthers implizieren eine kritische Stimme gegen das Axiom von Gottes Unveränderlichkeit und Leidensunfähigkeit." For Schneider, the main point has to do with the unprecedented depth to which Luther was willing to attribute the full experience of *Anfechtung* to Christ, an attribution that traditional christological commitments prevented others in the tradition from entertaining. With Schneider, it is not so much a matter of affirming the mutual communication between humanity and divinity, but a complete reconfiguration of the categories responsible for the question itself. Nevertheless, within this "reconfiguration," he is clear that God truly participates in experiences or activities associated with the humanity.

82. A few examples here include Jens Wolff, *Metapher und Kreuz: Studien zu Luthers Christusbild* (Tübingen: Mohr Siebeck, 2005), 426; Sibylle Rolf, "'Christum und nichts anders': die Kommunikation von Gott und Mensch und die Predigt des Evangeliums," *Luther* 80, no. 3 (January 1, 2009): 158n.26; Robert Kolb, *Martin Luther: Confessor of the Faith* (New York: Oxford University Press, 2009), 115; Jürgen Moltmann, *The Crucified God: The Cross of Christ as the Foundation and Criticism of Christian Theology*, trans. R. A. Wilson and John Bowden (Minneapolis: Fortress Press, 1993 [1974/German ed. 1973]), 232–33; and Ted Peters, *God—The World's Future: Systematic Theology for a Postmodern Era* (Minneapolis: Fortress Press, 1992), 206–209. Thomas Weinandy seems to presuppose more or less the same interpretation of Luther, but would evaluate the resultant shift rather differently. See Weinandy, *Does God Suffer?* (Notre Dame, IN: University of Notre Dame, 2000), 185.

in fundamental ways. These two claims are genetically related to one another according to the work of many authors. Luther's commitment to a reciprocal, communicative exchange of predicates between natures seems to demand an aggressive overhaul of the late medieval conceptualities. The doctrine of "suppositional carrying" permits only an "extrinsic" account of the relationship between divinity and humanity in Christ. This is the conceptual thicket that Luther must clear away in order for his own ideas to surface. The result is a dynamic and communicative Christology in which God suffers in God's very nature.[83]

A Soteriology of Requisite Divine Passibility

The previous section's documentation of the divergence reception's first "tier" of analysis has focused primarily upon "whether" and "how" Luther deviates from late medieval Christology according to recent major literature. This second section turns its attention to the question of constructive rationale. That is, if it is true that Luther is so intent upon securing the suffering of God in Christ, why is this commitment so important to him? What constructive role does the affirmation occupy within Luther's theological oeuvre? The answer, for a considerable number of scholars, is soteriological in nature. In other words, Luther insists upon reciprocal, communicative exchange because he presupposes that only a God who really suffers can really redeem.[84]

83. A recent essay that lays considerable emphasis upon the "communicative structure" of Luther's theology is Rolf, "'Christum und nichts anders,'" 150–69.

84. One reason for this trend is the fact that most scholars view Luther's Christology to be determined completely by soteriological concerns. Such a claim is often intended to differentiate Luther's theological style from medieval theology, which is often characterized, by contrast, as highly speculative.

The seeds of this view are already embedded in Nilsson's claim that Luther's Christology is soteriologically determined. This is a common refrain. Luther's predecessors are often denigrated for their love of abstraction. Luther, on the other hand, is not interested in the parlor games of philosophical contemplation. His is a soteriologically sourced Christology. Although Nilsson does not emphasize the point, it is only natural to expect that Luther's passibilist account of the *communicatio idiomatum* should be sourced by his account of redemption.[85] Subsequent interpreters of Luther's Christology make the connection explicitly. Ian Kingston Siggins insists that Luther's soteriology requires him to reject divine impassibility.[86] For Lienhard, divine impassibility is fundamentally incompatible with Luther's soteriological claim that Christ actually bears the sins of humanity.[87]

A common thread in these assorted analyses is the premise that Luther's reform of late medieval soteriology carried with it a recalibration of dogmatic norms. Florian Schneider approaches the

85. For Nilsson's comments on the centrality of soteriology in these matters, see Nilsson, *Simul*, 207, 227, 237, 243. A particularly clear statement appears on 257: "Diese Kommunikation in Christus zwischen Person und Natur, Natur und Natur, vom Menschlichen zum Göttlichen und vom Göttlichen zum Menschlichen, ist für Luther der entschiedende 'Artikel.'" The logic described above, though, does not emerge as forcefully in Nilsson as it does in later authors. In subsequent chapters I will criticize the implicit polemic against medieval Christologies that this narrative typically presupposes. It may be the case that Luther's leverages a different soteriology than his contemporaries, but it is not true to accuse them of utter abstraction.

86. Siggins, *Martin Luther's Doctrine of Christ*, 241. Siggins is a unique case because he argues that the overall shape of Luther's thought points in the direction of divine passibility, but laments the fact that Luther himself seems not to have realized this. In this respect, Siggins is among the most severe examples of the "new wine in old wineskins" interpretation, because he thinks Luther does not do away with the doctrine of divine impassibility in his discussion of the communication of attributes, but claims that he would *need* to do so in order for the more central emphases of his theology to function properly. In an ironic way, then, Siggins reinforces the accuracy of this chapter's sequential arrangement, but disagrees implicitly with the interpretations of Luther's Christology that correspond with it. His solution is to "fix" Luther in order to help him be more consistent with his own best ideas. See more on Siggins in the documentation of the third tier below.

87. Lienhard, *Luther*, 138. This is an odd claim. The vast majority of the confessional Protestant tradition accepted this theory of the atonement and still maintained a classical doctrine of divine impassibility. Lienhard could be right, but the history of dogma mitigates the prima facie plausibility of his argument.

coordination from a similar angle. For Schneider, the very shape of Luther's Christology is dictated by his newly forged doctrine of justification by faith. This includes the prerequisite that God meets human beings where they are, and thus shares completely in the forsakenness of their situation.[88] Luther's doctrine of Christ must therefore accommodate a fissure tearing through the divine being. So, each of these authors endorses the premise that Luther's understanding of soteriology requires a mutual, communicative exchange in which Christ's divine nature suffers.

The most explicit version of this coordination appears in the works of Johann Anselm Steiger and Dennis Ngien.[89] Steiger's essay "Die communicatio idiomatum als Achse und Motor der Theologie Luthers" builds upon the work of Schwarz, Nilsson, and Lienhard, making the now-familiar claim that Luther overturns the impassibilist veto which casts its shadow across patristic and medieval treatments of the communication of attributes.[90] Whereas John of Damascus, for instance, limits his discussion of reciprocal attribution in order carefully to proscribe the suffering of Christ's divinity, things are "entirely different" [*ganz anders*] for Luther. Unlike the Damascene and much of subsequent dogma, Luther deletes the impassibilist qualification and embraces a fully reciprocal exchange between natures.[91] The emphasis in Steiger's essay rests upon ways in which Luther extends the motif of exchange into a wide assortment

88. Schneider, *Christus Praedicatus*, 191: "Die Überwindung der Sünde in Christus uns zugute muß zunächst die Sünde nochmals schrecklich groß machen, so groß, daß ein Riß durch Gott selbst geht, daß er sich selbst in einem sich gegen ihn selbt richtenden Willen gegenübertreten muß."
89. This association is also advanced by the Erlangen theologian Werner Elert. See Volker Keding, "Wider das Apathieaxiom: Die theopaschitische Christologie des späten Elert und ihre Wirkungsgeschichte," in *Mit dem Menschen verhandeln über den Sachgehalt des Evangeliums: die Bedeutung der Theologie Werner Elerts für die Gegenwart*, ed. Rudolf Keller and Michael Roth (Erlangen: Martin-Luther-Verlag, 2004), 97.
90. For Steiger's citation of these authors, see his "Die communicatio idiomatum," 1n.1. For his insistence that Luther intensifies the *communicatio idiomatum* to include the suffering of the divine nature, see ibid., 3–5.
91. Ibid., 3.

of theological corridors. The first and most theological extension is soteriological in nature. According to Steiger, Luther's christological adjustment is geared toward a soteriology of communicative exchange wherein humanity receives a share in all that belongs to divinity, and vice versa.[92] A central ingredient of this exchange in Steiger's interpretation is the genuine sharing of God in the defects of human existence.[93]

Dennis Ngien builds upon Steiger's assessment. He agrees that Luther moves beyond a traditional doctrine of the *communicatio idiomatum* and embraces a relationship between natures that includes the suffering of the divine nature of Christ. Ngien defends this interpretation in an influential essay entitled "Chalcedonian Christology and Beyond: Luther's Understanding of the *Communicatio Idiomatum*."[94] The decidedly soteriological trajectory of Luther's revolutionary position becomes clear in the third section of Ngien's essay, "God's Suffering and Soteriology."[95] Here, Ngien mounts his argument largely on the basis of a section of Luther's 1539 treatise "On the Councils and the Church," where the reformer states:

> Unless God is in the balance and throws his weight as a counterbalance, we shall sink to the bottom of the scale. . . . If it is not true that God died for us, but only a man died, we are lost. But if God's death and God dead lie in the opposite scale, then his side goes down and we go upward like a light or empty pan. Of course, he can also go up again and jump out of his pan. But he could not have sat in the pan unless he became a man like us, so that it could be said: God dead, God's passion, God's blood, God's death. According to his nature God cannot die, but since God and man

92. "Dieses soteriologische Theologoumenon verdankt sich christologischer Reflexion; man könnte auch sagen: Luther hat die Christologie konsequent auf die Soteriologie angewandt, indem er beide Lehren synoptisch gelesen und die eine auf die andere angewandt hat." Ibid., 5–6.

93. Ibid., 5–7.

94. Ngien, "Chalcedonian Christology," 54–68. Ngien's point of view is that Luther maintains the traditional position at many points in his life, but that there are a handful of texts in his corpus that unambiguously move beyond it.

95. Ibid., 59–60.

> are united in one person it is correct to talk about God's death when that man dies who is one thing or one person with God.[96]

Ngien does not address in his discussion here the important qualifier "according to his nature God cannot die," which would seem, prima facie, to complicate the blatantly passibilist interpretation he assigns to this passage. Elsewhere, he addresses disclaimers of this kind by emphasizing Luther's distinction between concrete and abstract predicates, a response that echoes the work of earlier scholars surveyed above.[97]

The directness of Ngien's appropriation of this text warrants verbatim documentation:

> In order to redeem human beings from the power of death, *God has to co-suffer and co-die in Christ.* That is why Luther makes use of his image of the scale, to illustrate that God can go down, can rise and jump out of his pan. God lets himself be overtaken by death in the suffering and dying of Jesus, and yet he remains the victor over death. The divine nature was present throughout the earthly life of Jesus, and was not untouched by the whole affair of the incarnation. With this it becomes clear how closely the two-nature Christology and soteriology are linked in Luther's thinking. *It is a theological axiom that Christ be affected by suffering even according to the divine nature, otherwise salvation through Christ's suffering is inconceivable to him.*[98]

96. This section is copied from ibid., 59, where the author quotes *The Formula of Concord*'s rendering of WA 50:590. This same quote occupies a central place in Steiger's presentation in "Die communicatio idiomatum," 6–7.
97. Ngien, "Chalcedonian Christology," 62, 65. According to Ngien, and others already surveyed above, this distinction points to the fact that God only suffers in and through the incarnate unity with the human nature. *Outside* of the incarnation, or before it, divinity does not and cannot suffer. Thus, the emphasis in this explanation of the distinction rests upon a sequential or temporal analysis. When Luther says, "God cannot suffer," this is taken to mean that divinity *by itself* (in eternity)does not suffer, but this statement is not thought to mitigate the subsequent reality that divinity *does suffer* in and through the incarnation of Christ. Chapter 2, below, will address the adequacy of this interpretation.
98. Ibid., 59; emphasis mine.

Here we see that, for Ngien, Luther's reconfiguration of traditional Christology is soteriologically motivated. The theme of God's full and redemptive participation in the predicament of postlapsarian humanity stipulates the capacity of divinity to suffer. In short, a god who cannot suffer is necessarily other than the God who takes on flesh to redeem fallen humanity in Christ. The soterio-christological symmetry, which Ngien articulates so clearly, is an important binding thread that unites this chapter's sequential presentation of the divergence reception. What has emerged is a determinate, formal assumption pertaining to the internal organization of Luther's theological commitments. To summarize: the logic of his soteriology *requires* christological innovation. Luther's passibilism is no mere factoid; it identifies an animating feature of his theological vision.[99] Viewed retrospectively, the sequential thrust of the divergence thesis's cumulative argument could be summarized in the following manner:

> Luther's commitment to a soteriology of God's radical participation in the lowly estate of sinners requires as its internal presupposition the capacity of God's *nature* to suffer, or experience genuine vulnerability. This capacity is secured only insofar as the traditional proscriptions against divine suffering, which govern the traditional treatment of the *communicatio idiomatum*, are overcome. This trajectory stands in diametrical tension with late medieval conceptualizations of the

99. A notable exception here is Beer, who likewise argues for a christological divergence, but thinks the source of Luther's novelty lies not so much in a soteriology of divine solidarity, but in Luther's tendency to proliferate antithetical dualisms. As we have already explained, Beer is included here because he reiterates an interpretation of Luther's Christology that comports in many particulars with those scholars whose work points more neatly along the trajectory of the divergence reception. The organization of this chapter is not intended to suggest that every point along the way *must* point in the direction of a historicized doctrine of God. It would be more accurate to say, more modestly, that the interpretations charted here *have* been appropriated in this way; and, in many cases, that this trajectory has often been cited as a major motivating factor for the alleged christological divergence so many defend. Other appropriations of this "logic" are to be found in a number of systematic uses of Luther over the last several decades. Most conspicuous here is the work of Jürgen Moltmann, but his understanding of Luther's soteriological significance is by no means an isolated phenomenon.

> hypostatic union as an instance of "suppositional carrying." Such an approach begins with a procrustean, philosophical premise that divinity and humanity are incompatible with one another. Because this premise contradicts the fundamental impetus of Luther's soteriology, it must be jettisoned in favor of an unmitigated affirmation of *real* and *reciprocal* communion between God and man in the person of Christ.

It is this basic logical organization of Luther's theological commitments that has mediated to contemporary theology its general perceptions of Luther's ongoing significance. With this observation, we come to the third tier of the divergence thesis, which focuses upon the trajectory of Luther's christological legacy.

A Fundamentally New Doctrine of God

The account of Luther's thought that has materialized in the past two sections is pregnant with constructive theological potential. It provides an access point in and through which Luther's Christology fruitfully intersects contemporary streams of theological discourse. In particular, Luther's passibilism has proven attractive for theologians interested in doctrines of divine immanence. Luther is often identified as a hinge point in this area. The crucial task here is to demonstrate ways in which constructive appropriations of Luther's Christology presuppose the structure of commitments outlined in the previous two sections. In this third section, we will survey the broad contours of these contemporary appropriations. At stake in these conversations is the specification of Luther's significance today.[100]

100. This documentation is necessary for at least two reasons. (1) The historical task is often (if not always) reciprocal in nature. Interpretations make way for narratives of significance, and narratives of significance often encourage retrospective interpretations of figures on the plane they established. A full account of a reception, then, requires description of both cause (interpretation) and effect (significance) because the progression between these stages is seldom one-way. (2) For better or worse, the broader perceived significance of Luther's thought in relation to modern questions has served often as a framework for the interpretation of his thought. The particular conceptual extension examined in this section goes a long way in

Theological extensions of Luther's theology tend to include two central elements, which frame generic contemporary perceptions of his ongoing significance. In the first place, Luther's modern interpreters typically assume that he decisively repudiates classical accounts of the doctrine of God, with their putatively Greek specification of divine attributes.[101] There is considerable overlap on this point with the familiar, historical narrative of "Hellenization," which has so often functioned as an explanatory framework for making sense of early Christian doctrinal development.[102] Situated within this narrative, Luther emerges as a principled de-Hellenizer, an abject opponent of every attempt to define the being of God in the terms of classical theism.[103] For those in contemporary theology uneasy with a traditional concept of God, Luther thus seems rather understandably to be a congenial ally and model.

The second central element of the extension is positive in nature. It focuses upon the new doctrine of God, with which Luther supplants its philosophically corrupted precursor. What is generally regarded as central to Luther's alternative account is its stark recognition of God's passionate involvement in history. He acknowledges that God, like us (though not perhaps in exactly the same way), is conditioned by the events of salvation history and does not remain unchanged by God's association with them. Divine passibility is an emblematic

documenting the central claims responsible for recurrent assessments of Luther's fundamental theological contributions. All of this adds to the interpretive thicket that together constitutes the divergence reception as defined in this study.

101. I am thinking here, primarily, of immutability, simplicity, impassibility, and the like.

102. Theologians typically credit Adolf von Harnack with this framework. It functions also in the work of Albrecht Ritschl, Friedrich Loofs, and Wilhelm Bousset (among others).

103. The question of whether this characterization is fair to patristic or medieval modes of thought need not detain us here. For our purposes, the salient fact is that Luther has been interpreted frequently on the terrain of such a narrative. There is also some overlap here with Heidegger's influential critique of onto-theology, which is sometimes invoked by those concerned with developing theology beyond all metaphysics, and beyond the question of "being" altogether. Heidegger himself paves the way for such a reception. See, for instance, Merold Westphal, *Overcoming Onto-Theology: Toward a Postmodern Christian Faith* (New York: Fordham University Press, 2001), 4.

outgrowth of this insight. The constructive payoff for contemporary theology is an ostensibly more robust doctrine of divine immanence. In other words, the divergence thesis enables a theological extension of Luther's theology, which speaks to ongoing interest in the nearness of God. This extension is what I have in mind when I speak of the "third tier."

Premonitions of this "immanence extension" may be detected in Schwarz's seminal essay only on the basis of indirect inference. In his interpretation, Luther diverges from late medieval theology primarily because he adopts a christological first principle that forfeits all a priori conceptions of the divine being, a point of view that places Luther at odds with the nominalist penchant for beginning with a doctrine of divine-human incommensurability. In light of Schwarz's earlier comment that the nominalists faithfully redact the christological views of the early church, is it too much to conclude that he conceives of this shift as touching upon the most basic doctrinal assumptions of the early church? Does Schwarz understand classical Christian theism as a whole to be supervised by the very same a priori commitments that Luther would later overthrow? At the very least, we may observe that, for Schwarz, the central dividing line between Luther and the late medieval objects of his criticism is a fundamental one. Whereas the latter takes its starting point from pagan philosophy, Luther begins with the actual union of God and man in Jesus Christ, and thinks conceptually outward entirely on its basis. One must be careful here to not place words in Schwarz's mouth. The focus of his essay does not rest upon Luther's contemporary significance. Nevertheless, whether intentional or not, the reader is left with the implication that Luther, for the first time in the history of dogmatic development, called into question the Hellenistic philosophical inheritance, which had long supervised the unfolding of theological inquiry. It is precisely this conceptual shift, on Schwarz's account, which allows Luther to affirm fully the mystery of God's real union with humanity in Christ. The implication of all this is that Luther initiated a major set of adjustments to the traditional doctrine of God. Scholars writing in Schwarz's wake herald the extent and significance of these adjustments more vigorously than Schwarz himself does.[104]

One such scholar is Ian Kingston Siggins, who argues that the central, abiding trajectory of Luther's thought carries theology beyond the static God of the philosophers and embraces a more dynamic understanding of God's being. As already noted in previous sections, Siggins does not regard Luther to be entirely consistent on this point. The reformer's discussion of the *communicatio idiomatum*, for instance, remains diluted by traditional concepts that don't really cohere with his theological vision. So, for Siggins, although it is clear that Luther entirely rejects the doctrine of divine impassibility, his attempt to speak within the traditional christological categories sometimes leaves the awkward impression that he ascribes suffering only to the humanity. This is a point of view that Siggins regards as incoherent and probably Nestorian.[105] The terminological glitch is regrettable, but should not detract from the prevailing trajectories of Luther's theological emphasis. Siggins comments: "In short, even though Luther's presentation of the *communicatio idiomatum* is technically tenable, it creates an impression alien to his design. Fortunately, it is a minor incident in his biblical exegesis; and at most

104. Even Nilsson, who published his important book in the same year as Schwarz's essay, espouses a markedly starker appraisal of Luther's relation to the apparent Hellenism of the tradition's doctrine of God, although Nilsson, like several others, argues in favor of Luther's fundamental traditionalism in other respects. His ability to mount this "traditionalist" argument depends upon an ancillary relation between an alleged center of patristic Christology and the broader philosophical vocabulary through which this center was expressed. Such a strategy has been adopted by several other scholars who likewise seek to defend Luther's Chalcedonianism, though they still embrace the main elements of the divergence interpretation.

105. For the former concession, see Siggins, *Martin Luther's Doctrine of Christ*, 237. For the latter verdict, see 128.

points Luther is content to confess the unity of the natures on the ground that the biblical account means what it says."[106]

That Luther should speak in these traditional terms at all is accidental to his intentions. It should be seen as an inadvertent byproduct of the time in which he lived and not in any way central to his evangelical theology.[107] The explosive materials of Luther's theology lie, for Siggins, somewhat muted in nucleic dormancy. The radically new evangelical content never quite erupts. Had they done so, the restrictive structures of static orthodoxy would surely need to disappear or suffer major reconfiguration. The relation of all this to Siggins's interpretation of Luther's reconfiguration of the doctrine of God is visible in a particularly impassioned paragraph that shows up toward the end of his magisterial study:

> If only Luther had rigorously pursued his own counsel into the realm of dogma! But remnants of the philosophers' God persist, despite his radical insistence that whatever rational apprehension of God we may possess, it is to be abandoned for the lively knowledge of the God and Father of our Lord Jesus Christ. This should lead to a complete reworking of the truth enshrined in the sentence, "Christ maintained His Godhead unaltered when He became man." For it should mean that even what we know of God's unchangeability is determined by what we discover of it through faith in Christ. And this God is not the almighty incomprehensible First Cause of the schools, but a God whose mercy is from everlasting to everlasting. "Since that Day God speaks to us Himself through His Son and Holy Spirit. Now we hear a fatherly voice proclaiming sheer unfathomable, ineffable love and mercy, utterly nothing but blessing, nothing but goodness, sweetness, and love. *For that is what it means to be God.*"[108]

106. Ibid., 234. Note the latent assumption here that the traditional categories mitigate against what Scripture clearly affirms. This is an abiding conviction on the part of the various scholars who favor a divergence interpretation of Luther. To a large extent, the judgment is presumed rather than argued.
107. Ibid., 239: "Luther's struggles with the formal categories of Christological theory arise from traditional familiarity, not from evangelical concern; and he is therefore unsuccessful in reinterpreting the old orthodoxy in terms of his new and living faith."
108. Ibid., 240.

Siggins represents a minority voice in our survey. Like others within the before-outlined sequence, he insists that Luther rejects the doctrine of divine impassibility and strikes a preliminary blow against theology's long-tenured philosophical overlord. Siggins differs from many others, however, because he asserts this point in spite of Luther's treatment of the *communicatio idiomatum*, rather than on its basis. On Siggins's account, Luther is simply inconsistent. An unresolved fissure tears through the heart of his theology, separating its genuinely evangelical contents from the unexamined relics of a stale medieval Scholasticism.[109] Luther inaugurates a new, passibilist doctrine of God, but does not allow this revolutionary affirmation sufficiently to reshape his christological discourse.[110] He cracks the foundations of classical theism, but leaves conspicuous relics teetering precariously in their former place. The mixture is an unstable one. A purge would eventually become necessary. This has been the work of subsequent theologians more willing than Luther to extend the reformer's best, critical intuitions.[111]

Marc Lienhard's reflection upon Luther's transhistorical significance in this area is much the same. He is more specific, however, about what Luther contributes to modern theology and more optimistic about the extent to which Luther eventually overcame the internal fissure between old and new within the development of his thought.[112] On Lienhard's account, Luther's Christology is significant above all for its pioneering recognition of God's ontological historicity. This explosive insight confronts and

109. This internal fissure is illustrated by Siggins's statement that Luther's soteriological emphases cannot survive if the doctrine of impassibility is retained. Ibid., 241.

110. He will insist, for instance, that Christ suffers "only according to His humanity."

111. This interpretation bears a striking similarity to many of Luther's nineteenth-century interpreters. The reformation began as a movement, which should have precipitated a complete reworking of Christianity—a razing of the bastions. The effects were stalled, however, by an unfortunate lapse back into outmoded Scholasticism.

112. See, here, primarily, the section "Luther and the Modern Evolution of Christology" in Lienhard, *Luther*, 391f. On the "fissure" in Luther's thought according to Lienhard, see above.

moves beyond the essentially Platonic doctrine of God, which dominates the theological framework of Luther's predecessors and contemporaries.[113] In the modern period, theology has learned that "persons" are not entities defined by their possession of a "nature." Instead, persons are their "history." For Luther, then, the divine persons are simply identified with their economic interactions throughout salvation history.[114] Thus, Luther emerges in Lienhard's closing evaluation as an important precursor (perhaps the hinge point) leading up to modern trends in the doctrine of God such as historicism and the affirmation of divine suffering.

Axel Schmidt parses the significance somewhat differently, though Luther's Christology still points forward to decidedly modern frameworks in both theology and philosophy. Luther's account of the union of divinity and humanity in Christ, for instance, is proto-Hegelian. Luther describes the incarnation as a dialectical union of opposites. This is, in fact, his only recourse since he has jettisoned the classical distinction between persons and natures, which is intrinsic to Chalcedonian Christology. To be sure, Schmidt's appraisal of the innovation is decidedly pejorative, and in this he differs from many other scholars. In the end, he is skeptical whether Luther has the philosophical resources necessary for affirming a genuine union beyond mere juxtaposition. This reflects Schmidt's bias against trends in modern philosophy that others may celebrate. What is crucial here is simply that he shares the general scholarly opinion that Luther's adjustments to Christology carry with them a trajectory that leads forward into German Idealism.[115]

113. Ibid., 391–92.

114. Ibid., 393. This is a view echoed by a number of contemporary theologians writing in the wake of Karl Barth. One such example is Robert W. Jenson. For a helpful introduction to Jenson's thought, see Scott R. Swain, *The God of the Gospel: Robert Jenson's Trinitarian Theology* (Downers Grove, IL: InterVarsity, 2013).

115. See, for example, Schmidt, *Die Christologie in Martin Luther's Disputationen*, 323n.14.

Johann Anselm Steiger argues that Luther's treatment of the *communicatio idiomatum* only continued the historicization of metaphysics already implicit in the two-nature doctrine of the early church. Luther is significant because he carried this process into a position of more radical internal consistency.[116] The reformer's transformation of the early church's Greek metaphysics is thus interpreted with a nod toward Hegel, who would later take up Luther's theological mantle through his organization of history as the self-emptying of *Geist* ("Spirit"). Steiger is unique in the sense that he asserts here no fundamental breech with the patristic or medieval doctrine of God. The shift is not a revolution but, rather, a continuation of an ongoing process of metaphysical historicization.[117] Luther's significance, then, consists in the fact that he accelerates a preexisting philosophical transition. He precipitates a departure from the relatively prehistoricized account of God's being, which prevailed throughout the patristic and medieval periods. He nudges dogmatic development onward in the direction of modern conceptual frameworks (Hegel's in particular) that reflect upon the interrelatedness of God and man in Christ with a greater seriousness and internal consistency.[118]

Florian Schneider agrees. Because the unity of Christ's person is constituted by a linguistic concursus of contrary affections, Luther's view of the death of Christ is said to contain profound implications

116. Steiger, "Die communicatio idiomatum," 6: "Luther hat die metaphysische Ontologie der altkirchlichen Zwei-Naturen-Lehre soteriologisch gedacht und so die Metaphysik vergeschichtlicht und damit einen der Alten Kirche bereits begonnenen Vergeschlichtlichungsprozeß der Metaphysik konsequent vorangetrieben."

117. Ibid., 27–28.

118. A similar point of view that predates Steiger is an essay by Peter Hünermann, "Geschichte der Christologie: Geschichte Jesu Christi mit den Menschen?" *Theologische Quartalschrift* 164 (1984): 102–120. Hünermann also thinks Luther points the way forward in the direction of Hegel, but carries out his reconfiguration of Christology only incompletely. Luther's Christology of reciprocal exchange, it should be noted, is the logical link upon which this entire account of the reformer's perceived significance hangs.

for the very life of God.[119] In particular, Schneider's proposal highlights the fact that God also is qualified by the event of the incarnation and, in a certain way, actually dependent upon it for the final constitution of God's being.[120] "Through this linguistic activization and dynamization, Luther freed Christology from the labors [*Bemühungen*] of ancient metaphysics."[121] This conceptual liberation points the way forward to a more modern Christology with its openness to the historicity and passibility of God.[122]

The motif of an all-embracing break on Luther's part from a classical doctrine of God (as motivated by his Christology and soteriology) is perhaps nowhere stronger than in the recent work of Dennis Ngien. One finds inklings of the broader, synthetic narrative in the conclusion to his oft-cited essay "Chalcedonian Christology and Beyond," composed in 2004.[123] More developed, though, is the cumulative argument set out in the published version of Ngien's doctoral dissertation, *The Suffering of God according to Martin Luther's 'Theologia Crucis.'*[124] In this book, Ngien assesses the extent to which the suffering of God in Christ is constitutive of God's very being for Luther.[125] On Ngien's account, the doctrine of impassibility originates as the product of philosophical projection. It is a speculative conceptualization, which flatly contradicts the biblical testimony.[126] Luther, on the other hand, begins with Scripture and thus liberates theology from its "captivity to Hellenized or any *a*

119. Schneider, *Christus Praedicatus*, 184.
120. Ibid., 148. Schneider points here in a footnote to a comment by Eberhard Jüngel on the historicization of God's being.
121. Ibid., 354.
122. Ibid., 355.
123. In the last section, for instance, Ngien argues for a line of continuity between Luther and modern theologians such as Moltmann and Jüngel. See Ngien, "Chalcedonian Christology," 65.
124. Ngien, *Suffering of God*.
125. See a condensed version of Ngien's entire argument in ibid., 1–2.
126. See his characterization of theology before Luther in ibid., chs. 1 and 2.

priori theological formulations."[127] This means, first and foremost, that God reveals Godself to us in and through the sufferings of Christ, a suffering in which the divine nature clearly participates. Ngien helpfully summarizes the significance of this shift within Luther's theology: "Luther conceives the theology of the Trinity in such a way that it includes the Incarnation and Passion of God in Christ, not as an addendum but as ontologically constitutive of God."[128]

These various authors document the extent to which a divergence interpretation of Luther's Christology has funded constructive appropriations of the reformer's theological significance. Luther is regarded to be a tipping point in the history of dogma. He charts a trajectory that departs from classical accounts of the divine being and secures a historicized, theological ontology. What is most important to recognize here is the extent to which this appropriation depends and builds upon the divergence thesis, documented earlier in this chapter. In order to create the conditions necessary for an alternative reception, then, it is necessary to consider in subsequent chapters whether the three tiers of the divergence thesis represent a historically legitimate appraisal of Luther's theology.

An Agenda for Subsequent Examination

In light of the preceding documentation, a few critical questions present themselves as criteria against which to measure the divergence thesis's legitimacy as an interpretation and reception of Luther's Christology.

127. Ibid., 41.
128. Ibid., 151–52. Ngien concedes that Luther never argues that the Father suffers. Only the sufferings of the divine Son are ontologically basic to the life of the Trinity, in Ngien's view.

Does Luther reject suppositional carrying and displace it with an alternative conception of the hypostatic union?

The question is not whether Luther's Christology departs in any respect from late medieval Scholasticism. The focus here is, rather, more general. Medieval accounts of the hypostatic union are neither monolithic nor homogenous. There is considerable internal variety even among those theologians who affirm and make use of suppositional carrying as an explanatory mechanism. In one sense, to suggest that Luther continues in this line of analysis is to say very little, for the framework itself is subject to vast internal malleability.[129] And yet, the previous literature review suggests that much hinges upon this preliminary diagnostic question. Is there adequate textual evidence to postulate an unequivocal rejection of suppositional carrying?[130] Engaging this question will require use of a template. What are the central affirmations that characterize suppositional carrying as a general rendering of the hypostatic union? Which elements are essential to the concept in its broadest outline? As a

129. That is to say, while the theory does stipulate *some* things, there are many subsidiary questions that it leaves unaddressed—questions over which adherents of the theory in general can and do disagree.

130. This question need not directly engage the question of whether or not the rather critical presentation of Ockhamist Christology found in Schwarz is entirely correct, nor whether his pessimistic evaluation of the subsequent extrinsic relation between human nature and divine person represents an accurate depiction of late medieval thought. For a trenchant criticism of Schwarz along these lines, see Graham White, *Luther as Nominalist: A Study of the Logical Methods Used in Martin Luther's Disputations in the Light of Their Medieval Background* (Helsinki: Luther-Agricola Society, 1994), 271–80. There exists considerable diversity within medieval Scholasticism concerning the range of broader christological opinion with which the theory of suppositional carrying is paired. Schwarz comes close to acknowledging this internal variety in at least one place in his essay (ibid., 30): "Man kann die Intention der skotistisch-ockhamistischen Christologie anti-eutychianisch nennen und kann darin ein berechtigtes Bestreben erblicken, die in der Hochscholastik festgelegte Position der Subsistens-Theorie mit ihrem anti-nestorianischen Zug nach der Gegenseite hin abzusichern." Schwarz may intend by this statement strongly to differentiate a subsistence theory of the hypostatic union from later reflection upon Christ in terms of "suppositional carrying." Whether such a bifurcation is appropriate is a question we will explore in ch. 2.

subsequent exercise, we may then ask whether Luther remains within the general parameters of the theory, or whether he blazes his own solitary path.[131]

Does Luther's treatment of the communicatio idiomatum *apply "suffering" to the divine nature of Christ?*

This second question is relatively straightforward. Its adjudication requires an appraisal of Luther's treatment of the communication of idioms, especially in the works that flowed from his pen in the last fifteen years of his life. This focus upon Luther's mature theological output reflects the frequent emphasis among the scholars surveyed in the previous section on its internal development. Many interpreters acknowledge, for instance, that Luther articulates a relatively traditional doctrine of the *communicatio idiomatum* during the early years of his theological output.[132] It is only later in Luther's career that divine impassibility is expunged. This is an important concession. It concedes the fact that Luther retains traditional qualifications, which proscribe the suffering of Christ's divine nature for much of his life. In light of this concession, the majority of our attention will focus upon mature texts in which developmental accounts identify

131. This analysis will focus upon texts emphasized by Schwarz and other scholars as evidence of a fundamental divergence. To the extent that these texts reflect an ongoing commitment to suppositional carrying, the divergence thesis inevitably must crumble. Assessing the question is not simply a question of verbal acquiescence on Luther's part to medieval vocabulary, though that is surely a significant question. It will also be crucial for the next chapter to measure the extent to which Luther assumes characteristic entailments of the theory. A few examples of such entailments include: (1) an asymmetrical treatment of the relation between the person of Christ and the divine nature on the one hand, and the human nature on the other; (2) a use of "supposit logic" for specifying and adjudicating the truth-value of christological statements; (3) a denial that the person of Christ is a "composite"; and (4) a strategy of establishing the continuity of subjectivity between the eternal *Logos* and the incarnate Christ that depends upon a noncomposite understanding of the person.

132. Exceptions to this trend include the work of Erich Vogelsang and Florian Schneider.

an unambiguous departure from traditional norms. Like the first question, assessment here will require familiarity with late medieval patterns of christological speech. The alleged novelty of Luther's Christology in this respect hinges entirely upon whether certain of his predications stand outside the borders of medieval discourse.

Does Luther's soteriology depend *upon the divine nature of Christ suffering along with the humanity?*

This is a synthetic question. Critical assessment requires some apprehension of Luther's theological vision as a whole. The focus of chapter 4 isolates one aspect of this vision. It asks: Does Luther's soteriology require the suffering of Christ's divine nature? Many interpreters insist upon an affirmative answer to this question. On this account, Luther's soteriology lays considerable emphasis upon the genuine passibility of God in Christ. In order to assess this claim, chapter 4 will engage a set of crucial texts from Luther's corpus in which this passibilist, soteriological alignment purportedly surfaces. It will also draw more broadly upon a wide array of other texts, which provide substantive insights into the internal configuration of Luther's soteriological vision. Interaction with these texts will yield an alternative appraisal of Luther's theology as it pertains to the nature and purpose of God's involvement in the sufferings of Jesus.

The third tier of the divergence thesis rests upon the historical legitimacy of tiers one and two, and thus stands or topples entirely on their basis. Because of this, the present study will not labor the reader with any discrete discussion of an additional diagnostic question designed to secure the validity or invalidity of Luther's alleged reconfiguration of the doctrine of God. If the preliminary assertions of the divergence thesis are refuted successfully, it will simply be assumed that the "historicizing" reception of Luther's ideas is exegetically misguided. The final chapters will be occupied instead with the task of reimagining a contemporary appropriation of Luther's Christology no longer based upon the premise of seminal divergence.

Conclusion:
The Thesis Revisited

It is now possible to restate the central thesis of this study with greater specificity. The subsequent chapters will argue in favor of four implication-laden claims:

1. Luther's writings nowhere evince a fundamental rejection of the late medieval theory of suppositional carrying. On the contrary, careful examination of pertinent texts demonstrates an abiding acceptance of this general explanatory model.
2. Luther's doctrine of the *communicatio idiomatum* clearly and intentionally retains the doctrine of divine impassibility and nowhere endorses a *mutual* (that is, bidirectional) sharing of distinctive attributes between natures.
3. The internal configuration of Luther's soteriology presupposes and depends upon the impassibility of Christ's divine nature.

The fourth claim introduces a cumulative judgment, which draws upon the first three:

4. Luther's significance for modern doctrines of divine immanence has been widely misconstrued. His doctrine of Christ does not lend support for the contemporary promotion of a historicized

ontology of God's being, but points in a decidedly alternative direction.

It will be the task of subsequent chapters to substantiate each of these claims, and explore a few of the constructive implications that follow in their wake.

2

Detractor or Debtor?

Luther on the Late Medieval Metaphysics of the Incarnation

The "divergence thesis" has at its axis the contention that Luther executes a substantive reconfiguration of prevailing medieval accounts of the hypostatic union. This claim is the operative premise for all subsequent tiers of analysis, because it furnishes the conceptual point of departure that establishes critical divergence. It is the seam at which the fabric of antique metaphysics starts to tear apart, thus clearing space for a radically different alternative. Luther's "new" Christology is the stone that disrupts the placid waters of late medieval dogma. The significance of the initial impact becomes clear only as its embedded implications radiate steadily outward, reordering the very nature of theology itself. The shape of this narrative underscores the critical importance of the next two chapters. The analysis of Luther's Christology scrutinized therein stands at the very core of the "divergence thesis" as a whole. It is the *sine qua non* of the thesis's legitimacy, the evidentiary basis by which it succeeds or fails. The investigation that follows seeks to refute all elements which are essential to the core premise of seminal divergence. Such a refutation, if successful, will destabilize the foundation upon which prevailing receptions of Luther's Christology are built.

Because this first "tier" of the divergence thesis is twofold, its critical appraisal will be divided correspondingly into two major chapters. The present chapter measures the extent to which Luther accepts or rejects suppositional carrying as an appropriate model for speaking about the hypostatic union. The focus of the next chapter shifts to Luther's treatment of the *communicatio idiomatum*. In particular, it is concerned to assess whether Luther repudiates the doctrine of divine impassibility, and insists upon the suffering of Christ's divine nature. Both chapters will argue that the extent of Luther's novelty has been greatly exaggerated in recent scholarship.

Luther and His Late Medieval Context

Lying at the evidentiary foundations of the divergence thesis is an interpretation of Luther's Christology that pits him decisively over against late medieval conceptions of the hypostatic union. In particular, Luther is supposed to reject the Scholastic view that the unity of humanity and divinity may be understood as an instance of "alien suppositional carrying." Assessing the veracity of this interpretive claim will require some prior delineation of the medieval doctrine expressed on its own terms. This exercise is strangely absent from many of the texts surveyed in the previous chapter. The majority of Luther's modern interpreters are content to characterize late medieval Christology through pejorative monikers such as "Nestorian," "static," "abstract," or "speculative."[1] This tendency is problematic and obfuscatory. Characterizations of this sort presuppose a point yet to be proved, namely, that late medieval Christology is fundamentally bankrupt (for whatever reason), and that Luther does well to deviate from it.[2]

Reinhard Schwarz's essay, "Gott ist Mensch," is a salutary exception to this tendency. Its engagement with medieval texts is extensive and nuanced. And yet, even Schwarz's analysis is shaded by a decidedly derogatory posture.[3] Consequently, much of Schwarz's descriptive assessment is idiosyncratic when measured against the findings of contemporary medieval historiography.[4] This observation holds methodological importance for the next two chapters. It behooves present purposes to specify in advance what are the broad contours of the late medieval Christology from which Luther is alleged to depart. This specification will provide a reference point from which

1. See, for instance, Marc Lienhard, *Luther: Witness to Jesus Christ: Stages and Themes of the Reformer's Christology* (Minneapolis: Augsburg, 1982), 30, 387–89; Ulrich Asendorf, *Die Theologie Martin Luthers nach seinen Predigten* (Göttingen: Vandenhoeck & Ruprecht, 1988), 197; Vidar L. Haanes, "Christological Themes in Luther's Theology," *Studia Theologica* 61 (2007): 23–29; Florian Schneider, *Christus praedicatus et creditus: die reformatorische Christologie Luthers in den "Operationes in Psalmos" (1519–1521), dargestellt mit beständigem Bezug zu seiner Frühzeitchristologie* (Neukirchen-Vluyn: Neukirchener, 2004), 102–103; Athina Lexutt, "Christologie als Soteriologie: ein Blick in die späten Disputationen Martin Luthers," in *Relationen* (Münster: LIT, 2000), 205–207. To some extent, these authors document the importance of Schwarz's essay not only for creating broad perceptions about Luther's christological commitments, but also for establishing a lens through which medieval Christology is interpreted.
2. For a nuanced argument against the verdict that Ockham's philosophical commitments preclude his affirmation of Chalcedonian Christology, see Marilyn McCord Adams, "Relations, Inherence, and Subsistence; or, Was Ockham a Nestorian in Christology?" *Nous* 16 (1982): 62–75. For an examination of how this pejorative pattern of examination shapes the divergence thesis, see the discussion in ch. 5, below.
3. Reinhard Schwarz, "Gott ist Mensch: zur Lehre von der Person Christi bei den Ockhamisten und bei Luther," *Zeitschrift für Theologie und Kirche* 63 (1966): 289–351. Illustrations of this posture are provided in the section that follows.
4. For a devastating argument to this effect, see the interaction with Schwarz in Graham White, *Luther as Nominalist: A Study of the Logical Methods Used in Martin Luther's Disputations in the Light of Their Medieval Background* (Helsinki: Luther-Agricola Society, 1994), 271–80. I will also document several problematic aspects of Schwarz's analysis in light of the forthcoming survey of medieval Christology below.

to appraise the extent of Luther's dogmatic novelty. Limitations of space preclude comprehensivity.[5] The following sketch will concentrate instead upon the intent and intrinsic commitments that attend the doctrine of "suppositional carrying," broadly construed.[6]

A preliminary clarification is in order. Schwarz's tendency to refer to the "late medieval" or "nominalist" theory of suppositional carrying is potentially misleading. It could be taken to imply, for instance, that notions of Christ's human nature being carried by an alien *suppositum* (the divine person) are peculiar to "late" medieval Christology. Such is not the case. To be sure, nominalist thinkers make ample use of the descriptive model in the course of christological analysis. The doctrine itself, however, is much older than its appropriation among adherents of the *via moderna*. It is espoused by a far broader assembly of medieval theologians than the designation "late medieval" or "nominalist" can accommodate.[7] As we shall see, the concept of alien

5. This introduction does not attempt to make any substantive contribution to the study of medieval Christology. On the contrary, the description that follows is deeply indebted to the work of specialist literature. This indebtedness is intentional, as it will mitigate the risk for agenda-driven idiosyncrasy.
6. Chapter 3 will build upon this specification by engaging late medieval theories of predication, which carry christological reflection into concrete linguistic expression.
7. Because of this fact, we may dissociate ourselves from the closely related question of whether Schwarz's particularly severe presentation of the Ockhamist *reception* of this theory is accurate. This is because the endorsement of "suppositional carrying" is paired, in the history of medieval theology, with any number of variant attempts subsequently to specify the sort of relation that emerges between the divine person and human nature in the incarnation. Thus, even if we were to grant (1) that Schwarz's radically extrinsic interpretation of Ockhamist Christology is accurate; and (2) that Luther finds such a view offensive, we would still, on that account, not be justified in concluding that Luther obviously rejects the doctrine of "suppositional carrying" altogether, for the affirmation of the theory itself is broader than its particular appropriation in late medieval nominalism. This is not, however, *in any way* to concede the accuracy of Schwarz's interpretation of the Ockhamists. What I am trying to demonstrate here is that the underlying organization of Schwarz's argument in favor of his allegation that Luther rejects suppositional carrying constitutes a *non sequitur*, and that this fact has implications for the extent to which we must engage it on its own terms. The overall plausibility of his essay rests upon the following elements: (1) a radically extrinsic interpretation of Ockhamist Christology; and (2) an identification of this extrinsicism with suppositional carrying as such. Since Luther lays emphasis on the real *union* of divinity and humanity and criticizes doctrines of the incarnation that artificially "externalize" this relationship (that is, he rejects element 1), Schwarz's essay is able to argue plausibly that he also rejects suppositional carrying (on the

suppositional carrying originates as the product of a long-developing process of terminological refinement. It reflects an attempt to co-opt the vocabulary of antique philosophical terms in a way specifically calibrated for expressing orthodox Christology. In the language of Chalcedon, Christ is fully divine and fully human. He exists as a single person (*hypostasis* or *prosopon*) in whom those natures subsist inconfusedly, unchangeably, indivisibly, and inseparably.[8]

Expounding this doctrine within the prevailing philosophical vocabulary of the mid- to late-medieval period required of its practitioners an assortment of fairly complex, conceptual adjustments. A strictly Aristotelian account of the hypostatic union would terminate necessarily either in blatant contradiction (descriptive nonsense) or rank heresy (Nestorianism).[9] An important essay by

basis of the identification expressed in element 2). Although I think a good case can be made that Schwarz caricatures the Christology of late medieval nominalism (thus questioning the validity of element 1), the limits of space lead me to point out, more straightforwardly, that the identification of Ockhamist Christology (however extrinsic it may be) with suppositional carrying is false because many medieval theologians who were not Ockhamists assumed it to be true. This alone is sufficient to mitigate the major traction of Schwarz's argument. Again, for a criticism of element 1, that is, Schwarz's interpretation of Ockhamist Christology, see the afore-referenced section of White, *Luther as Nominalist.*

8. I am using Chalcedon as a baseline for orthodox Christology because this same approach is adopted by Marilyn McCord Adams and Allen Bäck in their fine work on medieval doctrines of Christ. However, there is a potential anachronism going on here. The reception of Chalcedon in the West is circuitous. Determinate knowledge of the council seems to have been obstructed by inadequate historical and textual information during the medieval period. These obstructions are mostly mitigated by the thirteenth century, but periodic clarifications were still in order even by the time Luther writes in the sixteenth century. For a discussion of the sources upon which Luther relied, especially in his 1539 treatise "On the Councils and the Church," see Dorothea Vorländer, *Deus incarnatus: die Zweinaturenchristologie Luthers bis 1521*, Untersuchungen zur Kirchengeschichte, Bd. 9 (Witten: Luther-Verlag, 1974), 34. See also Mark Edwards, *Luther's Last Battles: Politics and Polemics, 1531–46* (Ithaca: Cornell University Press, 1983), 93–96, esp. n.94. I am grateful to Gregorio Montejo for alerting me to the historical problems associated with speaking of the "reception" of Chalcedon in the medieval West without recognition of the circuitry involved in its transmission. For a helpful treatment of the major christological controversies leading up to Chalcedon, see John Anthony McGuckin, *St. Cyril of Alexandria: The Christological Controversy: Its History, Theology, and Texts* (Crestwood, NY: St. Vladimir's Seminary Press, 2004).
9. This is not to imply that medieval theologians sought intentionally to "Aristotelianize" theological discourse, or that their work is rightly understood in this light. It would be more accurate simply to acknowledge that their reflections upon traditional dogma took place

Marilyn McCord Adams explains why this is so.[10] According to McCord Adams, Aristotle's analysis of individual existents proceeds on the basis of a fundamental distinction between "primary substances" and "secondary substances." A "primary substance" refers to an individuated existent as such, whereas a "secondary substance" designates this existent's "whatness." It specifies what kind of thing this primary substance is. So, in the case of Socrates, a "secondary substance" analysis specifies the fact that Socrates is "human" (so, secondary substance = "humanity"), but the "primary substance" refers to the individual person of Socrates himself. This same distinction appears in alternative form in medieval discourse, with its language of *supposita* and *naturae*. Within this vocabulary, a *suppositum* refers to the primary substance, which "carries" (*suppono*) a generic secondary substance into individuated existence.[11] A *nature*, on the other hand, denotes the secondary substance, which is thus "carried."

Salient for the purposes of the present survey is McCord Adams's contention that for Aristotle there is always a one-to-one ratio between primary and secondary substances within an individual existent.[12] The man Socrates's secondary substance (his humanity) reflects essentially what he is (human). The notion that an individual

within a definite philosophical context that, in the mid- to late-medieval period anyway, was heavily influenced by Aristotle, and, as a result, their treatment of Christology in particular reflects a decisively Aristotelian vocabulary. The main point of this survey, though, is not how *Aristotelian* the medieval theologians are, but how extensively they calibrate and modify Aristotle's philosophy in order to express a traditional doctrine of the hypostatic union. For a succinct summary of the theological dilemma that emerges from Aristotle's views, see Marilyn McCord Adams, "What's Metaphysically Special about Supposits? Some Medieval Variations on Aristotelian Substance," *Aristotelian Society Supplementary Volume* 79 (2005): 30.

10. Ibid., 16. See also Marilyn McCord Adams, *Christ and Horrors: The Coherence of Christology*, Current Issues in Theology (Cambridge: Cambridge University Press, 2006), 110–14. I am relying, to a great extent, upon McCord Adams's description of this philosophical framework.
11. Another, brief explanation of this vocabulary appears in Armand Maurer, *Medieval Philosophy: An Introduction*, 2d ed. (Toronto: Pontifical Institute of Mediaeval Studies, 1982), 177.
12. McCord Adams, *Christ and Horrors*, 110f.

person (like Christ) could possess two natures, or secondary substances, would entail, for Aristotle, one of two logical consequences. On the one hand, insofar as Christ is truly just one primary substance or *suppositum* (as Chalcedon demands), the assertion that Christ simultaneously possesses two natures (or "secondary substances") collapses into sheer contradiction. No primary substance can be, as to its essence, two "kinds" of things simultaneously. As McCord Adams illustrates, "Beulah the cow" simply *cannot* be, at the same time and in exactly the same way, "Beulah the donkey."[13] For Aristotle, the notion of a two-natured *suppositum* would be tantamount to the self-contradictory idea of a "square-circle." In a strictly Aristotelian environment, the existence of two secondary substances simply entails two corresponding primary substances.

Under the constraints of this logical impasse, one could seek, then, to resolve the contradiction by embracing a second purely Aristotelian alternative and concede that Christ is actually somehow two persons or two supposits that exist beside one another, one divine and the other human. This option avoids contradiction to be sure, but resolves the problem (from the perspective of Chalcedonian orthodoxy, at least) in a decidedly heretical direction. Orthodoxy demands that Christ be one person. Otherwise, one invites a Nestorian bifurcation of Christ into two acting subjects. Since the two "strictly Aristotelian" options terminate in either contradiction (that is, simply asserting nonsense) or heresy (allowing the philosophical vocabulary to corrupt Christian content), it is understandable that the medieval theologians deemed this philosophical framework to require a bit of creative tweaking in order for it to comport with their theological intentions.[14]

13. Ibid., 110–11.

According to McCord Adams, it is Boethius (c. 480–525) who first attempts to apply the conceptual vocabulary of Aristotle's *Categories* beyond the realm of earthly existents, to which Aristotle thought their viability restricted.[15] Boethius extends Aristotle's descriptive grammar to characterize objects of theological reflection as well.[16] In order to do this, he suggests that Christian theology should conceptualize the union of God and man in Christ as a unique event in which the divine *suppositum* (that is, the second person of the Trinity) assumes to itself not a self-individuated human person, but an otherwise intact human nature. That is, while Boethius may not deny the general viability of Aristotle's prescriptive one-to-one ratio between primary and secondary substances, the incarnation represents for him at least one instance in which this otherwise predictable pattern is strangely interrupted. In the hypostatic union, the one primary substance (supposit) of the second person of the Trinity "carries" into discrete expression not only its own nature, but also the human nature of Christ, which would ordinarily be its own *suppositum*, but in this case depends upon the divine Word in a relation of "alien suppositional carrying."[17] Boethius evidently

14. The extent and depth of this conceptual tweaking goes beyond what we are able to detail here. For a more nuanced presentation, see McCord Adams, "What's Metaphysically Special about Supposits?" 15–52. See also idem, *Christ and Horrors*, 124.
15. We also see the influence of the Aristotelian inheritance in Boethius's definition of a person as an "individual substance of a rational nature." In this case, the term *substance* refers to the concept of a primary substance described above.
16. Boethius was a late patristic theologian whose work would later be highly influential for the scholastic theologians of the medieval West. My presentation of Boethius's significance depends here upon McCord Adams, "What's Metaphysically Special about Supposits?" 16, 22–25.
17. Speaking more accurately, the divine nature *is its own suppositum*. The distinction between primary and secondary substance as invoked here is not meant to imply the presumption of a generic category of "God-ness" in which the three persons of the Trinity share equally. To do so would suggest a "quaternity" and the theologians of both the patristic and medieval periods avoided such a connotation on both philosophical and theological grounds. As we have already mentioned, this way of describing the incarnation is actually impossible within a consistently Aristotelian framework. See McCord Adams, "What's Metaphysically Special about Supposits?" 32–33. See also idem, *Christ and Horrors*, 111: "Unmodified Aristotelian essentialism raises a problem for how a substance individual could have two substance-natures *essentially*, in such

views the Aristotelian framework as furnishing a useful vocabulary for articulating of the Christian confession that God became man in Christ within Chalcedonian parameters.[18]

This quasi-Aristotelian grammar would later become a mainstay in medieval reflection upon the person of Christ.[19] Amidst a host of other disagreements and differences, this general framework is shared by thinkers as diverse as Thomas Aquinas, Bonaventure, Duns Scotus, William of Ockham, Gabriel Biel, and a host of others. Speaking in a general sense, the broad intent of the mechanism is to speak of the incarnation in a way that respects four directive criteria: (1) a genuine union of two fully intact natures (divine and human); (2) within a single, undivided person; (3) without the entailment of blatant contradiction; and (4) without the entailment of any "ontological conditioning" or "fundamental change" to the divine nature.[20] The following working definition may be ventured:

> The medieval account of the hypostatic union as "suppositional carrying" reflects the attempt to articulate a Chalcedonian understanding of Christ (that is, two complete natures united in but one person) through a tailored application of Aristotelian philosophical vocabulary in which the self-suppositing divine nature is said to assume an intact human nature, which would, under normal circumstances exist on the basis of its own individuating self-supposition; but in this unique

a way that it could not exist without them. Unmodified Aristotelian essentialism rests here, because it doesn't envision any other way for a substance individual to have or be characterized by a substance-kind."

18. See McCord Adams's detailed presentation of how Scotus and Ockham explore this "exception" in her afore-referenced essay "What's Metaphysically Special about Supposits?" As she comments in an earlier essay, these complexities sprout from the distinction medieval explanations of the incarnation create between "being an individual created substance nature and being a suppositum of such a nature." Marilyn McCord Adams, "The Metaphysics of the Incarnation in Some Fourteenth-Century Franciscans," in *Essays Honoring Allan B. Wolter*, ed. William A. Frank and Girard J. Etzkorn (St. Bonaventure, NY: Franciscan Institute, 1985), 26.
19. This is not to imply universal acceptance.
20. On the use of qualification in medieval Christology as a means of bypassing contradiction, see Allan T. Bäck, "Aquinas on the Incarnation," *New Scholasticism* 56 (1982): 127–45; and idem, "Scotus on the Consistency of the Incarnation and the Trinity," *Vivarium* 36 (1998): 83–107. For a discussion of the fourth desideratum, see McCord Adams, *Christ and Horrors*, 125–27.

> case, is sustained instead by the *divine suppositum* in a relationship of *alien suppositional carrying*. Medieval versions of this account are additionally supervised by a consistent desire to avoid: (1) the proliferation of blatant contradiction; and (2) the suggestion that the divine nature (or divine person) incurs ontological change as the result of this unique relationship.[21]

This synopsis provides us with a heuristic definition of suppositional carrying. The model is not microdeterminate. Considerable space remains for internal variation on various aspects of christological inquiry.[22]

This is precisely the point at which Schwarz's essay stumbles. He overstates the extent to which the explanatory model of suppositional carrying predetermines a host of theological conclusions and presuppositions. For instance, Schwarz operates on the assumption that this theory only leaves space for a rather anemic account of actual union. On his reading, suppositional carrying begins with the premise that humanity and divinity are philosophically estranged from one another.[23] Schwarz's overdeterminate rendering of

21. I emphasize the qualifier *medieval* here, because both Richard Cross and Marilyn McCord Adams defend a doctrine of suppositional carrying for use in modern theology, but suggest it be paired with a doctrine of God no longer bound to the presupposition of divine impassibility. Thus, my claim here (and in ch. 1) is not that it is *impossible* to affirm suppositional carrying and not retain a doctrine of divine impassibility. My argument is based upon the fact that Schwarz and others interpret Luther's alleged rejection of divine impassibility to require an overthrow of the medieval doctrine of the hypostatic union. In response, I mean simply to prove that: (1) Luther does not reject suppositional carrying; and that (2) his articulation of it, unlike Cross and McCord Adams, retains the traditional doctrine of divine impassibility that, in the medieval period, supervised the modalities of its expression. The argument, then, is intentionally cumulative. Merely disproving Luther's rejection of suppositional carrying would not entail his retention of divine impassibility—a point both Cross and McCord Adams's constructive work demonstrates. This is not intended to function as a *comprehensive* definition of the theory itself, but to establish its broadest boundaries. Our definition is considerably less determinate than the one presumed by Schwarz, but his interpretation of Luther's Christology would still place Luther at odds with our broader characterization (especially with respect to the fourth criterion). Whether or not this interpretation is accurate will be the question pursued in a subsequent section of this chapter.
22. Consider, for instance, the extent of variation painstakingly chronicled in Richard Cross's book *The Metaphysics of the Incarnation: Thomas Aquinas to Duns Scotus* (New York: Oxford University Press, 2002).

suppositional carrying is rhetorically compelling. It encourages his readers to agree that Luther *must* have rejected late medieval models to the extent that he insists upon a genuine and robust union between God and man in Christ. On Schwarz's account, the deviation appears obvious because his idiosyncratic interpretation of suppositional carrying practically prohibits this affirmation.

But Schwarz's pejorative presentation of suppositional carrying assumes too much. The contrast only works if we accept the strange premise that medieval theologians accepted a descriptive model altogether incapable of substantively affirming the incarnation. A broader and less agenda-driven account of suppositional carrying creates space for a renovated appraisal of the relation between Luther and his late medieval teachers. The following section pursues this reappraisal. It seeks to evaluate whether or not Luther actually departs from suppositional carrying as specified above. This question will be adjudicated not only on the basis of explicit statements about the theory from his writings, but also by discerning the extent to which Luther honors the directive criteria identified above as representative of generic "medieval intent."[24]

Luther and Suppositional Carrying

At the headwaters of the divergence thesis's evidence is a specific set of texts in which Luther seems explicitly to take up cudgels against the doctrine of suppositional carrying by criticizing one of its essential elements. Without question, the most important text in

23. See Schwarz, "Gott ist Mensch," 293–98.
24. Again, I am not claiming here that the fourfold definition provided above furnishes a comprehensive summation of medieval christological intent. Instead, it seeks to articulate the broad commitments to which medieval theologians understood themselves responsible, and emphasizes especially those aspects of these commitments to which divergence interpreters would ordinary assume Luther to object.

this respect comes from the disputation "De divinitate et humanitate Christi," held at the University of Wittenberg in February of 1540.[25] The original composition of this disputation was provoked by the opinions of one Caspar Schwenckfeld (1489–1561), a so-called radical reformer, who insisted that that it is erroneous to refer to Christ as a "creature."[26] Luther takes exception to Schwenckfeld's criticism and responds as one motivated to quell its apparently burgeoning influence. He responds to Schwenckfeld's criticisms in the disputation by concentrating on questions of theological language and christological rules of predication. From this semipolemical vantage point, Luther also reflects upon the nature of the hypostatic union, whose ontological uniqueness is the source of the linguistic complexity he hopes to clarify.[27]

Luther's fundamental response to Schwenckfeld is that his criticisms miss their mark. They presume a doctrinal meaning that the phrase "Christ is a creature" does not actually convey. Schwenckfeld errs in this way because he does not understand christological speech, which is always prone to misinterpretation when dogmatic intent is wholly ignored. Even an author whose intent is identifiably orthodox can have his words twisted into the defense of rank heresy. Such ambiguity will always exist, in Luther's judgment, because human speech can never perfectly encapsulate or reflect its theological subject matter. In order to document this

25. Martin Luther, "De divinitate et humanitate Christi," WA 39/II:92–121.

26. Schwenckfeld also seems to have asserted the noncreatureliness of Christ's glorified *humanity*. For more on Caspar Schwenckfeld, see Mitchell Tolpingrud, "Luther's Disputation Concerning the Divinity and the Humanity of Christ" *Lutheran Quarterly* 10 (1996): 151; Paul L. Maier, *Caspar Schwenckfeld on the Person and Work of Christ: A Study of Schwenckfeldian Theology at Its Core* (Assen: Van Gorcum, 1959); R. Emmet McLaughlin, *Caspar Schwenckfeld, Reluctant Radical: His Life to 1540*, Yale Historical Publications 134 (New Haven: Yale University Press, 1986). For Luther's precise treatment of christological predication, see chapter 3.

27. Thus, not unlike the medieval theologians surveyed above, the question of language and "proper predication" is inextricably linked with Luther's understanding of Christology in general.

phenomenon, he furnishes a litany of statements from traditional sources, which enlist descriptive language that carries with it latent connotations or trajectories that could be deemed theologically problematic. It is from this litany of examples that the main evidence in favor of Luther's explicit rejection of suppositional carrying is derived. In theses 46 through 48, Luther remarks:

> 46. But none have spoken more awkwardly [*insulsius*] than the Nominalists [*Moderni*], as they are called, who of all men wish to seem to speak most subtly and properly.
>
> 47. These say that the human nature was sustained or "supposited" by the divine nature, or by a divine supposite.
>
> 48. This is said monstrously and nearly forces God as it were to carry or bear the humanity.[28]

It is not difficult to understand why this text has been utilized so often to corroborate the claims of the divergence interpretation. Luther clearly identifies the medieval framework of suppositional union (thesis 47) and criticizes the image it evokes as monstrous [*portentose*] (thesis 48). What room is there, beneath the weight of this harsh repudiation, to suggest that Luther maintains any kind of allegiance to the late medieval christological framework appropriated during the years of his theological education? His comments here seem to establish the very opposite.

28. I am using in this section Christopher Brown's excellent translation of the Luther's 1540 disputation, http://www.iclnet.org/pub/resources/text/wittenberg/luther/luther-divinity.txt (italics mine). Another translation of this disputation in English is found in Mitchell Tolpingrud, "Luther's Disputation Concerning the Divinity and the Humanity of Christ," *Lutheran Quarterly* 10 (1996): 151–78. When available, this chapter will make use of broadly available translations of Luther's works in English, and furnish pertinent sections from the original text in the footnotes. WA 39/II: 95: "46. Nulli vero insulsius loquuntur, quam Moderni, quos vocant, qui omnium volunt subtilissime et propriissime loqui videri. 47. Hi dicunt, humanam naturam sustentari seu suppositari a divina natura, seu supposito divino. 48. Hoc et portentose dicitur et cogit pene Deum velut portare vel gestare humanitatem."

Such is the straightforward assumption of scholars who identify in Luther a fundamental christological divergence. Theses 46–48 practically provide the methodological premise of Reinhard Schwarz's essay. Because he assumes this text clearly demonstrates that Luther does reject late medieval Christology, Schwarz focuses upon explaining for his reader what exactly about suppositional carrying Luther finds so offensive.[29] Others, like Beer and Schmidt, suspect Luther implicitly to reject the late medieval model based upon their analysis of other elements in his theology, but turn to this quote for a final verification of the theological "breach" they allege.[30] In both cases, whether enlisted as a premise to get the argument off the ground in the first place, or as final confirmation of an interpretation advanced on the basis of other factors, theses 46–48 occupy a crucial position in the scholarly defense of the divergence thesis. But are Luther's comments here as unambiguously dismissive of "suppositional carrying" as it first appears? A reconsideration of the argument in light of its context furnishes reason to question the "rejection reading," despite its prima facie plausibility.

The broad intent of Luther's argument in this section of the disputation is to suggest and illustrate the fact that christological speech conveys, by virtue of its unique subject matter, a correspondingly unique significatory content, even though this new content is communicated through the very same vocabulary used in ordinary discourse. As a result of the underlying shift in semantic reference, one must be careful to avoid drawing the mistaken conclusion that theological language necessarily behaves or functions in the same way as its enlisted words and concepts function within mundane spheres of description. Schwenckfeld's reaction to the

29. Schwarz, "Gott ist Mensch," 301–302. See esp. n.43 in this respect.

30. Theobald Beer, *Der fröhliche Wechsel und Streit: Grundzüge der Theologie Luthers* (Leipzig: St. Benno-Verlag, 1974),413; Axel Schmidt, *Die Christologie in Martin Luthers späten Disputationen* (St. Ottilien: EOS Verlag, 1990), 234.

phrase "Christ is a creature" illustrates what can happen when this significatory transition of meaning is insufficiently appreciated. For Luther, Schwenckfeld errs because he interprets the term *creature* to connote a thing separated from divinity, as it often does when enlisted within an ordinary sphere of discourse. The glaring problem, of course, is that no (orthodox) Christian writer of the past defines the "creatureliness" of Christ in this manner.[31] It is malicious, according to Luther, to criticize theological statements on the basis of ancillary linguistic connotations that their authors do not intend.

The unique referential object of christological speech renders all human vocabulary and grammar finally inadequate to bear witness to its intended content. The mystery of the incarnation exceeds the grasp of reason and language. Because of this basic semantic incapacity, one could distill all manner of heretical meanings from even the most circumspect analogies and explanations, even when the intended meaning is soundly orthodox. Luther does not think that all descriptions are thereby rendered equally valid, but insists that the evaluation of christological speech must always account for intent.[32] After all, even an apparently orthodox formulation of words could conceal heterodox content, if the underlying descriptive intent or meaning deviates from the catholic faith.[33] Luther urges caution and insists that the use and analysis of christological speech always

31. WA 39/II:94: "21. Nam creatura veteris linguae usu et in aliis rebus significat rem a divinitate separatam infinitis modis. . . . 27. Qui enim dicunt, Christum esse creaturam, veteris linguae usu, id est, separatam, nulli unquam fuerunt christiani." Luther points out in the next thesis that an ordinary meaning of "creature" would be applied to Christ only by Arius and those who follow his teaching.

32. Luther acknowledges the importance of accurate description, and urges that only the most careful analogies be used among those uneducated in the faith.

33. Ibid., 96: "61. Tanta est simplicitas et bonitas Spiritus sancti, ut homines sui, dum falsa loquuntur grammatice, vera loquuntur sensu. 62. Tanta est versutia et malitia sathanae, ut homines sui, dum vera loquuntur grammatice, id est, verbis, mendacia loquantur theologice, id est, sensu. 63. Hic potest dici: Si mentiris, etiam quod verum dicis, mentiris; e contra, si verum dicis, etiam quod falso dicis, verum dicis. 64. Hoc est, quod dicitur haereticum esse, qui scripturas aliter intelligit, quam flagitat Spiritus sanctus."

requires a somewhat flexible analysis, which takes into account the intrinsic deficiencies that attend the application of ordinary vocabulary to transcendent subject matter. The identification of intent is a mooring principle of interpretation. The attentive listener refuses to allow the unintended connotations of an author's enlisted vocabulary to derail him from it.[34]

In order to concretize the importance of this kind of receptive flexibility, Luther provides a series of illustrations containing statements from past theologians, each of which attempts to speak coherently about the union of God and man in Christ. The unintended theological connotations that attend these various examples demonstrate, for Luther, the way in which the theologian's task must always limp and struggle along with analogies and vocabulary intrinsically inadequate to it. The intent of the illustrations is to document how theologians whose meaning Luther deems orthodox can nevertheless be interpreted in heterodox ways if one is inclined to quibble over the various unintended trajectories of their descriptive vocabulary.[35]

It is within this series of illustrations that one finds Luther's oft-referenced remark about the notion of "suppositional carrying" being somehow "monstrous." Given the overarching intent of this section, it now appears rather unlikely that Luther's point here is to counsel the rejection of this doctrinal model as a whole. Such a conclusion would capitulate to Schwenckfeld's inordinate policing of theological language on the grounds of its unintended heretical connotations, the very practice Luther seeks here to criticize![36] No, the main trajectory

34. For more on the precise matter of Luther's new theological language, see the subsequent discussion and attendant footnotes associated with Luther's 1539 "Disputation concerning the Passage 'The Word Became Flesh'."

35. Ibid., 95: "49. Sed omnes illi recte et catholice sapiunt, ideo condonanda est illis incommoda locutio. 50. Quia rem ineffabilem volebant effari, deinde omnis similitudo claudicat nec unquam (ut dicunt) currit quatuor pedibus."

of Luther's discourse highlights a methodological posture shared with his medieval predecessors, namely, that the analogical vocabulary of theological inquiry ought not be pushed too far, or carried outside the carefully proscribed boundaries of its explicitly intended use.[37] At most, Luther's comments about late medieval Christology reflect his recognition that the metaphor of "carrying" contains problematic resonances of meaning that ought carefully to be avoided. The pertinent question regarding thesis 46 and following, then, is not: Should the doctrine of suppositional carrying be rejected? Instead, we ought to ask: What unintended resonances of meaning does this description create? Why does Luther think that these resonances are theologically problematic? Does his caution comport with standard medieval qualifications, or does his critical analysis betray a fundamentally new theological trajectory?

These are the real questions that must occupy our attention. Advocates of a divergence interpretation will clearly insist that something disruptive and implicitly revolutionary is at work in Luther's comments here. For Beer and Schmidt, Luther's critical comments ultimately manifest the reformer's fundamental aversion to nonsoteriologically determined metaphysics, thus confirming their suspicion that he implicitly dismisses the distinction between "person" and "nature" altogether.

For Schwarz, the comments illustrate Luther's rejection of late medieval Christology as a docetic corruption.[38] Each of these

36. The reader will also note that two other analogies from this section are admitted by Luther to suggest unwanted consequences, but are a consistent and favored component of Luther's christological vocabulary elsewhere; namely, the analogy of fire and iron, and of body and soul.
37. See, for instance, Cross, *Metaphysics of the Incarnation*, 78.
38. Schwarz, "Gott ist Mensch," 301–302: "Es ist praktisch der Vorwurf des Doketismus, den Luther gegen die ockhamistische Christologie erhebt. Das Menschsein Gottes in Christus kann seines Erachtens nicht mit Begriffen wie sustenare oder suppositare humanam naturam gedeutet werden." Schwarz develops this interpretation on the basis of an earlier christological disputation of 1539. This disputation, and Schwarz's interpretation of it, will be addressed later in the present chapter.

renderings depends upon a perception of Luther's theological sensibilities as distilled from elsewhere in his thought. Neither appeals directly to the 1540 text as such in order to defend its construal of how Luther thinks the language of "carrying" is potentially problematic. The result is a hermeneutical spiral, which creates the impression of evidentiary progress, but actually only defers the issue in question to texts located elsewhere in Luther's corpus. If these "corroborating texts" themselves depend upon a determinate "divergence rendering" of these several theses (utilized as either the cornerstone or capstone of the divergence reading as a whole), then advancing a divergence reading of the 1540 disputation on their basis introduces a circular logic that tries to assume what it first must prove.[39]

But is the mere fact of Luther's concern about the language of "carrying" evidence of novelty? Graham White argues that the opposite scenario is more likely. In his book *Luther as Nominalist*, White contends that Luther's critical remarks in this section of the disputation comport rather seamlessly with a blatantly medieval (in fact, specifically nominalist) constellation of theological and philosophical concerns.[40] The latent risk with the language of "carrying," when applied to the incarnation, is that such an image suggests that the divine person would become a composite entity in doing so. On the late medieval account, such an implication is

39. That is, it risks creating a logical relationship of symbiotic dependency between the two following statements: (1) the 1540 disputation communicates a rejection of suppositional carrying *because ancillary factors in Luther's theology show this to be true*; and (2) ancillary factors in Luther's theology portend a rejection of suppositional carrying, *because the 1540 disputation shows this to be true*. The only way to address this potentially circular form of argument is to investigate each evidentiary component and ask whether either (separately or together) demonstrates the rejection of suppositional carrying attributed to it. If these components fail to demonstrate such a rejection, then the methodology will be shown to be misleading, and it may be concluded that Luther's explicit affirmation and use of supposit vocabulary elsewhere should not be dismissed so hastily as an accidental discursive residue denuded of its original theological content.

40. For White's interpretation of the 1540 disputation, see White, *Luther as Nominalist*, 231–98.

problematic for a number of reasons. At the very least, it seems to imply that the immutable, impassible, and simple divine Son is the passive recipient of ontological conditioning. In order to bypass this implication, nominalist theologians were cautious when using "compositional" language to delimit carefully its meaning so as to proscribe any unintended semantic consequences. As White points out, theologians writing in the tradition of Ockham tend to exercise particular diligence in this regard.[41]

Interpreted in this way, Luther's complaint about suppositional carrying expresses a theological sensibility which he learned under the tutelage of the very medieval theologians that Beer, Schmidt, and Schwarz assume him so ruthlessly to criticize! In White's interpretation, Luther's derision of suppositional carrying as "monstrous" reflects a theological intent wholly consonant with the Christology of late medieval nominalism. The broader context of Luther's comment buttresses the accuracy of this view. Throughout the section, Luther furnishes a series of examples, which create the false impression that Christ is a composite entity.[42] If White's construal of Luther's intent is accurate, then one could advance the case, contra Schwarz and others, that Luther is, in fact, nowhere *more*

41. Ibid., 254–55. For more on the language of "composition," see below.
42. Thesis 45 is especially clear in this regard, which immediately precedes Luther's depiction of suppositional carrying. WA 39/II:95: "35. Nulli enim fuerunt unquam patres aut doctores, qui non improprie sint locuti, si dicta eorum cavillari velis 36. Sedulius poeta christianissimus canit: Beatus autor seculi servile corpus induit, idque per totam ecclesiam. 37. Cum nihil possit magis dici haereticum, quam humanam naturam esse vestem divinitatis. 38. Non enim vestis et corpus constituunt unam personam, sicut Deus et homo constituunt unam personam. 39. Tamen piissime sensisse Sedulium, caetera carmina probant evidentissime. 40. Eadem ratione haereticum esset vulgatum illud: Tota trinitas operata est incarnationem filii, sicut duae puellae tertiam induunt, ipsa simul sese induente. 41. Ita scholastici aliqui, dum divinitatis et humanitatis habitudinem sentiunt similem esse unioni formae ad materiam, non possent defendi. 42. Alii contra esse habitudinem similem materiae ad formam, multo ineptius, si iudicentur rigide, loquuntur. 43. Neque illa consisteret, ubi divinitatem igni et humanitatem ferro similant, etiamsi sit pulcherrima similitudo. 44. Neque illam ferre liceret, quam Athanasius ponit: Sicut anima rationalis et caro unus est homo, ita Deus et homo unus est Christus. 45. Omnes enim negant, Christum esse compositum, etsi constitutum affirmant."

medieval in his christological predilections than when he cautions against the unwanted "composite" connotations that attend the language of suppositional "carrying"![43]

But is White correct? The opening theses of Luther's argument lend significant reason to think so. In this section, Luther enlists the distinction between concrete and abstract predication as a way of clarifying the way in which certain ascriptions must be applied to Christ.[44] While a nuanced discussion of this distinction's significance for Luther's treatment of the *communicatio idiomatum* must be deferred until the next chapter, certain aspects of his discussion are crucially important here, because they manifest an underlying asymmetry within Luther's Christology, which mirrors medieval, theological intent.

Luther is rather specific in this section of the disputation that, because the person of Christ cannot be identified with "humanity," the application of human predicates to Christ must always observe the semantic restriction that such applications take place "in the concrete." That is, they refer to the person of Christ, on account of something that truly belongs to Christ (his humanity). Christ, however, is not identical either with his humanity, or humanity in general. What is most telling is Luther's subsequent admission that this restrictive distinction no longer applies when divine predicates are in view, at least not in the same way. "In the divine predicates or attributes there is not a difference of this kind between the concrete

43. White's interpretation carries the advantage of contextual sensitivity since thesis 45 deals directly with the risk of some christological language to imply a composite doctrine of Christ. In light of this fact, one is led to question how likely it is for Luther to worry in one moment about implying composition, and in the next to jettison the very conceptual vehicle through which this connotation is avoided. For more on the complex question of whether Christ is a composite, see below. Ibid., 95: "45. Omnes enim negant, Christum esse compositum, etsi constitutum affirmant."

44. This distinction between abstract and concrete predication is a fairly prominent medieval semantic device enlisted to distinguish between property ascriptions that refer either to the person of Christ (concrete), or to one of his two natures (abstract).

and the abstract."[45] Luther's eschewing of this distinction as it concerns divine predicates reflects the fact that, unlike the incarnate Son's contingent relation to his humanity, Christ is identical with his divinity, just as the doctrine of suppositional carrying insists him to be.

A composite rendering of this text would only be "feasible," in other words, if Luther endorsed a symmetrical application of the abstract/concrete distinction. In that case, neither humanity nor divinity would relate to Christ in a relation of identity, because the person of Christ would itself be understood as the mutually conditioned byproduct of union. Luther forecloses this symmetry, however, and thus evidently understands the person of Christ to be coextensive with the divine nature, which assumes to itself a human nature. This exegetical intuition secures further corroboration in argument 28 of the public disputation's published transcript. Here, Luther attends in greater detail to the assertion that Christ is a creature, the very affirmation that makes Schwenckfeld uneasy. In his response, Luther tangibly reflects an ongoing retention of the doctrine of suppositional carrying: "But when we call Christ a creature, *we understand the divine person which assumed a human nature.* Nor is the creature in Christ the subject [*suppositum*], not even according to philosophy, but something assumed. Christ, being created, is not separated from God. Therefore he is not a creature in the old sense of the word."[46] So, although theses 46–48 may

45. Trans. Christopher Brown. WA 39/II:93: "9. In divinis praedicatis seu idiomatibus non est differentia talis inter concreta et abstracta."

46. Trans. Christopher Brown; emphasis mine. WA 39/II:118a: "Nos autem dicentes Christum creaturam intelligimus divinam personam, quae assumpsit humanam naturam. Non est autem suppositum, neque in philosophia, illa creatura in Christo, sed assumpta. Christus creatus non est separatus a Deo. Ergo non est creatura in vetere significatione." Theobald Beer, somewhat strangely, refers his reader to this text as further evidence that Luther rejects the idea of a divine suppositum entirely. Beer, *Der fröhliche Wechsel*, 408n.83. Beer overlooks the fact that Luther is referring here to the fact that the *human* nature is not a *suppositum*, the salient fact that complicates the semantics of the word *man* as applied to Christ, since ordinary usage of the term

create the initial impression that Luther rejects suppositional carrying, consultation of the larger context yields that Luther intends nothing of the sort. To the contrary, the christological disputation of 1540 only manifests the extent to which Luther continues to presuppose the medieval doctrine's fundamental accuracy. The existence of any divergence on his part must be demonstrated elsewhere.

Another source of evidence for the divergence interpretation consists in texts where Luther enlists specific christological vocabulary that appears to reflect a "composite" account of Christ's person. For instance, Luther will refer to the hypostatic union as a *compositus* (composition) or *additus* (attachment). He also occasionally enlists semantically related terms such as *copulatio* (coupling), *constitution* (constitution), or *coniunctio* (joining), all of which seem to denote either a unitive theory of dialectical aggregation (Beer and Schmidt), or suggest that the person is itself somehow ontologically constituted by the union of natures (Schwarz and Lienhard).[47] If proven to carry either of these meanings, this vocabulary would indeed clearly contradict the doctrine of suppositional carrying, at least in its medieval form of articulation.[48]

The rhetorical force of this argument is rather clear. It exploits an indisputable characteristic of Luther's christological discourse, namely, his occasional tendency to describe the hypostatic union with vocabulary that seems to connote a "parts ontology" of the incarnate person of Christ.[49] The fact that Luther even goes so far

does refer to a human *suppositum*. This point is pursued at greater length in the 1539 disputation discussed below. Beer's ability to quote this text in defense of his position is a function of the truncated form in which it appears in his discussion. From this response of Luther, he cites only the following: "Es gibt kein Suppositum, auch nicht in der Philosophie."

47. For the various citations highlighted in this respect, see Schwarz, "Gott ist Mensch," 304–305nn.55–57; Beer, *Der fröhliche Wechsel*, 327, 333, 400–401, 404n.81, 406–408; and Schmidt, *Die Christologie*, 237, 248.

48. On the distinction between union and aggregation, see McCord Adams, *Christ and Horrors*, 125.

as to refer to Christ explicitly as a *compositus* appears to cement the inevitable conclusion advanced by advocates of the divergence thesis that he clearly rejects the late medieval doctrine of suppositional carrying. For how can the incarnate Christ ontologically be identified entirely with the divine *Logos* (as this doctrine insists) if Christ is said to be a composite of divinity and humanity? Doesn't such a designation entail the allocation of some degree of constitutive force to the human nature with respect to the personal subsistence of Christ? Isn't this exactly what Luther means to express by saying that the one person is a composite, that is, constituted in some way by both divinity and humanity?

Such is the understandable appeal of those who argue for some version of the divergence interpretation. They contend that this vocabulary paints a picture of Christ's being that simply cannot exist within the framework of suppositional carrying since it entails a compound ontology of the incarnate person, rather than identifying the incarnation's active subject with the immutable, simple, and impassible divine *Logos*, who assumes the human nature to himself in a relation of suppositional dependency. The salient difference between these two perspectives has to do with whether the assumption of the human nature is viewed to be ontologically "informing" so far as the identity of the incarnate person is concerned. The strength of this construal as an interpretation of Luther's vocabulary depends *entirely* upon the assumption that the word *compositus* (and others like it) unambiguously conveys the meaning assigned to it by advocates of the divergence thesis. It must be the case that utilization of such terms necessarily denotes a rejection of suppositional carrying *ipso facto*.[50] This assumption, however, is demonstrably inaccurate.

49. One example of this language is to be found in a text from Luther's 1532 interpretation of Psalm 45; see WA 40/II:517b.

In fact, the language of Christ as a "composite" is a fairly consistent aspect of medieval, theological vernacular. Luther's use of the term *compositus* is not nearly so revolutionary as many of his modern interpreters suggest. To be sure, theologians of the mid- to late-medieval period sought rather assiduously to avoid any suggestion that the person of Christ is somehow ontologically constructed by the union of divinity and humanity. Neither were the medievals willing to entertain notions of unity on the order of mere aggregation such as one finds in the interpretation of Luther's Christology advanced by Beer and Schmidt. And yet, many theologians of the medieval period make use of the language of "composition" as a way of expressing certain aspects of Christ's unique identity.[51]

According to Walter Principe, the medieval tradition is indebted primarily to John of Damascus for its use of composition language.[52] His works from the seventh and eighth centuries are referenced rather extensively in Peter Lombard's *Sententiae*, the standard theological textbook of the medieval period.[53] This led to a fairly

50. Here, as in the case of the 1540 disputation, divergence interpreters seek to buttress the plausibility of their interpretation on the basis of other texts that seem to endorse their overall point of view. In some cases, Luther's use of this vocabulary is confirmed to denote divergence on the basis of the 1540 text itself. This sort of interconnectivity of interpretive claims makes the task of analyzing and evaluating the central argument in favor of divergence somewhat slippery. A careful reader will find herself directed (somewhat sporadically) back and forth between a number of (allegedly) mutually reinforcing interpretive judgments. The initial impression created by this approach leaves the reader with a sense that whatever claim is advanced in the main text is buttressed by clear texts taken from elsewhere in Luther's writings. I have tried already in this chapter to show a few ways in which this impression is misleading, since the texts cited are often far more ambiguous than their use as documentary support would seem to suggest. In many cases, the textual interpretations these footnotes presume to be true are themselves dependent upon the interpretive claim advanced in the main argument their citation is intended to justify. In an attempt to break through this potential circularity, this chapter attempts to parse apart each of the centrally constitutive analytical and interpretive components that together recommend the veracity of the divergence thesis, and assess their demonstrative value seriatim.
51. This is not to deny the fact that many medieval theologians were also hesitant about this language to the point of advising strongly against its use altogether.
52. Aquinas, for instance, specifically cites John of Damascus in the *sed contra* section of *ST* IIIa, q. 2, a. 4.

broad appropriation on the part of other medieval theologians. For instance, the twelfth-century theologian Hugh of St. Cher regularly refers to Christ as a composite person. Principe explains:

> Hugh of Saint-Cher is a strong defender of the concept of the *persona composita*; for him it is an expressive way of stating that through and in the union of the Son of God is really, physically united to human nature, and to a human nature itself composed of body and soul. For him—and in this he differs from Alexander of Hales—the composition evoked by the phrase is to be thought of as exclusively in the human nature; taken as a whole, the phrase *persona composita* indicates that the divine person is truly united to and physically present in a composite human nature. The Incarnate Word is not, however, to be thought of as a whole composed of several parts; if body and soul may be said to be parts of the Son of God, they are so only in the sense that the simple divine person, who adds nothing to his own being by the union, unites to himself a human nature itself composed of parts.[54]

So, although the language of composition is applied to the person of Christ, the intended meaning is actually restricted to the human nature, since the incarnate Word is itself not capable of any composition or change.[55]

A similar qualification is to be found in the work of Thomas Aquinas in the thirteenth century, in the *tertia pars*'s second question, article 4. Aquinas explains:

53. Walter H. Principe, *William of Auxerre's Theology of the Hypostatic Union*, The Theology of the Hypostatic Union in the Early Thirteenth Century, vol. 1 (Toronto: Pontifical Institute of Mediaeval Studies, 1963), 87. For specific citations, see n.55.

54. Walter H. Principe, *Hugh of St. Cher's Theology of the Hypostatic Union*, The Theology of the Hypostatic Union in the Early Thirteenth Century, vol. 3 (Toronto: Pontifical Institute of Mediaeval Studies, 1970), 147. Philip the Chancellor adopts a similar position. See Walter H. Principe, *Phillip the Chancellor's Theology of the Hypostatic Union*, The Theology of the Hypostatic Union in the Early Thirteenth Century, vol. 4 (Toronto: Pontifical Institute of Mediaeval Studies, 1975), 145.

55. Thus highlighting once again the normative status of the fourth criterion included in the original designation of medieval intent provided above.

> The person or hypostasis of Christ can be viewed in two ways. As it is in itself, it is completely simple, just as is the nature of the Word. But considered under the aspect of person or hypostasis, which means subsisting in some nature, the person of Christ subsists in two natures. Hence, although there is a single subsisting reality there, the style of subsisting is double. He is thus called a composite person [*persona composite*] in that the one reality subsists in two natures.[56]

Like Hugh of St. Cher, Aquinas affirms that Christ is a composite, but immediately qualifies the sense in which this description must be interpreted. Michael Gorman argues, for instance, that Aquinas makes it rather clear that the divine nature (which he understands to be equivalent with the divine Word) is not in any way changed through the event of the incarnation. God does not undergo any process of "becoming" as the language of composition could be taken to imply.[57]

Even many of the late medieval nominalists, whom Luther is assumed categorically to reject, continue to defend the descriptive value of the statement that Christ is a composite, so long as this language is properly qualified. Nicholas of Oresme, for instance, whose tractate on the communication of idioms (c. 1361) appears to have framed many of the late medieval debates on that topic, explicitly affirms that Christ may be called a composite, but insists that this may be said only according to the humanity.[58] Oresme carefully proscribes any notion that the joining of divinity and

56. *ST* III, q. 2, a. 4. Thomas Aquinas, *Summa theologiae: Latin text and English translation, introductions, notes, appendices, and glossaries* (Cambridge, UK: Blackfriars, 1964). For a helpful discussion of this article, see Michael Gorman, "Christ as Composite according to Aquinas," *Traditio* 55 (2000): 143f. See also Cross, *Metaphysics of the Incarnation*, 51–61, 197–98; and Eleanore Stump, "Aquinas' Metaphysics of the Incarnation," in *The Incarnation: An Interdisciplinary Symposium on the Incarnation of the Son of God*, ed. Stephen T. Davis, Daniel Kendall, SJ, and Gerald O'Collins, SJ (New York: Oxford University Press, 2002), 206–207.
57. On this, see Gorman, "Christ as Composite," 148–52.
58. Ernst Borchert, *Der Einfluss des Nominalismus auf die Christologie der Spätscholastik nach dem Traktat "de communicatione idiomatum" des Nicolaus Oresme*, Beiträge zur Geschichte der Philosophie des Mittelalters 35, 4/5 (Münster i. W. 1940), 15.

humanity somehow "makes" or "forms" the person of Christ as discrete parts ordinarily constitute a whole.[59] Despite these caveats, however, the use of "composition terminology" is approved for carefully proscribed christological use. Theologians in the tradition of Ockhamism admittedly tend to be rather hesitant in this regard, although Scotists are apparently less so.[60] Now we come to the main point of this brief survey: If compositional christological vocabulary is deeply engrained within the fabric of medieval theological discourse, then why should its appearance in Luther's writings be identified as an obvious novelty?

Axel Schmidt directly acknowledges the existence of medieval precedent, and concedes the attendant implication that compositional language does not necessarily evince a composite account of Christ's person in the revolutionary ways previously described.[61] Why is it, then, that Schmidt is so quick to accuse Luther of doctrinal deviation, when he exonerates patristic and medieval antecedents on the same body of evidence? The reason, of course, is because Schmidt already assumes that Luther rejects suppositional carrying. Luther's meaning must lie elsewhere because the fact of his divergence is presupposed on the basis of other factors. Here again, the occasional circularity of the argument for divergence manifests itself. What ordinarily would not count as clear evidence of a deviation from suppositional carrying (the mere use of compositional language) is admitted as such, because Luther is thought elsewhere (that is, in his late christological disputations) to embrace this deviation explicitly.[62] Theobald Beer,

59. For a description of Oresme's articulation of this principle, see ibid., 111. For the text of Oresme's explanation, see the edition of his tractate in the appendix of ibid., 7–8. This is a qualification that is later taken up by the late medieval theologian Pierre d'Ailly, among others. For an overview of its reception in later theology, see White, *Luther as Nominalist*, 255.

60. Ibid., 254. White's interpretation of the 1540 disputation leads him to suggest that Luther actually sympathizes far more with the caution of the Ockhamists than with the comparatively more unguarded use of compositional language enlisted in Scotist Christology.

61. Schmidt, *Die Christologie*, 249n.87. It is only fair to assume that Beer, Schwarz, and Lienhard are similarly aware of these antecedents.

although less forthright in his admission of medieval precedent for this compositional vocabulary, marshals the "composite evidence" in a similar way, by using the already-analyzed theses from the 1540 disputation as hermeneutical confirmation for his interpretation.[63] But if the 1540 disputation provides no such corroboration, then the secondary argument evaporates along with it. A careful exegesis of the 1540 text therefore kills two evidentiary birds with one stone.

Another source of evidence used to defend the divergence interpretation consists of texts in which Luther is alleged to embrace a symmetrical account of divinity and humanity as they relate to the person of Christ. Such an account differs from the standard medieval point of view, as we have already explained, because it refuses to differentiate between the distinct ways in which Christ relates to his divine nature on the one hand, and to his human nature on the other; preferring instead simply to assert their union in a more straightforward fashion.[64] The result of such symmetry is a composite doctrine of Christ in which both divinity and humanity exert a common constitutive role in the ontological makeup of the incarnation's acting subject. It should be clear why such a view is understood by advocates of the divergence interpretation to grate against the doctrine of suppositional carrying. For Schwarz, the symmetry of Luther's position is the heart of the reformer's anti-docetist correction of nominalist Christology. By according the

62. See ibid., 249.

63. Beer, *Der fröhliche Wechsel*, 405.

64. As described in previous sections of this chapter, the asymmetrical account of this relation in medieval Christology derives from the fact that whereas Christ simply *is* divine (that is, the person of Christ is identical with the preincarnate divine *Logos*), Christ is human only in the sense that the divine person has assumed into suppositional dependency a fully intact human nature. This suppositional dependency does not carry with it any notion of ontological conditioning for the medievals, even though they will still insist that the relation of "personal carrying" is sufficient for securing the validity of the incarnation. Although Schwarz does not specifically invoke this language, it is clear from his account that he understands Luther to reject this prohibition against ontological conditioning—a correlate of his composite doctrine of Christ's personhood.

human nature an equally ontologically determinative status in the existence of the theandric person, Schwarz understands Luther to override the philosophical axiom of late medieval Scholasticism, which stipulates an unbridgeable gap between divinity and humanity. For Schmidt and Beer, on the other hand, the symmetry of Luther's position provides evidence that, although he sometimes speaks as if he retains a traditional distinction between "person" and "nature," the actual contents of his christological explanation betray the traditionalist façade. The result of the distinction's practical betrayal is that Luther is forced to affirm the unity of divinity and humanity on a univocal metaphysical plane, thus necessitating his composite doctrine of the hypostatic union (through juxtaposition or aggregation). The result is a dialectical Nestorianism with oddly monophysite resonances.

Some of the evidence marshaled in favor of this allegedly "symmetrical" christological vantage point depends upon texts far more ambiguous than their use by advocates of a divergence interpretation would seem to suggest. Schwarz, for instance, lays special emphasis upon Luther's rather emphatic endorsement of the statement that "God is man," and implies that such a statement alone demonstrates an obvious fundamental departure from late medieval Christology. Schwarz reaches this conclusion because, on his account, the doctrine of suppositional carrying allows its practitioners to speak of the incarnation only in a far more logically circuitous and tentative way. Luther's forthrightness in these statements, accordingly, is taken as indication that he cuts through arcane metaphysical qualifications, which actually denude the doctrine of the hypostatic union of its fundamental content.[65] Luther is alleged

65. Schwarz, "Gott ist Mensch," 303–304, 307–308: "Dass Gott Mensch geworden ist, dass der Schoepfer und das Geschoepf in Christus dieselbe Person ist, gerade darauf baut die Theologie." Schwarz assumes that no medieval theologian could say such a thing, an assumption that the next chapter shows to be utterly unfounded. Despite this fact, one finds permutations of this

to stress a degree of identity between the divinity and humanity of Christ, which intrinsically overrides the asymmetrical distinctions ingredient to the doctrine of suppositional carrying. Luther's zeal for the reality of the incarnation leads him to transgress traditionally erected metaphysical borders.

In a parallel line of argument, Schmidt and Beer allege Luther's apparent elision of the distinction between persons and natures on the basis of his strident, and apparently unprecedented, identification of divinity and humanity in Christ. Taking up a designation rather common in recent literature, Beer and Schmidt suggest that Luther's Christology depends upon the existence of a radical union of opposites; and by this they mean to suggest that Luther's doctrine of the hypostatic union entails a fundamental contravention of ordinary reason and simply contradicts the rules of philosophical grammar (that is, the rule of noncontradiction).[66] Although many scholars appraise the resultant propositional paradox this creates in a positive light, for Beer and Schmidt it represents a desperate and ultimately fruitless attempt on Luther's part to secure a conceptually durable explanation of the hypostatic union.[67] This attempt is fruitless,

claim scattered across contemporary interpretations of Luther's significance. In its least guarded form, these interpretations make it seem as if Luther is the first theologian in the history of Christendom *actually* to affirm the doctrine of the incarnation.

66. See, for instance, Schmidt, *Die Christologie*, 202, 244–45. Schmidt's main evidence is that Luther asserts creator and creature to be one. Schmidt's rationale behind a decisively novel interpretation of this assertion (for surely he is aware that Christian theologians had been saying similar things long before Luther was born) is again the 1540 disputation, which, in his mind, expunges the possibility that this union could be envisioned in terms of a "personal" union. In other words, Luther must be trying simply to force a unity on the same ontological plane. Here again, though, if the interpretation of the 1540 disputation is incorrect, then this evidence also fails.

67. The alleged paradox has its roots in Luther's alleged attempt to engage divinity and humanity on the same ontological plane. Whereas the doctrine of suppositional carrying provides a kind of internal differentiation that parses this relationship, the "coincidence of opposites reading" rejects this asymmetrical arrangement and tries to stand the divine nature and human nature on an equal playing field. The resulting account of union makes it plausible to wonder how it is possible to maintain *both* sets of Chalcedonian proscriptions at the same time, even though most authors will insist this to be the case. Here I would tend to agree with Schmidt and Beer

because it implicitly forfeits the necessary distinction between persons and natures that any such explanation would require. The so-called identity of opposites Luther advocates is only a counterfeit simulacrum of orthodox Christology. It enables a hollow affirmation of union, which masks beneath its veneer a quasi-Nestorian fissure between divinity and humanity.[68]

In both instances, the argument depends upon the notion that Luther asserts something that is clearly impossible to affirm within a medieval frame of reference, with its decidedly asymmetrical account of the incarnate person of Christ.[69] Neither set of textual evidence succeeds, though, in establishing that something this radically new must be read into the data, nor even that it is exegetically plausible to posit such novelty. In fact, a consideration of Luther's allegedly innovative language in relation to its medieval context once again seriously attenuates the likelihood of such an interpretation. For Schwarz's argument in this area to succeed, it would need to be true that late medieval Christology is incapable of affirming the dogmatic assertion that "God is man." But doesn't such an interpretation

that there seems to be a necessary choice between either a kind of monophysite mixture of divinity and humanity such that the only differentiation available would be analeptic in nature (that is, one that must recall the prior differentiation that no longer perdures in any *actual* once the incarnation has taken place), *or* the union itself must be a mere juxtaposition or perhaps agential coordination of two fundamentally separate entities (thus, Nestorianism). Schmidt and Beer's problem, in my view, is not so much in their theological analysis of this view, but in their failure to see that *Luther* does not endorse it. It is understandable, on the basis of the literature predating their work that they would draw the conclusion that they do, but this study hopes to demonstrate some key ways in which this reading is inadequate.

68. This is an inadvertent Nestorianism. Luther does not intend to affirm two subjects, but the conclusion is entailed by his rejection of a substantive distinction between persons and natures.

69. The claim between these two groups is once again remarkably similar, despite the fact that they argue for radically different appraisals of Luther's alleged innovation. Schmidt, for instance, agrees with Schwarz's point that Luther is arguing for a degree of unification between God and man that is simply beyond the capacity of medieval Christology to affirm. Whereas Schwarz thinks this fact proves Luther's correction of late medieval docetism, Schmidt thinks his proposal terminates in philosophical nonsense and places Luther in the unintended conundrum of having to vacillate between either sheer juxtaposition of natures (Nestorianism) or a divine-human mixture (monophysitism).

strangely presuppose that Luther's Scholastic predecessors can't uphold the doctrine of the incarnation? Surely such a view is the product of Schwarz's own anachronistic prejudice, rather than the result of historical exegesis of late medieval views interpreted on their own terms. In any case, there is simply no evidence to commend the conclusion that Luther's statement, "God is man," implies a fundamental departure from the doctrine of his Scholastic teachers.

In reality, one finds that the phrase "God is man," along with others expressing appreciably more radical content, is the explicit object of late medieval assent, albeit always under the supervisory conditions of very specific qualifications.[70] Schwarz himself tacitly recognizes this to be true, as reflected in his detailed treatment of Gabriel Biel's interpretation of "God is man."[71] The pertinent question, then, is not whether such a statement ("God is man") is affirmed (for all orthodox theologians of the time period surely intend to uphold the doctrine of the incarnation!), but how it is interpreted. Schwarz seeks to dissociate Luther from his late medieval environment, not because one explicitly affirms the incarnation while the other explicitly does not, but because he thinks the late medieval doctrine of suppositional carrying impedes this genuine affirmation, and understands Luther's apparent rejection of it to provide a much needed conceptual course correction.

70. See the discussion of this phrase provided in Cross, *Metaphysics of the Incarnation*, 185–89.

71. Schwarz, "Gott ist Mensch," 322f. The products of this survey are the pessimistic account of nominalist Christology that we have already suggested form the baseline of comparison against which Schwarz adjudicates Luther's relationship to suppositional carrying. Space precludes a point-by-point analysis of Schwarz's view here. The question that concerns us is whether Luther's own view of this statement entails a rejection of suppositional carrying as specified above. For a devastating criticism of Schwarz's interpretation of Biel, see White, *Luther as Nominalist*, 271–80. White's argument in this respect provides further corroboration of the fact that Schwarz's diagnosis of Luther is incorrect, since he has skewed the data by advancing an inordinately pejorative account of Biel, only then to prove on its basis that Luther moves beyond it.

If this is the case, though, then the mere statement "God is man" in Luther's writing hardly counts as evidence one way or the other. Its presence is decidedly ambiguous so far as the question of Luther's alleged divergence is concerned. Like theses 46–48 of the 1540 disputation, as well as Luther's use of compositional vocabulary, its demonstrative value relies entirely upon a verification of the divergence thesis based upon additional factors. The same verdict applies to texts in which Luther is understood to embrace a doctrinally unprecedented understanding of the hypostatic union in terms of a "coincidence of opposites," as Schmidt and Beer contend. The colorful christological language thought to furnish evidence for this view is identifiable within the patterns of patristic and medieval discourse, and as such, cannot bear the demonstrative weight the divergence interpretation seeks to assign to it.[72] In short, neither proves a "symmetrical" account of Christ's person, as it might initially seem.

Perhaps most important to a "symmetrical" interpretation of Luther's Christology is a divergence appraisal of Luther's 1539 "Disputation concerning the Passage: 'The Word Was Made Flesh.'"[73] Rather like the 1540 text, the disputation of 1539 hinges on a question of theological language.[74] Theses 4–7 of the disputation

72. One very early instance of such juxtaposition of opposites occurs in the writings of Ignatius of Antioch. Note, for instance, the following christological reflection as quoted in Thomas Weinandy, "Ignatius of Antioch," in *The Zondervan Handbook to the History of Christianity*, ed. Jonathan Hill (Oxford: Lion, 2007), 51: "Very Flesh, yet Spirit too; Uncreated, and yet born; God-and-Man in One agreed, Very-Life-in-Death indeed, Fruit of God and Mary's seed. At once impassible and torn by pain and suffering here below: Jesus Christ, whom as our Lord we know." Bernard of Clairvaux (1090–1153) is also rather fond of juxtaposition of opposites language. See, as an example of this, the texts referenced in Walter Allgaier, *Der "froehliche Wechsel" bei Martin Luther; eine Untersuchung zu Christologie und Soteriologie bei Luther unter besonderer Beruecksichtigung der Schriften bis 1521*, unpub. dissertation (Erlangen-Nürnberg, 1966), 119.

73. WA 39/II:1–33. English translation available in LW 38:235–77.

74. For a helpful overview of the central themes covered in this disputation, see Reijo Työrinoja, "Proprietas Verbi: Luther's Conception of Philosophical and Theological Language in the Disputation: Verbum caro factum est (Joh. 1:14), 1539," in *Faith, Will, and Grammar: Some*

introduce a statement, which Luther assumes to have originated from the Sorbonne faculty in Paris, which argues that truth is exactly the same, whether articulated in theology or philosophy.[75] Luther makes it rather clear, even at the outset of his argument, that he regards this seamless understanding of the relation between disciplines as grossly deficient. Much of the disputation is occupied with an attempt to demonstrate why such a view is unsatisfactory, and to argue in favor of a preferable alternative. Luther's efforts along these lines are complex, and the development of his argument touches upon a range of far-reaching issues, many of which lie outside the scope of this chapter. At the heart of his counterproposal is his insistence that theological and philosophical speech must be parsed into two distinct spheres of discourse, both of whose contents agree generally with "truth" in a final sense (thus avoiding any notion that these "spheres" are mutually contradictory), but reflect upon the peculiar objects of their analysis in different ways and according to different

Themes of Intensional Logic and Semantics in Medieval and Reformation Thought, Schriften der Luther-Agricola Society, no B 15 (Helsinki: Vammalan Kirjapaino Oy, 1986), 143–78; and White, *Luther as Nominalist*, 124–80.

75. WA 39/II:3–4: "4. Sorbona, mater errorum, pessime definivit, idem esse verum in philosophia et theologia. 5. Impieque damnavit eos, qui contrarium disputaverunt. 6. Nam hac sententia abominabili docuit captivare articulos fidei sub iudicium rationis humanae. 7. Hoc erat aliud nihil, quam coelum et terram includere in suo centro aut grano milii." For a discussion of the actual historical document to which Luther may be referring, see Työrinoja, "Proprietas Verbi," 145–46. See also Stefan Streiff, *"Novis linguis loqui": Martin Luthers Disputation über Joh 1,14 "verbum caro factum est" aus dem Jahr 1539* (Göttingen: Vandenhoeck & Ruprecht, 1993), 72–90. Streiff argues on p. 41 of the same book that Luther means to attack a central tenet of scholastic theology in general. White and Työrinoja both suggest, on the contrary, that the discussion Luther is taking up is one over which there was much diversity of opinion throughout the late medieval period. In this light, both Streiff and Schwarz appear hasty in their attempt to distill here a fundamental shift over against medieval dogma in general.

rules of speech.[76] This overall proposal is reflected in the theses that circumscribe the disputation as a whole:

> 1. Although the saying, "Every truth is in agreement with every other truth," is to be upheld, nevertheless, what is true in one field of learning is not always true in other fields of learning.[77]
>
> 40. We would act more correctly if we left dialectic and philosophy in their own area and learned to speak in a new language in the realm of faith apart from every sphere.
>
> 41. Otherwise, it will turn out that, if we put the new wine in old wineskins, both of them will perish; this is what the Sorbonne did.
>
> 42. In articles of faith, the disposition of faith is to be exercised, not the philosophical intellect. Only then will we truly know what this means: "The Word was made flesh."[78]

76. That Luther wants to avoid contradiction is rendered clear in his claim in thesis 1 that one must uphold the notion that all truth agrees with truth. WA 39/II:3: "1. Etsi tenendum est, quod dicitur: Omne verum vero consonat, tamen idem non est verum in diversis professionibus." The semantic yield of Luther's proposal manifests itself in the notion of a "new language" or "grammar" whose words continue to signify the same objects as in their more mundane usage, but do so in a different way or with a new modality. Although interpretations of this phenomenon in Luther's thought are legion, suffice it here to suggest that Luther's concern is to reserve some continuity of meaning between "new" and "old" in order to bypass the kind of sheer equivocation that would cause theology to degenerate into linguistic nonsense, while, at the same time, insisting that this signification operates in a new way as the result of its referential transition upon a unique and transcendent object. Although Luther's occasionally sharp distinction between philosophy and theology has made it appear plausible to a handful of scholars that his thought produces a "double theory" of truth, such a construal succeeds only to the extent that the first aspect of this tension is either ignored or seriously downplayed. How exactly Luther balances his position between the Scylla of seamless univocity and the Charybdis of pure equivocation, and whether or not the result is logically tenable are not questions that may occupy our attention here. For a helpful treatment of the theme of "new" and "old" language in Luther's theology, and its relation to univocation and equivocation, see White, *Luther as Nominalist*, 177–79, 299–348; and Streiff, *"Novis linguis loqui."* Streiff, however, is dependent upon Schwarz for his construal of Luther's relation to late medieval Christology.
77. LW38:239. WA 39/II:3: "1. Etsi tenendum est, quod dicitur: Omne verum vero consonat, tamen idem non est verum in diversis professionibus."
78. LW38:242. WA 39/I:5: "40. Rectius ergo fecerimus, si dialectica seu philosophia in sua sphaera relictis discamus loqui novis linguis in regno fidei extra omnem sphaeram. 41. Alioqui futurum est, ut vinum novum in utres veteres mittamus, et utrumque perdamus, ut Sorbona fecit. 42. Affectus fidei exercendus est in articulis fidei, non intellectus philosophiae. Tum vere scietur, quid sit: Verbum caro factum est."

For the sake of focus, the following discussion will seek to provide neither a nuanced analysis nor evaluative appraisal of this programmatic proposal. It will ask, more modestly, what the disputation reveals about Luther's relation to late medieval Christology—the very question treated so prevalently by "divergence interpretations" of this text.[79] Such a concentration does not stray too far, though, from the central concern of Luther's argument. Christology occupies an important place in the argument, because Luther thinks it especially clear that the purported univocity of the Sorbonne's statement shipwrecks itself on the shoals of christological description. The centrality of this contention is clear already in theses 2 and 3, where Luther remarks:

> 2. In theology it is true that the Word was made flesh; in philosophy the statement is simply impossible and absurd.
>
> 3. The declaration, "God is man," is not less but even more contradictory than if you would say, "Man is an ass."[80]

79. For a treatment of the broader issues at stake (for instance, Luther's understanding of the relation between theology and philosophy), see the pertinent discussions in Työrinoja, "Proprietas Verbi," 143–78; Streiff, *"Novis linguis loqui"*; White, *Luther as Nominalist*; Christine Helmer, *The Trinity and Martin Luther: A Study on the Relationship between Genre, Language and the Trinity in Luther's Works, 1523–1546* (Mainz: P. von Zabern, 1999); and Bengt Hägglund, *Theologie und Philosophie bei Luther und in der Occamistischen Tradition; Luthers Stellung zur Theorie von der doppelten Wahrheit* (Lund: C. W. K. Gleerup, 1955).

80. LW 38:239. WA 39/II:3: "2. In theologia verum est, verbum esse carnem factum, in philosophia simpliciter impossibile et absurdum. 3. Nec minus, imo magis disparata est praedicatio: Deus est homo, quam si dicas: Homo est asinus." Despite Schmidt's suggestion that such juxtapositions show how Luther simply wishes to bulldoze philosophical distinctions altogether; or Schwarz's contention that Luther simply casts aside the restrictive framework of bad philosophy, we must observe that Luther is *far* from unique here. The very same line of thought is entertained, for instance, by the late medieval scholastic Gabriel Biel. See Gabriel Biel, Wilfrid Werbeck, Udo Hofmann, Martin Elze, Renate Steiger, Hanns Rückert, and Volker Sievers, *Gabrielis Biel collectorium circa quattuor libros Sententiarum: Liber tertius*, Gabrielis Biel Collectorium Circa Quattuor Libros Sententiarum (Tübingen: J. C. B. Mohr [Paul Siebeck], 1979), 174. Biel is acknowledging the objection that it seems absurd to affirm the incarnation, because in philosophy God and man are "*termini disparati.*" This mirrors the progression of Luther's argument in a 1537 sermon on John 3 that we will investigate in chapter 3.

How exactly Luther thinks the Sorbonne's account of theology and philosophy flounders christologically is made clear in the published record of the ensuing academic debate provided in the Weimar edition of Luther's works.[81] These texts show the heart of his criticism to be an accusation that the Sorbonne can sustain a univocal coordination of theology and philosophy regarding the statement "God is man" only if it admits two, basically equivocal, designations of the term *man*. Ordinarily, the term *man* refers to a human nature or a rational animal, which subsists as its own supposit. A "man," in other words, is a human secondary substance, which is carried into individually subsistent existence on account of its own nature alone.[82] This definition, however, simply does not work if transitioned univocally into the theological sphere. The incarnate Son of God simply is not a "man" in this philosophical sense since, on the scholastic account anyway, Christ is "human" only in the sense that the divine person assumes a human nature into a relation of alien suppositional dependency.[83]

It is therefore rather misleading to claim complete univocity of meaning between the following two statements: (1) "Socrates is a man"; and (2) "Christ is a man." The assertion of complete significatory univocity is inappropriate in this context because an important transition of meaning differentiates the function of the term *man* in both cases.[84] Albeit ostensibly slight in its extent, such

81. The Weimar edition preserves three written accounts of the proceedings. The discussion above will seek to avoid drawing any significant conclusions from aspects of one version or another whose contents are clearly idiosyncratic in comparison with its counterparts.

82. Marilyn McCord Adams points out that, in late medieval discourse, a "man is a nature composed of body and intellectual soul that is sustained by no suppositum or it is a suppositum that sustains such a nature composed of body and intellectual soul." See McCord Adams, "Relations, Inherence, and Subsistence," 69. The human nature of Socrates, in other words, *is* its own suppositum according to this description; see her further discussion on 72.

83. WA 39/II:10b.

84. This differentiation does not affect the truth value of the statement "Christ is man" in Luther's mind because it rightly names the fact that Christ, like all other human beings, is in possession of a completely intact human nature. This fact, though, does not necessarily mean that Christ

a differentiation of meaning forecloses the validity of any syllogism whose premises depend upon a consistently stable definition of the term *man*. If all this is true, Luther argues, the initial, programmatic statement affirming a seamless harmony of discursive meaning across the disciplinary boundary of theology and philosophy succeeds only by cannibalizing itself. The thesis of undisturbed univocity, in other words, depends in its execution upon an equivocation of terms. Such, in rather broad outline, are the grounds upon which Luther criticizes the Sorbonne statement.

The salient question, for the purposes of this study, is what Luther's critical view of the Sorbonne statement suggests about his relation to the Christology of late medieval nominalism. Authors who interpret the disputation as evidence in favor of a divergence insist that Luther's argument reflects a fundamental rejection of suppositional carrying. For Schwarz, the complaint about equivocation is itself intended primarily to express Luther's dissatisfaction with a nominalist account of Christ's humanity as a nonpersonal, ontologically noninforming accident somehow carried along by the divine *Suppositum*.[85] The problem with such a view, in Schwarz's construal, is that it fails to

relates to his human nature in exactly the same way that ordinary human beings do, a caveat buttressed by late medieval accounts of the incarnation in terms of alien suppositional carrying. Once this caveat is acknowledged, though, a theologian is faced with a significant methodological choice. Either one will try to ambiguate the ordinary meaning of the word *man* so as to include the unique instance in which the divine person assumes to itself a human nature in an attempt to achieve a thorough-going discursive symmetry between theology and philosophy; or, one will admit the different *way* in which Christ is called man, thus leaving relatively undisrupted the integrity of philosophical discourse, while at the same time finding a way to uphold and talk about the unique event of the incarnation. Marilyn McCord Adams illustrates rather helpfully how currents in late medieval theology and philosophy contributed to the urgency of this question specifically in relation to the vocabulary of supposits. See McCord Adams, "What's Metaphysically Special about Supposits?" Luther's treatment of the Sorbonne statement in the 1539 disputation appears to have far more to do with these methodological concerns, rather than with any attempt on his part to suggest the fundamental bankruptcy of late medieval Christology in general. To the contrary, it is precisely *because* Luther retains a late medieval point of view that he suggests a totally univocal position to be problematic.

85. That is, the notion that Christ's humanity is not expressed personally in the sense that the *divine* Supposit is identified with the person of Christ.

secure the genuine "truth value" of the incarnation. To be sure, the nominalists think that suppositional carrying enables the confession that God became man, but Schwarz deems the semantically circuitous way in which they qualify this statement to terminate in a kind of semantic illusion or betrayal. That is, although the medieval theologians find a way to enable assent to the doctrine of the incarnation, the actual contents of their view can really only affirm that "God is God" and "man is man."[86] All of this amounts, for Schwarz, to a theological equivocation of massive proportions. In light of this analysis, Schwarz understandably assumes that Luther's pervasive rant against equivocal language accordingly has as its final target a nominalist understanding of the incarnation in terms of suppositional carrying. Framed in this manner, Luther's argument would proceed basically as follows:

1. If a seamless continuity exists between theological and philosophical spheres of discourse, then all theological statements must fall within the boundaries of predetermined philosophical possibility.
2. If theological statements must fall within these restrictive boundaries, then the incarnation must be construed in such a way that avoids any true unity of infinity (God) with the finite (man).
3. But if the incarnation is interpreted in this way, then theology is forced into a logically futile attempt to affirm union (the doctrine of the incarnation) while at the same time actually denying it.
4. The result is an interpretation of the statement "God is man" (suppositional carrying) that denudes this confession of its actual content.

86. See Streiff's representation of Schwarz's argument in Streiff, *"Novis linguis loqui,"* 62.

5. Thus, what begins in an attempt to secure the univocity of signification between philosophical and theological discourse terminates in an *equivocal* explication of the incarnation.
6. Therefore, it is inappropriate to assert a seamless continuity between theological and philosophical spheres of discourse.

The problem with this construal is that Luther's complaint against equivocation in the 1539 disputation does not sprout from his underlying rejection of suppositional carrying, but emerges precisely because he accepts a late medieval account of the metaphysics of the incarnation as normative. By missing this aspect of the disputation, Schwarz's interpretation distorts, and very nearly inverts, the actual intent of Luther's critique. So far as the christological application of the Sorbonne's statement is concerned, Luther regards its claim in favor of a seamless continuity between theological and philosophical discourse as misleading not because such a view terminates in an unacceptable Christology, but because it artificially cloaks important (medieval) christological distinctions that he assumes to be valid. One clear illustration of this phenomenon is to be found in arguments 3a and 4, as recorded in the "C" account of the public debate.[87]

The objection to which Luther responds in this section is the assertion that the term *man* is, in fact, attributed univocally of God (that is, the second person of the Trinity), and that one may therefore licitly refer to God as a "thinking animal."[88] Luther's concern in this response is not to confute or criticize the proposed predication that

87. Public disputations at the University of Wittenberg were often recorded by hand by student attendees. The above sentence alludes to the fact that several 'versions' exist for some of the debates. Differences between the various transcripts are frequently minimal. In this particular case, the account labeled as the 'C' version is the source, which provides access to the theological rationale, which buttresses Luther's argument as reflected in the disputational theses. The particular section of this transcript corresponds with theses 3 and 4 of the published disputation.
88. As a caveat, it may be observed that the adjudication of statements such as this one (which may appear rather strange) is a persistent custom of nominalist Christology, especially in its extensive discussions regarding the communication of attributes. For more on this practice, see chapter 3.

God (in Christ) is a rational animal, but focuses instead upon the major premise understood to get this predication off of the ground, namely, the assumption that the term *man* is applied to God univocally—that is, in the same way that it is applied to human beings other than Christ. Luther addresses the point as follows:

> When I speak of God as man, I cannot deny that he is a thinking animal; here the Scholastic theologians have admitted that Christ was a rational animal and man. However, they distinguish senses of the word "man" and say that it is equivocal, so that, when it refers to anyone of the human race apart from the incarnation, it designates a person subsisting by himself. This is a philosophical meaning. It has another meaning when it is said about Christ. Here one does not interpolate that fictitious philosophical concept of a person. For here a new word is coined, designating the divine person sustaining our human one, as a white person signifies a man who maintains whiteness.[89]

It is crucially important for the purposes of this section to explicate the significance of what Luther is arguing here. Assumed in his response is the observation that an ordinary meaning of the term *man* cannot be applied without modification to the incarnate person of Christ. The reason for this is that an ordinary application of "man" designates not a human nature, but a human person. That is, it refers to a self-subsisting entity or *suppositum*. But this cannot apply to Christ, Luther continues, because Christ is not a self-subsisting human nature, but a divine person carrying a human nature. Thus, while we may observe that the term *man* continues to denote an entity possessing an intact human nature (otherwise Luther would be forced to reject the truth value of the statement that Christ is

89. LW 38:271. WA 39/II:10c: "Quando dico Deum hominem, non possum negare, quod et sit animal sensitivum; hic theologi scholastici concesserunt, quod Christus esset animal rationale et homo. Distinxerunt autem homines, et significat aequivocum, ut, quando significat aliquem de genere humano extra incarnationem, significat personam per sese subsistentem. Haec est significatio philosophica. Alia est, quando de Christo dicitur. Hic non supponit illam fictam personam philosophicam. Hic enim fit novum vocabulum significans personam divinam sustentantem nostram humanam, ut albus significat hominem sustentantem albedinem."

a rational animal), the relation of this human nature to the person in which it subsists differs rather markedly from ordinary usage. Whereas "man" usually refers to a human person, as applied to Christ it signifies a divine person, albeit one that sustains a genuine human nature.

The main point we must glean from this discussion is that Luther's complaint is emphatically not that the doctrine of suppositional carrying introduces an unacceptable equivocal representation of the incarnation, as Schwarz alleges. To the contrary, it is precisely because Luther endorses the metaphysical qualifications embedded within this doctrine that he counsels against cloaking these significatory qualifications underneath a misleading veneer of purported univocity of meaning.[90] The progression of Luther's logic, then, may be summarized as follows:

1. If the articulation of truth is exactly the same in theology and philosophy, then the common terms applied in each must share complete univocity of significatory meaning.
2. If a completely univocal application of terms unites theological and philosophical spheres of discourse, it would need to be

90. Schwarz justifies the transition of Luther's accusation of "equivocation" against the Sorbonne onto late medieval Christology on the basis of Luther's reference to Gabriel Biel in WA 39/II: 11c–12c: "Univoce homo sumptum non verum est in theologia, sed in philosophia. Quando vero aequivoce non subsistit syllogismus 4 terminorum, sic ipsi Parisienses distinguunt, et tamen dicunt, idem esse verum in philosophia et theologia. Cur ergo distinguunt? Si esset idem, deberet etiam esse univocatio, idem verbum, eadem significatio. Nescientes ergo, quid dicant, tamen distinguunt a philosophia theologiam. Alii sumpserunt hominem univoce, ut Gabriel, ille incurrit in hunc syllogismum: Omnis homo est creatura. Occam voluit, non esse univocum, sed aequivocum, ut aliud sit humanitas in Petro, aliud in Christo. Homo in philosophia secundum naturam suam non significat filium Dei aut personam divinam. Hoc idem est, quod nos dicimus: communicatio idiomatum. Syllogismus non admittitur in mysteriis fidei et theologiae. Philosophia est error in theologia." Schwarz's interpretation of this text wrongly locates its significance. Luther's point is not to encourage the rejection of medieval Christology on the grounds that it perpetuates an equivocation. On the contrary, it is precisely because Luther accepts the doctrine of suppositional carrying that he feels he must resist the claim that theological and philosophical speech are univocally related to one another. For more on the term 'man' within late medieval discourse, see White, Luther as Nominalist, 161–62.

true, for instance, that the theological confession "Christ is *man*" expresses the exact same content as it does when the term *man* is applied to any other rational animal.

3. This does not follow, though, since in the case of Christ, "man" denotes a *divine* person carrying a human nature; whereas in other discursive settings it denotes a *human* person subsisting in itself.
4. Therefore, the articulation of truth cannot be exactly the same in theology and philosophy.

The turning point in this logical sequence arrives in step 3, where Luther acknowledges a differentiation of meaning precisely because he takes it for granted that the Scholastic conception of the incarnate Christ as a divine person carrying the human nature is normative. Interpreted in this way, Luther's argument presents itself as more of a plea for discursive honesty, than as a revolutionary assault against late medieval Christology writ large. Schwarz's argument to the contrary represents a misconstrual of Luther's christological views. Luther's complaint against the Sorbonne statement is funded, not by his implicit rejection of late medieval Christology as equivocal in its account of Jesus' humanity, but by his fundamental presupposition of the doctrine of suppositional carrying as a valid explanation of the hypostatic union.[91]

Perhaps somewhat paradoxically, Axel Schmidt's treatment of the 1539 disputation actually reinforces this criticism of Schwarz, even

91. This interpretation, namely, that Luther's complaint against the Sorbonne statement arises *because he accepts suppositional carrying*, and not because he rejects it, is collaborated by other sections of the recorded debate, and is reflected in versions "A" and "B" as well as the quote from the "C" version provided above. See, for example, WA 39/II: 16a: "Ego capio hominem dupliciter uno modo pro substantia corporali per se subsistente, alio modo pro persona divina sustentante humanitatem. Est hoc, quaeso, theologiam et philosophiam conciliare, cum distinguis, imo hoc ipso, quod univoca distinguifices?" Luther also cites scholastic christological distinctions as evidence against the argument that "man" is applied to God univocally. See WA 39/II:10b.

though he also purports to find in the disputation evidence of divergence. Schmidt acknowledges that Luther's explicit discussion of the person of Christ in this disputation mirrors the late medieval account. This fact perplexes him because he has already concluded that Luther rejects late medieval Christology. Schmidt's solution to the resultant evidentiary quandary is to suggest that two irreconcilable strands exist within Luther's theology, and that each of these strands manifests itself in the 1539 text. Schmidt admits the presence of a conservative element in which Luther retains a basically medieval description of the hypostatic union. In making this concession, Schmidt inadvertently controverts the validity of Schwarz's interpretation of the disputation, as described above. In addition to the "conservative element," however, Schmidt also isolates a "progressive" strand in Luther's argument, which contradicts his apparent traditionalism. This strand is visible, Schmidt insists, in Luther's analysis of syllogisms within the disputation. Here we find an unresolved fissure between theology and philosophy, which Schmidt identifies as the source of Luther's doctrinal idiosyncrasies.[92]

Whereas late medieval thinkers customarily refute heretical syllogisms through an analysis of premises, Luther appears in this disputation simply to discard the validity of syllogistic reasoning altogether. Schmidt concludes from this approach that Luther understands the doctrine of the incarnation simply to contradict philosophical reason, thus yielding, as it were, a double account of truth. Christologically speaking, the result of all this is to forfeit any need for a distinction between persons and natures, since this differentiated analysis (once introduced in order to bypass philosophical contradiction) is no longer necessary. In any case, even if Luther desired this distinction, his antipathy toward even a

92. For Schmidt's argument to this effect, see Schmidt, *Die Christologie*, 202–10; 220–27. For the language of a progressive versus conservative strain, see 201, 283–84.

ministerial role of philosophically derived distinctions would bar its actual use. Thus, Luther is forced simply to assert a dialectical union of man and God in a way that contravenes reason. Thus, although Luther tries to speak like a late medieval theologian in certain respects, his antipathy toward philosophy introduces a bifurcation of thought that bears doctrinal fruit in an aggregate doctrine of Christ's person.

Schmidt's appraisal of the 1539 disputation suffers, though, from a number of exegetical deficiencies. Perhaps most glaring is that the entire trajectory of his interpretation depends upon the fact that, while it concedes Luther explicitly to assert one thing to be true (suppositional carrying/distinction between person and nature), it must make the case that the ancillary discursive furniture of Luther's argument implicitly proscribes his doing so. In other words, it is a construal that depends on adjudicating what Luther must be saying, at the direct expense of what Luther actually says. He overstates, for instance, the extent to which Luther's analysis of syllogism unambiguously denotes a wholesale rejection of philosophical reasoning within theology. Reijo Työrinoja, for instance, argues that the way in which Luther arbitrates syllogistic legitimacy within the theological sphere continues to reflect standard late medieval practice.[93]

Whether or not Työrinoja's interpretation turns out finally to be convincing is not a question we have space to arbitrate here. However, does it not seem far preferable to interpret Luther's intent in a way that comports with his affirmation of suppositional carrying elsewhere in the disputation rather than postulate the existence of two radically incongruent trajectories of christological discourse within

93. See the discussion in Työrinoja, "Proprietas Verbi," 143–78. For a helpful discussion of the artificial way in which Luther's view of philosophy has been polarized in much recent scholarship, see Helmer, *The Trinity and Martin Luther*, 50–56.

the same text? Schmidt's "solution," in other words, can count only as an exegetical avenue of last resort. The exegesis on which his view depends succeeds only by destroying the coherency of the text itself, that is, by presuming within it the existence of an irresolvable fracture of meaning. Ironically, adopting this approach violates a principle of reasoning famously defended by the very thinkers whose Christology Schmidt thinks Luther rejects, namely, that "plurality should not be posited without necessity."[94]

Conclusion

At the beginning of this chapter, we observed the fact that each of the major advocates of divergence acknowledges there to be texts in Luther's corpus, both early and late, that express at least superficial acquiescence to the language of suppositional carrying.[95] Despite the fact that this concession plausibly implies an ongoing acceptance of suppositional carrying as an explanation of the hypostatic union, advocates of the divergence thesis argue rather forcefully that Luther in fact decisively rejects this account in favor of a "composite" doctrine of Christ. They advance this argument on the basis of the following interpretive claims:

1. Luther explicitly rejects suppositional carrying as "monstrous" in his 1540 "Disputation on the Divinity and Humanity of Christ."
2. Luther clearly utilizes compositional descriptive vocabulary, which reflects an irreducibly different doctrine of Christ's person than the one endorsed in late medieval Christology.

94. See the reference to this phrase in Armand Augustine Maurer, *The Philosophy of William of Ockham in the Light of Its Principles* (Toronto: Pontifical Institute of Mediaeval Studies, 1999):51n.116.
95. Schwarz, "Gott ist Mensch," 305, 335–36n.156; Beer, *Der fröhliche Wechsel*, 406; and Schmidt, *Die Christologie*, 234–35, 241–43.

3. Luther asserts a degree of unity between divinity and humanity in Christ not possible for the doctrine of suppositional carrying to secure.
4. Luther's 1539 "Disputation Concerning the Passage: 'The Word Was Made Flesh'" establishes a rejection of suppositional carrying either: (1) by deriding this doctrine as an equivocal affirmation of the incarnation (Schwarz); or (2) by creating an antithetical relation between philosophy and theology to the extent that the distinction between person and nature is effectively destroyed (Schmidt).

In the course of this section's discussion, we have suggested that each of these claims fails as a valid interpretation of the pertinent textual data. The context of the comments in the 1540 disputation demonstrates Luther's focus to be upon the unintended consequences of semantic assertions he otherwise accepts to be valid, a point reinforced by the fact that the theses directly preceding those in question express primary concern about the implication of Christ being a composite being. The compositional language that Luther does invoke elsewhere falls well within the ordinary parameters of medieval discourse, and thus fails as clear evidence for any dramatic divergence. Similarly ambiguous are the various places in Luther's writing where he registers a robust affirmation of the union between God and man in Christ. Claims of this kind can count as evidence of divergence only if it is assumed that similar expressions of unity are simply impossible within a late medieval christological framework, an assumption belied by the actual christological discourse of the period. Finally, the 1539 disputation's central complaint against the Sorbonne's implicitly equivocal position is sustained, not by Luther's underlying rejection of suppositional carrying, but by his continuing assumption that this mode of christological explanation is normative, a fact made rather clear by Luther's designation of the "man" Christ as a *persona divina sustentante humanitatem* ("a divine person sustaining humanity").[96] Since all of this evidence lacks demonstrative force, we must accept the transparent indications elsewhere in Luther's writing that he continues to affirm the doctrine of suppositional carrying, and reject the argument that this verbal assent is merely illusory in nature.

96. WA 39/II:16a.

3

The Suffering of God in Christ

A Sixteenth-Century Breakthrough?

We now turn our focus to the second stage of the divergence thesis's first tier of analysis. The issue directly in question throughout is Martin Luther's conception of God's participation in the sufferings of Christ. A specific appraisal of this conception is crucially important to the divergence thesis as a whole. The core of this appraisal is an emphasis upon the uniqueness of Luther's treatment of the communication of idioms. Unlike the preceding theological tradition, Luther is alleged to insist upon a "reciprocal exchange" between Christ's natures. This means that there is a direct participation of humanity in divine properties and a direct participation of the divine nature in human limitations such as suffering. It is this second aspect that is deemed especially important. What may seem initially to be only a small and therefore inconsequential conceptual adjustment turns out to be, as it were, the modern camel poking its nose into the medieval theological tent.

For once the predicational asymmetry characteristic of a classical understanding of the *communicatio idiomatum* is destabilized, an entire constellation of theological assumptions appears ripe for reformulation.

First to go, obviously, is the doctrine of divine impassibility itself, since an impassibilist doctrine of God could not accommodate reciprocal, communicative exchange. This preliminary course correction, however, is but one small part of a much more profound recalibration, which theoretically recasts the nature of God's relationship to the world. This "recalibration" is precisely the doctrinal dividend advocates of the divergence reception generally understand Luther's christological adjustment to enable. Because of this christological adjustment, Luther is supposed to clear away space for a more adequate conceptualization of God's immanent involvement within the created order. The legitimacy of this "reception" depends rather directly upon the interpretive judgment that Luther's doctrine of the *communicatio idiomatum* includes a participation of the divine nature in the sufferings of Christ's humanity.

But does Luther predicate "suffering" of the divine nature of Christ, as divergence advocates are so wont to insist? This is the critical question posed here. At the outset, we must acknowledge that Luther's understanding of the communication of attributes differs in at least one important respect from many patristic and medieval antecedents.[1] For Scholastic thinkers of the medieval period, the *communicatio idiomatum* refers primarily, if not exclusively, to the predication of divine and human attributes to the single person of

1. Whether or not there exists significant patristic precedent for Luther's point of view is not a question that may detain us here. Certainly, there are many patristic theologians who envision a divinization of Christ's humanity that takes place as the result of communicative exchange. It remains a question for future study whether and how these precursors might relate to Luther's own view, developed hundreds of years later within a different intellectual context.

Christ. Luther often describes the communication of idioms along these traditional lines, but there are also instances where he introduces a second sort of application. In these contexts, the *communicatio idiomatum* describes the participation of Christ's human nature in predicates that belong properly to his divine nature. An obvious example of this appears in Luther's defense of Christ's real presence in the Lord's Supper on the grounds that the humanity of Christ could share in the attribute of divine omnipresence.[2]

The question this chapter addresses is not whether Luther occasionally interprets the communication of idioms as a sharing between Christ's two natures, but whether this sharing is presented by him as "bidirectional." Is there, along with the human nature's participation in the divine majesty also a real participation of Christ's divinity in the suffering vulnerability of his humanity? Theologically speaking, a great deal hinges upon the arbitration of this question. In terms of Luther's relation to his context, one may note the fact that, although his endorsement of a divine-to-human communication of attributes is admittedly somewhat "unique" against the backdrop of medieval christological opinion, this view by itself need not destabilize traditional accounts of the doctrine of God. There is nothing outrageously controversial about Luther's assumption that the human nature of Christ is both passible and mutable. In this sense, the idea that Christ's humanity could be "altered" or "elevated" in some respects through the hypostatic union does not fall prey to

2. For a thorough discussion of ubiquity, see Jörg Bauer, "Ubiquität," in *Creator est Creatura: Luther's Christologie als Lehre von der Idiomenkommunikatiofirsn*, ed. Oswald Bayer and Benjamin Gleede, Theologische Bibliothek Töpelmann, bd. 138 (New York: Walter de Gruyter, 2007), 186–301. The capacity of Christ's human nature to be in more than one place at the same time is not the only application of this communicative principle in Luther's Christology, even if confessional debates later in the sixteenth century tended to focus in upon it. The present survey accepts this aspect of Luther's Christology, but will not expend additional space seeking either to verify or expand upon its degree of importance within Luther's theology as a whole. The following chapter will, however, reflect upon the soteriological significance of a "one-way" communication of attributes between natures.

the same theological and philosophical restrictions that apply in the case of the divine nature. To speak of an ontologically conditioning participation of the humanity in the majesty of God initiates no essential contradictions so far as longstanding conceptions of "human nature" are concerned.[3]

To speak of an ontologically conditioning participation of divinity in the death and suffering of humanity, however, fundamentally contradicts longstanding conceptions of divinity. That is, a two-way rendering of the communication of idioms entails severing a number of conceptual moorings intrinsic to the classically developed doctrine of God, a point outlined earlier. The salient question here is whether Luther endorses, in addition to his ordinary analysis of the *communicatio idiomatum* as a reference to the mutual application of predicates to the single person of Christ, a one-way or two-way doctrine of communicative sharing between Christ's humanity and

3. That is, insofar as this "ontological conditioning" avoids the implication that Christ's genuine humanity is somehow dissolved or transformed through metamorphosis into something other than really human. Luther clearly rejects such a view, predominantly in his complaints against the radical reformer Caspar Schwenckfeld in his 1540 "Disputation on the Divinity and Humanity of Christ." There are important precedents, moreover, in both patristic and medieval contexts, for christological views that exploit the mutability of Christ's humanity and do so without any implication that Christ ceases thereby to be human in any sense. For the patristic period, see the description of Gregory of Nyssa's "transformational Christology" in John Behr, *The Nicene Faith: Part 2*, Formation of Christian Theology, vol. 2 (Crestwood, NY: St. Vladimir's Seminary Press, 2004), 436–51. In the medieval period, at least Johannes of Mirecourt is willing to entertain the possibility of a human body being present in more than one place at a time. He advances this possibility not on the basis of the communication of idioms, but through recourse to the *potential absoluta Dei*. The very fact that such a thing is viewed as possible, though, shows that spatial circumscription is not viewed to be as essential to human nature as, for instance, impassibility is to the divine nature. Even in their most wildly speculative moments, the nominalist theologians do not suggest that it would ever be possible for *divinity* to suffer. Ernst Borchert, *Der Einfluss des Nominalismus auf die Christologie der Spätscholastik nach dem Traktat "de communicatione idiomatum" des Nicolaus Oresme*, Beiträge zur Geschichte der Philosophie des Mittelalters 35, 4/5 (Münster i. W. 1940), 84. It also seems fair to say that any christologically oriented doctrine of divinization entails some form of intrinsic human mutability. This, at least, would seem necessary if there is truly to be a genuine participation of human beings in the majesty and splendor of divine nature. For more on patristic openness to the teleological malleability of human nature, see Kathryn Tanner, *Christ the Key* (Cambridge: Cambridge University Press, 2010), 39f.

divinity. In what follows, I will argue that Luther clearly endorses a "one-way" communication of attributes, a position that he makes clear by his unwavering proviso that the divine nature does not and, indeed, cannot suffer.[4]

Passibilist Semantics

Luther often affirms some version of the statement that, in Christ, "God suffers." For some scholars, this fact alone establishes the emergence of something irreducibly novel within the reformer's theology. Paul Althaus, for instance, points to a text from Luther's 1540 "Disputation on the Divinity and Humanity of Christ," which states: "What Christ has suffered should also be attributed to God for they are one."[5] According to Althaus's assessment, this text conveys a clear commitment on Luther's part to dei-passionism, and thus entails a departure from the traditional doctrine of divine impassibility.[6]

4. This view will be shown in subsequent chapters to possess important implications for characterizing the basic shape of Luther's soteriological vision. It will also be deemed rather important for the task of responsibly appropriating Luther's christological witness in a contemporary theological context. In addition to the fundamental concern of this chapter to specify Luther's understanding of divine suffering, however, we must also acknowledge the subsidiary purpose of this investigation is to corroborate the thesis already advanced that Luther retains a medieval doctrine of suppositional carrying as the underlying metaphysic through which he makes sense of the hypostatic union. This corroboration is possible because the nature of Luther's predication theory provides a crucial insight into the conceptual substructure of his doctrine of Christ. His analysis of various "predicates" provides, as it were, a looking glass into the way in which the reformer conceptualizes the hypostatic union. The importance of this fact, for our purposes, is that it affords an opportunity to test ch. 2's claims vis-à-vis Luther's retention of the doctrine of suppositional carrying. In particular, we may test the previously advanced contention that Luther continues to assume an "asymmetrical" doctrine of Christ's person by measuring the extent to which such a view is manifest in a similarly asymmetrical predication structure. Does Luther distinguish, in other words, the application of divine and human attributes through a clearly differentiated mode of analysis? Although the abiding focus of this chapter will fall upon the first and primary objective, namely, triangulating Luther's precise views of divine suffering, the discussion will also furnish additional evidence in support of the claims advanced in ch. 2.
5. Paul Althaus, *The Theology of Martin Luther*, trans. Robert C. Schultz (Philadelphia: Fortress Press, 1966), 197n.44. Althaus quotes here from WA 39/II:121.

Althaus is not at all unique in drawing such a conclusion.[7] The initial plausibility of his interpretation melts away, however, under the heat of closer scrutiny.

A "dei-passionist interpretation" of texts like the one Althaus cites is misleading because it presupposes a degree of novelty that does not exist. The mere application of human attributes to "God" does not represent anything qualitatively new for patristic and medieval modes of discourse. Perhaps most conspicuous in this regard is the well-known Chalcedonian endorsement of the Marian term Θεοτόκος ("bearer of God"), a designation that unambiguously stipulates the application of human predicates not just to "Christ," but to "God" as well.[8] This same pattern of predication appears in the more blatant claim of canon 10 of Constantinople II (553) which insists that one of the Trinity has suffered for us.[9] Those patristic thinkers who endorse statements of this kind, it bears clarifying, intend no implicit rejection of divine impassibility. Theologians such as Cyril of Alexandria may insist, for instance, that God is "wrapped in swaddling bands," or that "God bleeds" and "dies," without budging on the underlying presupposition of divine impassibility.[10]

6. By this term, Althaus means to differentiate Luther from the early church heresy of "patripassionism," since Luther asserts only the suffering of the divine *Son*, and not the Father as well. This distinction appears rather frequently in the explanation of Luther's commitment to divine passibility.
7. See, for instance, Bernard Lohse, *Luther's Theology: Its Historical and Systematic Development*, trans. Roy A. Harrisville (Minneapolis: Fortress Press, 1999), 230.
8. Richard Price and Michael Gaddis, *The Acts of the Council of Chalcedon*, vol. 3, Translated Texts for Historians 45 (Liverpool: Liverpool University Press, 2005), 179–80.
9. Gilles Emery, OP, "The Immutability of the God of Love and the Problem of Language Concerning the 'Suffering of God'," in *Divine Impassibility and the Mystery of Human Suffering*, ed. James Keating and Thomas Joseph White (Grand Rapids: Eerdmans, 2009), 31.
10. For a thorough treatment of Cyril's Christology, see John Anthony McGuckin, *St. Cyril of Alexandria: The Christological Controversy: Its History, Theology, and Texts* (Crestwood, NY: St. Vladimir's Seminary Press, 2004), 175–226. See also Paul L. Gavrilyuk, *The Suffering of the Impassible God: The Dialectics of Patristic Thought*, Oxford Early Christian Studies (New York: Oxford University Press, 2004), 135–71.

Medieval authors continue these modes of christological predication. Scholars who emphasize the obvious centrality of the *communicatio idiomatum* in Luther's theology have sometimes failed to reflect adequately upon the extent to which this centrality is itself likely a product of the late medieval environment in which the reformer was educated, rather than an innovation of his own fabrication. Fourteenth-century theological discussion, in particular, is rife with interest and rigorous debate over the theory and practice of christological predication.[11] Insufficient emphasis upon, or awareness of, the intellectual milieu, stretching especially between the fourteenth and sixteenth centuries, has sometimes led scholars to assign an inordinate degree of novelty to aspects of Luther's christological discourse that are, in fact, rather prosaic once situated in the framework of a late medieval setting.

Robert Kolb, for instance, avers that Luther's affirmation of christological doctrine introduces "dramatically non-traditional expressions," such as: "'Mary makes broth for God,' Mary suckles God with her breasts, bathes God, rocks and carries God, and Pilate and Herod crucified and killed God, 'the infant Christ, lying in the cradle, suckled by the Virgin Mary, created heaven and earth.'"[12] How exactly the "nontraditional" character of such statements ought to be situated is not something Kolb neatly specifies for his reader. In

11. A dated, but still invaluable, window into the complexities of this discourse is available in Borchert, *Der Einfluss des Nominalismus*. Awareness of this fourteenth- and fifteenth-century literature makes the ordinary custom of introducing Luther's Christology predominantly in relation to fifth-century debates between Cyril and Nestorius appear historically unhelpful. To be sure, Luther is aware of these patristic debates, but his own point of access into the doctrine of Christ is the late medieval setting in which he lived and breathed. Thus, the practice of referring to Luther as Cyrillian or hyper-Alexandrian, while perhaps illuminating in some respects, represents a historically tendentious mode of classification. Luther's textual valorization of Cyril and denigration of Nestorius and Eutyches in such texts as his 1539 "On the Councils and the Church" is far from unique within the medieval period.
12. This amalgamation of quotes provided is in Robert Kolb, *Martin Luther: Confessor of the Faith* (New York: Oxford University Press, 2009), 112. See the appropriate citations to Luther's texts in n.18. It is somewhat unclear how Kolb situates the significance of this quote.

the context of his main argument, the emphasis seems to fall upon the fact that Luther appropriates a broadly traditional (that is, patristic) Christology, but does so through creative and nontraditional vocabulary.[13] Thus, Kolb emphasizes the conceptual continuity Luther's statements have with the Council of Ephesus's much earlier affirmation that God lay in Mary's womb.[14] A few pages later, however, Kolb argues that, for Luther, the divine nature shares in attributes of the human nature, thus registering his ostensible assent to a two-way understanding of the *communicatio idiomatum*.[15] The overall thrust in Kolb seems to be upon Luther's unique emphasis upon the radical union between God and man in Christ.[16] The dramatic novelty he attributes to Luther's speech, though, could certainly be taken to suggest the introduction of a foreign element in Luther's appropriation of the tradition.

Such an implication is pursued less ambiguously, for instance, in the recent work of Johann Anselm Steiger. Steiger calls attention to similar statements in Luther's writings, gleaned, in his case, from the reformer's 1539 treatise "On the Councils and the Church" and also from a sermon preached in December of 1525. Of these texts, Steiger remarks: "Since, on the basis of the *communicatio idiomatum*, all things that apply to the human nature of Christ are also applied to the divine nature, Luther can preach that the Creator was born (*nascitur creator*) and that the Word of God lay in a manger."[17] The operative

13. In point of fact, many of these same, purportedly "new," phrases show up in patristic literature. See, for instance, the discussion in Cyril of Alexandria, *On the Unity of Christ*, ed. John Anthony McGuckin (Crestwood, NY: St. Vladimir's Seminary Press, 2000), 47.
14. Ibid., 112–13.
15. Ibid., 115.
16. Kolb leans rather heavily upon Marc Lienhard's construal of Luther's Christology throughout his discussion. Whether or not he shares Lienhard's understanding of Luther's new ontology of Christ's person, and fundamental trajectory beyond divine impassibility is not discussed explicitly. See Kolb, *Martin Luther*, 110n.4, 111nn.5, 11, 112n.14, 113n.21, 115n.32, 116nn.35, 36, 40, 117n.43.
17. Johann Anselm Steiger, "Die communicatio idiomatum als Achse und Motor der Theologie Luthers: Der 'fröhliche Wechsel' als hermeneutischer Schlüssel zu Abendmahlslehre,

assumption that funds this analysis is a key semantic equation. Steiger assumes that attributing human predicates to God is more or less identical with attributing those predicates to the divine nature per se. It is this "semantic equation" which leads Steiger to conclude that Luther departs from an axiomatic commitment to divine impassibility.[18] The inference, however, is logically premature and altogether unlikely once the linguistic complexities of late medieval discourse are taken into account.[19]

A few examples of late medieval discourse demonstrate rather easily the prevalence with which blatantly human predicates are assigned to God because of the hypostatic union. Petrus of Palude (c. 1275–1342), for instance, affirms that, in Christ, God "sees," "eats," and "suffers."[20] Robert Holcot (c. 1290–1349) claims, a bit more controversially perhaps, that one may say that God can be deceived or even die, on account of the humanity of Christ.[21] In a similar vein,

Anthropologie, Seelsorge, Naturtheologie, Rhetorik und Humor," *Neue Zeitschrift für systematische Theologie und Religionsphilosophie* 38, no. 1 (January 1, 1996): 4: "Da aufgrund der communicatio idiomatum alle Dinge, die von der menschlichen Natur Christi gelten, auch seiner göttlichen zugeeignet werden, kann Luther predigen, daß der Schöpfer geboren wird (»nascitur creator«) und daß das verbum Dei in der Krippe liegt." The English translation provided above is taken from Steiger, "The *Communicatio Idiomatum* as the Axle and Motor of Luther's Theology," trans. Carolyn Schneider, *Lutheran Quarterly* 14 (2000): 127.

18. Steiger provides an example of this "regulation" in the work of John of Damascus, who occasionally speaks *as if* there were a fully reciprocal exchange of attributes between natures, but proscribes this possibility through his ongoing commitment to divine impassibility. Luther's unflinching ascription of human predicates *to God* indicates, for Steiger, that Luther fundamentally rejects this inconsistency: "Ganz anders jedoch Luther." He does not address, however, whether or not Luther similarly proscribes the suffering of the divine nature, as we shall in fact argue in what follows. Steiger, "Die communicatio idiomatum," 3–4.
19. So, by "semantic equation," I refer to Steiger's evident assumption that "the Creator is born" is simply equivalent to "the divine nature is born"; or that "God suffers" entails "the divine nature suffers." To assume this semantic equation is to overlook the thorough and meticulous ways in which theology since the patristic period has distinguished these two types of claims. In light of this tradition, of which Steiger is undoubtedly aware, one is forced to ask why a statement that can just as easily be found among patristic or medieval proponents of divine impassibility ought to be enlisted as clear evidence of an entirely different meaning when found in Luther.
20. Borchert, *Der Einfluss des Nominalismus*, 79.
21. Ibid., 85. Adam Wodeham (c. 1295–1358) likewise affirms the statement that "God died," although specifies the sense in which this is true. For him, this statement signifies that the human body with which the divine hypostasis is joined dies. The salient point, then, as we shall

Heinrich Totting of Oyta (c. 1330–1397) insists that the actions and sufferings of the humanity must apply to the divine suppositum on account of the *communicatio idiomatum*. On this basis, he affirms that "God suffered, died and moved about spatially."[22] Nicholas Oresme (1323–1382) assents to a similar point of view, stating that, in Christ, God is born of the virgin, suffers, and dies.[23] Luther's own exposure to the peculiarities of this late medieval semantic analysis is a function of his Scholastic training, in which he perused and commented upon several authors whose work reflects similar patterns of predication application. William of Ockham (c. 1287–1347), for instance, explains that the Son of God is incarnate, died, and suffered, and likewise that a "man created the stars."[24] Gabriel Biel (c. 1420–1495) advances a similarly direct application of human predicates to "God." In his commentary on the third book of Lombard's *Sententiae* he asserts that, in Christ, "*God* is temporal, corruptible, passible, mortal, etc.," and that *man* is "God, eternal, infinite creator, etc."[25]

Luther's ascription of suffering to God is hardly a major innovation.[26] By insisting that God suffers or dies, Luther is, in fact,

discuss below, is not whether such statements are affirmed, but *how* they are affirmed. In this case, the qualificatory discourse is essential for apprehending the meaning behind the assertion in question. Ibid., 86.

22. Ibid., 96. Michael Aiguanis also affirms the statement: "A creature bore the creator." Ibid., 87.
23. Ibid., 110.
24. Marilyn McCord Adams, "Relations, Inherence, and Subsistence; or, Was Ockham a Nestorian in Christology?" *Nous* 16 (1982): 68. Here in Ockham's statement we see the way in which the limits of the *communicatio idiomatum* are tested also by applying divine attributes or actions to Christ understood as a human being or as "man."
25. Text cited in Borchert, *Der Einfluss des Nominalismus*, 151: "Exemplum primi, ut quod concretum divine nature, scilicet deus, predicator de concreto humane nature scilicet homo, et econverso, dicendo, homo est deus, deus est homo, homo est eternus, infinitus creator, etc. Deus est temporalis, corruptibilis, passibilis, mortalis, etc. Exemplum secundi, Christus est deus, Christus est homo, etc. Dicitur notanter concretorum, quia abstracta naturam non predicantur de seinuicem." Important here is Biel's distinction between abstract and concrete statements. A great deal hinges, so far as the topic of this study is concerned, upon how exactly Luther makes use of this distinction, and whether he actually vests it with his own new meaning. For further discussion of this important text from Biel, see below.
26. One example of how this presumed novelty functions in the context of theological argument appears in Eberhard Jüngel's essay "Vom Tod des lebendigen Gottes: ein Plakat." *Zeitschrift Für*

taking up a pattern of christological description with a long and distinguished history. This point must be emphasized. Many scholars insist that Luther endorses divine passibility because they assume that these sorts of predications would have been unthinkable within a late medieval frame of reference. The empirical data belies the operative assumption. Statements such as "God suffers" or "God lies in a manger" do not require or evince a major reconfiguration of the *communicatio idiomatum*. Neither does it necessarily indicate a rejection of divine impassibilty. The strength of a divergence reading lies elsewhere.

Complexifying Modes of Christological Qualification

In the late medieval period, christological statements of the sort surveyed in the previous section are almost always accompanied by a highly refined qualificatory semantics. This discourse is intended to specify the intended sense of a christological statement, and thus to rule out potential confusions. The statement "God suffers," for instance, is often qualified with the phrase *secundum humanitatem* ("according to the humanity"), thus specifying the intended sense.[27]

Theologie Und Kirche 65, no. 1 (January 1, 1968): 93–116. Jüngel detects major christological shifts at work in Luther's disagreement with Zwingli over the real presence of Christ in the Eucharist. On 103–104, he turns his attention specifically to the *communicatio idiomatum* and comments, "Später trägt Luther seine Lehre von der communicatio idiomatum noch pointierter vor und weiß sich mit ihr von der Tradition (Zwinglis und der Scholastik) geschieden: »Hoc idem est, quod no dicimus: communicatio idiomatum.« »Hoc idem«—das ist die Behauptung, das Wort »Mensch« bezeichne den Gottessohn oder die göttliche Person. Und entsprechend kann es nun heißen: »Vere dicitur: Iste homo creavit mundum et Deus iste est passus, mortuus, sepultus etc.« So wird die Rede vom Tode Gottes möglich." The great irony of this last observation is the fact that Jüngel's cited examples are not at all unusual for medieval christological discourse. It is, rather, *because* of his exposure to medieval texts that Luther affirms of Christ that "this man created the stars," and "this God died and was buried." The dispossession of novelty severely mitigates the viability of Jüngel's reception of Luther's significance, which he develops in the remainder of the essay.

27. I.e., God suffers according to the humanity assumed by the *Logos* in the incarnation, and not according to the divine nature, which is impassible.

The real question, then, is not whether Luther ever applies human predicates to "God," but whether he continues along the grain of late medieval qualifications specifying the impassibilist sense of such expressions.

Texts by Luther, which seem to eschew these qualifications, should be regarded as the strongest evidence for the divergence thesis.[28] Dennis Ngien, for instance, points to a sermon on the Gospel of John preached in 1537, in which Luther states: "the two natures dwell in the Lord Christ, and yet He is but one person. These two natures retain their properties, and each also communicates its properties to the other."[29] Here we have a genuine instance in which Luther's language appears to exceed the scope of patristic and medieval semantic parameters. By suggesting that each nature communicates its own peculiar properties to its counterpart, Luther seems to commit himself to a two-way doctrine of the *communicatio idiomatum*, a view that would naturally include, by extension, his assent to a sharing of Christ's divinity in the sufferings of his humanity. Ngien also identifies texts to a similar effect in Luther's 1540 "Disputation on the Divinity and Humanity of Christ," as well as in a late installment of Luther's *Table Talk*.[30] Because Ngien's treatment of these texts is most

28. The most astute advocates of the divergence thesis recognize this. Dennis Ngien, for instance, acknowledges what we have argued in the previous section. Thus, although Luther affirms the statement that "God suffers" throughout his life, Ngien admits that much of Luther's corpus reflects a traditional understanding of the *communicatio idiomatum*. See the various citations provided in Ngien, "Chalcedonian Christology and Beyond: Luther's Understanding of the Communicatio Idiomatum," *Heythrop Journal* 45 (2004): 54–58. Ngien concedes not only that Luther retains the traditional view, but does so at least as late as 1544, the year before he died. The same concession appears in Lienhard's work, albeit in less forthright fashion. See, for instance, Marc Lienhard, *Luther: Witness to Jesus Christ: Stages and Themes of the Reformer's Christology* (Minneapolis: Augsburg, 1982), 169–71.

29. LW 22:491–92. Quoted in Ngien, "Chalcedonian Christology and Beyond," 59. The original text for this sermon is to be found in WA 47:199: "Jhr wisset, das do sej die Communicatio Idiomatum, das in dem herrn Christo sein zweierlej naturn und doch nur eine Person, und das diese zwo naturen furen und behalten, ja mit einander teilen ire eigenschafften."

30. WA TR 6:68. "Das aber von der Communication, Mittheilung einer Eigenschaft der Natur gesagt und beweiset ist (nehmlich, daß geborn werden &c. der göttlichen Natur auch zugeeigent und von ihr gesagt wird per communicationem idiomatum), dasselbige soll auch

specific and extensive, the following discussion will focus upon his exegesis as representative of the divergence reading in its clearest and most concentrated form.

Ngien's interpretation possesses an undeniable prima facie legitimacy, at least so far as the 1537 text from Luther's sermon on John is concerned. To be sure, the possibility for alternative exegetical renderings has sometimes been clouded by an excessive predisposition toward the identification of disruptive novelty in Luther's christological semantics as a whole.[31] Yet, it remains the case that these texts seem legitimately to point in the direction of a bidirectional doctrine of the communication of attributes. This preliminary concession notwithstanding, the following discussion will argue against Ngien's interpretation of these texts and suggest that, once situated in broad context, Luther's intent turns out rather explicitly to retain an ongoing commitment to the doctrine of divine impassibility.

The crux of the issue, so far as a divergence interpretation is concerned, resides in Luther's apparent insistence upon the ascription of human predicates not simply to the one person who happens to

verstanden werden von der Communication und Mittheilung der andern Eigenschaften, als leiden, sterben, begraben werden &c. Wiewol sie eigentlich der menschlichen Natur gebühren und zustehen, doch gibt sich die göttliche Natur in Christo drunter und leidet &c. auch nach dem Spruch Pauli Röm. 8: (1, 331) "'Wir müssen dem Ebenbilde des Sohns Gottes gleich werden'" &c. Jtem: "'Der seines eigen Sohns nicht verschonet, sondern hat ihn für uns dahin gegeben &c.'" Und in der ersten Epistel zun Corinth. am 2. Cap.: "'Denn wo sie die (Herrlichkeit) erkannt hätten, hätten sie den Herrn der Herrlichkeit nicht gecreuziget.'" Jtem zun Philippern 2: "'Jesus Christus, ob er wol in göttlicher Gestalt war, denn er war Gott gleich, doch nahm er Knechtsgestalt an, ward gleich wie ein ander Mensch und an Geberden wie ein Mensch erfunden, erniedriget sich selber, und ward gehorsam bis zum Tode, jazum Tode am Creuz.'" Deßgleichen singet die Kirche: "'Vita in ligno moritur'" (das Leben stirbt am Holz &c.). Darüm soll man gewiß gläuben, daß Alles, so der menschlichen Natur in Christo eigentlich zusteht und widerfährt, dasselbige wird auch communicirt, zugeeignet und gegeben der göttlichen Natur. Also daß recht und wahrhaftig gesagt wird: Gott wird geborn, gestillet oder gesäuget, lieget in der Krippen, frieret, gehet, stehet, fället, wandert, wachet, isset, trinket, leidet, stirbt &c." Ngien also thinks Luther's 1539 treatise "On the Councils and the Church" recommends this two-way position. Because of its explicitly soteriological frame of reference, however, we will defer investigation of this text until the next chapter.

31. As in the case of the texts discussed in the previous section.

be the divine Son (something for which there is extensive patristic and medieval precedent), but also to the divine nature itself. Such an insistence seems not only to forgo, but actually bulldoze, the qualificatory discourse enlisted within medieval Christology to protect the impassibility and immutability of Christ's divinity. And indeed, this is precisely the conclusion that divergence interpreters wish to draw. There is good reason to question the viability of this interpretation, however. In his 1537 sermon on John 3, for instance, Luther also insists that Christ's divinity and humanity both "retain their properties."[32] What can such a proviso communicate, if Luther intends by the previous statement to indicate a two-way communication of attributes between natures? If, for instance, the divinity of Christ is impassible by nature, and retains this property even in the event of the incarnation, how can it also be true that Christ's divinity shares in the sufferings of the humanity? Wouldn't that be self-contradictory?

To be sure, there are ways to reconcile this apparent tension of meaning within a divergence rendering of Luther's Christology. One could say, for instance, that the divinity retains its own properties in the sense that its sufferings stem not from a condition of existence intrinsic to itself, but from its union with the humanity of Christ. In that sense, though the divinity is rightly said to suffer, it does not suffer on account of its own peculiar properties, but solely through its participation in the properties of the human nature to which it is hypostatically joined. In this explanation, the tension of meaning embedded within Luther's statement resolves itself in favor of its latter half, namely, the ostensible affirmation of a two-way communicative exchange between Christ's humanity and divinity. If we limit ourselves entirely within the parameters of the two sentences Ngien

32. WA 47:199.

cites, then the plausibility of this hypothetical "resolution" cannot be denied.[33]

Equally plausible, however, is an interpretation of Luther's statement that resolves the apparent tension of meaning in favor of the statement's first half, namely, the governing qualification that each nature retains its own discrete properties.[34] In either case, one must admit that the precise form of Luther's language presents some degree of awkwardness, or at least inexactitude. That is, whether Luther intends by his statement to communicate either the impassibility or passibility of Christ's divinity, the verbal formulation he adopts to express himself is not immediately transparent to his underlying intent. Standing on its own, the textual tension simply remains, an exegetical obstacle with which the would-be interpreter must wrangle.

Earlier texts from Luther's career furnish reason to entertain the possibility that the intent of his ostensibly "two-way" language may actually fall within the parameters of characteristic medieval intent. One such text is taken from Luther's 1528 "Confession concerning Christ's Supper," in which Luther harshly criticizes Ulrich Zwingli's use of a rhetorical device (alloeosis) as a means for interpreting christological grammar. In the context of this larger criticism, Luther turns to the question of divine suffering to illustrate his point: "Now if the old witch, Lady Reason, alloeosis' grandmother, should say that the Deity surely cannot suffer and die, then you must answer and say: That is true, but since the divinity and humanity are one person in Christ, the Scriptures ascribe to the divinity, because of this personal

33. It could also be argued that impassibilty simply never was a genuine property of divinity, and therefore does not need to be "retained." This option, however, is much more difficult to sustain, since Luther often states rather forthrightly that God cannot suffer. Interpreters like Ngien must find a way to explain these statements.

34. The tension is apparent, because Luther's language in these statements is also understandable from within a medieval frame of reference. We will provide evidence to this effect in the closing portion of this chapter.

union, all that happens to humanity, and vice versa. And in reality it is so."[35] This text is remarkably similar to the 1537 sermon text cited above by Ngien. In the statement from 1528, Luther insists that everything pertaining to the humanity must be ascribed to the divinity of Christ. Strictly speaking, this way of summarizing the *communicatio idiomatum* swerves indeed from the ordinary intent of late medieval Christology, since the latter restricts the application of all christological predicates to the one person of Christ, who is both God and man. The medieval view prohibits the extension of these predicates to "divinity" as such, a term that ordinarily denotes the divine nature. On the basis of this text alone, then, one could justifiably suspect Luther to define the communication of attributes in terms of a two-way exchange between Christ's two natures, thus buttressing a divergence interpretation of his thought.

To advance such a view on the basis of this text, however, turns out to be an overly hasty misconstrual of Luther's position. Luther specifically prohibits the notion of a two-way communication within this text. He does so through qualifactory elucidations, which accord rather seamlessly with the ordinary medieval view of the *communicatio idiomatum*: "Indeed, you must say that the *person* (pointing to Christ) suffers, and dies. But this *person* is truly God, and therefore it is correct to say: the Son of God suffers. Although, so to speak, the one part (namely, the divinity) does not suffer, nevertheless the *person*, who is God, suffers in the other part (namely, in the humanity)."[36] In

35. LW 37:210. WA 26:321a: "Ob nů hie die allte wettermecherynn fraw vernünfft der Alloeosis grosmutter sagen würde / Ja die gottheit kan nicht leiden noch sterben /Soltu antworten / Das ist war. Aber dennoch weil Gottheit vnd menscheitynn Christo eine Person ist / so gibt die schrifft / vmb solcher personlicher einickeit willen auch der gottheit / alles was der menscheit widderferet / vnd widderümb / Vnd ist auch also ynn der warheit"

36. LW 37:210 (emphasis mine). WA 26:321a: "Denn das müstů ia sagen / Die person(zeige Christum) leidet stirbet / Nů ist die person warhafftiger Gott / drumb ists recht geredt / Gottes son leidet Denn ob wol das eine stuck (das ich so rede) als die gottheit nicht leidet / so leidet dennoch die person / welche Gottist / am andern stucke / als an der menscheit."

this series of qualifications, Luther makes it quite clear that his initial statement does not endorse the suffering of the divine nature, even though that is surely how it first appears. His point is, rather, that the one person of Christ is the acting subject of human predicates, and that this person is, at the same time, fully divine. This clarification is evident not only on the basis of Luther's direct application of all predicates here to the person of Christ rather than to the divine and human natures, but also because he specifically stipulates that Christ does not suffer in his divinity, but only in his human nature.[37] Luther's complaint against Zwingli is not that he rejects the suffering of the divine nature. He is concerned that the semantic analysis, summarized by the rhetorical term *alloeosis*, eschews the unity of Christ and speaks as if divinity and humanity act as their own discrete subjects.[38]

37. Luther continues to make this point clear through a number of analogies that stipulate how a predicate may be attributed to a given subject on account of one "part," while that same predicate is not true of another "part." LW 37:211: "Just as we say: the king's son is wounded—when actually only his leg is wounded; Solomon is wise—though only his soul is wise; Absalom is handsome—though only his body is handsome; Peter is gray—though only his head is gray. For since body and soul are one person, everything that pertains to the body or the soul, yes, to the least member of the body, is correctly and properly ascribed to the entire person. This is the way people speak throughout the world, not only in Scripture, and it is the truth. For the Son of God truly is crucified for us, i.e. this person who is God. For that is what he is—this person, I say, is crucified according to his humanity." WA 26:321a-322a: "Gleich als man spricht / des koniges son ist wůnd so doch / allein sein bein wund ist / Salomon ist weise /so doch allein sein seele weise ist Absalom ist schone / so doch allein sein leib schon ist Petrus ist graw / so doch allein sein hewbt graw ist Denn weil leib vnd seele eine person ist / so wirds der gantzen person recht vnd wol zugeeigent / alles was dem leibe odder seele / ia dem geringsten gelied des leibs widderferet // Dis ist die weise zu reden ynn aller wellt / nicht allein ynn der schrifft / Vnd ist dazů auch die warheit / Denn ynn der warheit ist Gottes son fur vns gecreutzigt / das ist / die Person / die Gott ist / Denn sie ist / Sie (sage ich) die person ist gecreutzigt nach der menscheit."
38. LW 37:211: "But this damned alloeosis exactly inverts the matter and changes it so that it ascribes to the parts what Scripture assigns to the whole person." WA 26:322a: "Aber die verfluchte Aleosis keret solchs stracks vmb / vnd wil wechseln vnd den stucken zu eigen / das der gantzen persone ynn der schrifft zugeeigent wird." Whether or not Luther's interpretation of Zwingli's Christology is accurate is a question we need not examine here. Our concern extends only to what Luther felt it necessary to say of Christ vis-à-vis the communication attributes.

Because Luther's publication against Zwingli appears approximately nine years before the text cited above from his 1537 sermon on John 3, it cannot count in any direct way as contextual evidence constraining Luther's probable meaning in the latter. This concession notwithstanding, the text from 1528 surely attenuates the prima facie legitimacy of Ngien's interpretation of the 1537 text and others like it.[39] It is at least worthwhile to ask: If Luther can invoke these ostensibly "two-way" descriptions in one instance and specify that he intends by them simply that the attributes of both natures are applied to a single acting subject (the person of Christ), why should it be concluded so abruptly that their appearance elsewhere must indicate a genuine, bidirectional communication of attributes in which the divine nature suffers?[40] The 1528 text illustrates the possibility of an interpretive alternative that ought to be considered. The key question thus becomes: Which interpretation comports best with Luther's overall argument within the sermons on John that were preached in the late 1530s?

In the case of the specific statement Ngien gleans from Luther's 1537 sermon on John 3, it is important, first of all, to situate Luther's discussion of the communication of attributes in relation to the larger theological question his sermon addresses. The Scripture text in this instance is John 3:35, which reads: "The Father loves the Son and

39. Ngien cites the 1528 text and seems to concede that it expresses a traditional point of view. However, he fails to notice or acknowledge that this earlier text employs the very same "two-way" language that he will later argue to demonstrate the suffering of divinity in the 1537 sermon.

40. The difficulty stems from the fact that Luther seems occasionally to use the term *divinity* to refer narrowly to the divine nature, and at other times as a way of referring to the divine person who becomes incarnate. Thus, in the 1528 text, when he insists upon divinity or deity suffering, he is referring to the fact, as the medievals also emphasize, that the Scriptures ascribe suffering to God because the single person who is God suffers according to his humanity. One possible root for this ambiguity is the fact that, in late medieval Christology, the divine nature simply is the divine person, whereas the same mode of identification is not possible when one is speaking of the human nature. This is a possibility we will later have occasion to explore in relation to a significant text from the late medieval Scholastic Gabriel Biel.

has placed all things in his hands." On the basis of this text, Luther poses an interesting theological problem for consideration. "Now the question arises again: How do we harmonize these two facts: that He is Lord over all and that at the same time He is a human being? If He is God, how could God give Him all? If He is God, He has always possessed everything."[41] On the basis of these questions, Luther is afforded the opportunity to reflect at some length upon the issue of christological speech. In particular, he is forced to grapple with how one may licitly refer human predicates (in this case, the fact that Christ "receives" something) to an acting subject who is divine. The question itself betrays Luther's ongoing indebtedness to a classical frame of reference vis-à-vis the doctrine of God. Its operative assumption resides in his underlying assumption that part of what it means for God to be God is that God cannot properly be said to receive something, since this would suggest not only a preexisting defect on the part of the divine being, but also God's innate capacity to experience change. If Luther did not deem these implications to be theologically unacceptable, there would be no reason for the question he poses to arise in the first place.

Luther addresses his question by appealing to the doctrine of the communication of attributes, reminding his hearers that the unity of God and man in Christ is such that human predicates are ascribed to God and vice versa. It is from this section that Ngien gleans his primary evidence for a reciprocal exchange of properties between the divinity and humanity of Christ. A brief survey of a few examples will again demonstrate why such an interpretation possesses some degree of prima facie plausibility. Luther's preliminary summation of the doctrine surely leaves the door open for Ngien's construal: "You

41. LW 22:491. WA 47:199: "Hie ist nun ein Frage: wie wil sichs reumen, so ehr ein Herr ist uber alles, und ist gleichewohl auch mensch? So ehr den Gott ist, wie hatt ehr ihme alles gegeben? ist ehr Gott, so hat ehrs zuvor alles."

know about the communication of properties: two natures dwell in the Lord Christ, and yet He is but one person. These two natures retain their properties, and each also communicates its properties to the other."[42] In a subsequent elaboration of his point, Luther even seems to corroborate the divergence thesis directly by specifically endorsing the application of Christ's human sufferings to his divine nature.

> The two natures, the human and the divine, are inseparable. They are so united in one Person that the properties of the one nature are also attributed to the other. For instance, mortality is peculiar to human nature; now that the human nature is united in one Person with the divine, death, exclusively the attribute of the human nature, is also ascribed to the divine. Now we can say: "God became man, God suffered, and God died."[43]

Here it is important to recall, however, that Luther's overarching concern in this section is to reflect upon how certain attributes or actions, which are clearly human in derivation, may be applied to the person of Christ who is also divine. The difficulty involved with this, as we have already noted, stems from the ontological distinction separating divinity and humanity, which Luther seems to acknowledge as valid. The overall shape of Luther's argument

42. LW 22:491–92. WA 47:199: "Jhr wisset, das do sej die Communicatio Idiomatum, das in dem herrn Christo sein zweierlej naturn und doch nur eine Person, und das diese zwo naturen furen und behalten, ja mit einander teilen ire eigenschafften." This is the primary text Ngien cites, as already documented above. We must also cite in Ngien's favor Luther's subsequent summary: "Since His incarnation the two natures are united; and the divine nature confers its properties on the human, and, vice versa, the human on the divine" (LW 22:493). "Do ehr aber nun mensch ist, do tragen die zwo naturen ir eigenschafft zusamen, und gibt die gottliche natur der menschlichen ire eigenschafft, und hinwidder die menscheit auch der gottlichen natur" (WA 47:200).

43. LW 22:492. WA 47:199: "Gleich wie die zwo naturen, die menscheit und Gottheit, unzertrennet sein, sondern also vereiniget in einer person, das was von einer natur geredet wirdt der andern auch zugeschrieben, als sterben ist menschlicher natur eigen, do ist den die menschliche natur vereiniget in einer person mit der Gottheit, das der todt, der doch allein der menschlichen natur wirdt zugesprochen, auch der Gottheit zugeeigent wirdt, und dan gesagt wirdt: gott ist mensch worden, Gott hat gelidden und ist gestorben."

that emerges from this acknowledgment may be summarized in the following statement: Although unbroachable polarities between humanity and divinity seem to proscribe any mutual predicational transfer, the union of God and man in Christ is such that the application of human properties 'to God' is licit, and indeed necessary.

Luther explicates this line of reasoning in an important paragraph of his sermon:

> Since the two natures are united in one Person, the effect is that the properties are also united. Admittedly, the properties of the divine nature have nothing in common with human nature. I shall go beyond this and say that there is still less relation between God and man. Yet these two natures are so united that there is only one God and Lord, that Mary suckles God with her breasts, bathes God, rocks Him, and carries Him; furthermore, that Pilate and Herod crucified and killed God. The two natures are so joined that the true deity and humanity are one. Now if the true God dwells in Christ, who was born of Mary, that is, the God who made and created all, we must say that the deity and the humanity joined not only their natures but also their properties, except for sin.[44]

Structurally, we can observe that the progression of thought encapsulated within this paragraph is comprised of four implicit components:

1. *Preliminary Concession*: The properties of divinity and humanity are irreducibly different from one another.

44. LW 22:492–93. WA 47:200: "Den die zwo naturen sind in einer person vereiniget, drumb sind die folge und eigenschafft auch vereiniget. Und ist war, das die eigenschafft der gottlichen natur rejmet sich nicht mit der menschlichen natur, und ich wil noch mehr sagen: Gott und mensch rejmet sich noch weniger, und dennoch sind die zwo naturen also vereiniget, das do Ein Gottund Herr sej, das Maria Gott seuget mit ihren brusten und Gott badet, wieget und hebet, item Pilatus und Herodes Gott gecreutziget und todtgeschlagen haben, und reimen sich die zwo naturn also zusamen, das die ware gottheit und menschheit ein dieng ist. So nun ein warhafftiger Gott in Christo ist, der geborn ist aus Maria, das ist: der alles gemacht und geschaffen hat, so mus man sagen, das sie nicht allein ihr natur zusamen gefast und getragen haben, sondern auch ihre eigenschafften, ausgenommen die Sunde."

2. *Apparent Semantic Implication*: This irreducible difference renders it ostensibly impossible and therefore improper to apply human properties to a divine subject (as John 3:35 apparently does by suggesting that Christ "receives" something).
3. *Salient Theological Reality*: Yet, God and man are united in the person of Christ.
4. *Semantic Recalibration*: Therefore, divine properties may be spoken of man, and human properties of God.

The crucial question has to do with whether and how Luther ascribes validity to components one and two of this fourfold progression. To what extent do these qualifications retain legitimacy after the union of God and man in Christ? In what ways must the new, christologically defined semantic context still respect the ontological gap between divinity and humanity with which Luther begins his discussion? Is the gap merely displaced?

For Ngien, Luther's Christology presupposes a genuinely diachronic ontological shift, which narrows the gap between divinity and humanity. Whereas, in his preincarnate state, the eternal Son is indeed incapable of suffering per se, this property of divinity "adjusts" in the event of the incarnation. Once united with a human nature capable of suffering, the divine nature becomes a genuine participant in creaturely passibility. We are labeling this interpretation "diachronic" because the properties of divine being undergo a sequentially mediated transformation. This transformation is precisely what creates the fundamentally new semantic context to which Luther now appeals.[45] The original polarity between divinity and humanity is overcome (or at least attenuated) through an

45. In order to bypass the implication here that the divine Son or the Trinity becomes "something else" in this process, Ngien suggests that the being of God is constituted in such a way that this event is always included. See Dennis Ngien, *The Suffering of God according to Martin Luther's 'Theologia Crucis'* (Vancouver: Regent College Publishing, 2005), 151–52.

ontologically conditioning event in which attributive proscriptions formerly appropriate (components one and two) forfeit their ongoing viability when once God actually becomes man.[46] Within this view, the predicational restrictions reflected in Luther's original question (How can God be said to "receive" something?) possess validity only in the sense that they used to be true.[47] The obsolete ontological realities they express, however, must not be allowed to qualify christological discourse in the present. The notion that divinity cannot suffer is true when the divine being is conceived in its anterior, preincarnate status. It becomes inapplicable once God assumes human flesh, however. Luther's solution to the question of how God can "receive" something, according to Ngien's interpretation, is to emphasize a diachronic contrast between "divinity-by-itself" and "divinity-in-union-with-humanity." The conceptual tension is resolved by the "reality-altering" event of the incarnation, which distinguishes these two discrete objects of semantic reference.[48]

A diachronic interpretation capably preserves the viability of the divergence thesis, but is it faithful to Luther's actual point of view? Subsequent qualificatory discourse within Luther's sermon on John

46. Here we have another expression of the deep interconnectivity between chapter 2 and the present chapter. Ngien's construal of Luther's proposed semantic shift presupposes a doctrine of the hypostatic union that is ontologically conditioning so far as the divine person is concerned. Although he does not name it as such, this view points strongly in the direction of a "composite" doctrine of Christ's person.

47. Or, perhaps, they are true only when treated in a context (perhaps philosophy) that abstracts from the reality of the incarnation. Of course, this would still represent a diachronic shift because, although philosophy may speak in this way, Luther is not reticent to insist that God truly has become man. In that sense, philosophy no longer could be seen to refer to "the real," but to a set of circumstances (separation of divinity and humanity) that no longer exist. Ngien gestures in this direction by seeing the "abstract" as the purview of philosophy, and the "concrete" as pertaining to theology. See Ngien, *Suffering of God*, 82.

48. Again, Ngien does not want to make of the preincarnate and incarnate Son two persons. Nevertheless, his arbitration of Luther's qualificatory discourse depends upon Luther granting at least some previous validity to statements such as "God cannot suffer" that no longer attains because of a diachronic ontological shift mediated by the event of the incarnation. For more on Ngien's treatment of this discourse, see below.

3 suggests not. This discourse reflects what could be termed a "synchronic" application of attributive proscriptions.[49]

> Throughout his entire Gospel John speaks of Christ as a true and natural human being, and also as divine. Here he refers to Christ, who was born, was baptized, and has disciples, as a real human being; at the same time he declares that all that is God's alone was given into His hands. He employs the term "given to Him," *which again applies to the human nature.*
>
> Thus the two natures are united in one Person, and there are not two Christs. Therefore, when you hear it said that God gave all things into Christ's hands and that He raised Him from the dead, *remember that this is spoken of Christ as man.* Then again, when we hear the expression: "He is seated at the right hand of God the Father," bear in mind that the human nature is united with the divine. To be in heaven and to be on earth are one thing, just as to be crucified and to live are one thing. . . . If you are perplexed by the statement that Christ died and that He is alive, you might find it still stranger to hear that Christ is God and man in one Person, that Christ died on the cross as a man, and that He nonetheless remains Christ in eternity.
>
> You must learn to brush aside all such doubts and misgivings. We are also called Christians because we acknowledge Christ in His doctrine. How can anything be given to Him? *According to His deity, He does not receive anything*; but God gave all to Christ inasmuch as God and man are one Person.[50]

49. That is, a mode of qualification, which retains components one and two of the afore-outlined argument even after the event of the incarnation (at the very least, Luther denies that divinity undergoes any diachronic change).
50. LW 22:493–94 (emphasis mine). WA 47:200–201: "Und redet Joannes durch sein gantz Euangelium von Christo als einem pur lautern menschen und widerumb &c. Alhier redet ehr von Christo, der geborn und getaufft ist, und der discipulos hat, als der warhafftig ein naturlicher mensch ist, und dennochs gibt ehr ihme alles in seine Hende, das gott allein gehoert, und dennochs spricht ehr: ihme gegeben. Das stehet einem menschen zu. Also sindt die zwo naturen vereiniget in einer person, das do nicht zwene Christus sind. Drumb wen du horest einen spruch von Christo, das im Gott alles in seine hende gebe und ihnen von den todten erwecke, Solches ist dan von Christo geredet als einem menschen. Widerumb saget man: ehr sitzet zur rechten hand gottes des vaters, Do wirdt vereiniget die menschlich natur mit der Gottheit, und ist dan gecreutziget werden und leben ein dieng, undten und droben sein ein dieng, wie wir droben im 6. cap. auch gesagt haben. Stost dich das nun fur den kopff, das Christus gestorben sej und lebe, viel mehr solt dich das seltzam duncken, das Christus Gott und mensch sej eine Person, das Christus am Creutze stirbet als ein mensch und bleibet doch

What we find in these paragraphs is an elaboration of Luther's underlying point about christological speech, which he expresses through differentiated, specificatory predicate analysis. The point of such analysis is to identify the specific 'part,' 'property,' or 'component' by virtue of which a given predication is truly, or validly, applied to Christ.[51] In this case, Luther is clear that it is according to Christ's human nature that he is said to receive all things from God. He also clarifies by way of specificatory restriction the implication this analysis is intended to proscribe, namely, that the ascription of these human properties and activities proceeds "according to His deity."

This discourse problematizes Ngien's interpretation, because it reflects Luther's ongoing assumption that "divinity" cannot directly receive gifts, suffer, or die, even in the case of the incarnate Christ. As in his 1528 "Confession concerning Christ's Supper," Luther's point in the 1537 sermon is, rather, that the one person, who is both divine and human, is the attributive recipient of properties belonging to both natures. Because of this fact, one may freely affirm the Johannine text, which describes Christ (who is divine) as receiving all things from God, without implying that this ascription applies directly to the Son's divinity. The specificatory discourse enlisted to explain this point makes it clear that Luther does not think this christologically oriented semantic shift entails the passibility of the divine nature. To the contrary, such an implication seems overtly to be disallowed.

Christus in ewigkeit. Also solt ihr Euch gewehnen, das ihr richtig hindurch gehet durch alle ergerniss, und wir heissen auch drumb Christen, das wir ihnen erkennen aus seiner lehre. Wie kan im dan etwas gegeben werden? Nach der Gottheit nimpt ehrs nicht, sondern weil Gott und mensch eine person ist, do hat ehr Christo gegeben."

51. These nouns appear in quotation marks because none is strictly appropriate for referring to the humanity of Christ as understood by Luther or his medieval predecessors. Here we find ourselves within the same dilemma engaged so prolifically during the medieval period, namely, what language can be used to refer to an object that is, by definition, entirely unique?

Luther attends to similar qualifications in a number of other sermons on John 1–4, all of which were preached between the years of 1537 and 1540, during Johannes Bugenhagen's (1485–1558) visitation errand to Denmark. A brief sampling of this peripheral evidence will reinforce the conclusion that Luther does not think the divinity of Christ is ontologically conditioned by the actions and properties that are properly derived from his humanity. For instance, in an explanation of John 1:4, "In Him was life," Luther calls attention to the enduring invulnerability of Christ's divinity throughout his passion: "Therefore He does not die according to His divine nature and come back to life; He is life, not only in Himself, but everything that lives has life in Him and through Him, especially man."[52] More closely reminiscent of Luther's comments on John 3:35 is an earlier homiletical reflection upon John 3:12: "No one has ascended into heaven but He who descended from heaven." Luther admits how strange it appears to say of a person who is God (and thus omnipresent) that He "descended."[53]

> How can reason harmonize the declaration that He descended and yet dwells above, that He ascended again and yet was continuously above in heaven? No human heart or mind can conceive such a thought. Reason says that it is impossible for one to descend from heaven and yet remain in heaven at the same time. Therefore we Christians are regarded as extremely stupid people to believe things that are impossible and diametrically opposed to reason.[54]

52. LW 22:30. WA 46:561: "Darumb stirbet er nicht nach seinem Goettlichen wesen und wird widerumb lebendig, sondern er ist das Leben, nicht allein in jm selber, sondern alles, was da lebet, das hat das Leben in jm und durch jn, sonderlich der Mensch." This section from John 1 is also a very important of Luther's soteriological application of two-nature Christology, a point we will explore at some length in ch. 4.
53. It is worth noting that this is the same question Peter Lombard raised several centuries earlier in book 3, distinction 22, question 4 of his *Sentences* (upon which Luther composed marginal notations during his study while in Erfurt). Luther's treatment of the question coincides almost exactly with Lombard's analysis, which relies heavily on Augustine. See Peter Lombard, *The Sentences, Book 3: On the Incarnation of the Word*, trans. Giulio Silano (Toronto: Pontifical Institute of mediaeval studies, 2008), 96–97.
54. LW 22:322. WA 47:51: "Das ist das Zeugniss und die seltzame predigt, die allein Christo

In an attempt to reconcile this tension, Luther allocates a significant amount of his subsequent discussion to the matter of christological predication and the communication of attributes. Here again, the salient point Luther stresses is the fact that Christ is one person existing in two natures, and that this theological reality carries with it unique semantic implications.

> But there is only one Son; and yet there are two natures, which gave Mary the right to say: "This Son Jesus, whom I bore and suckled on my breasts, is the eternal God, born of the Father in eternity, and also my Son." And God says likewise: "Mary's Son is My only Son." Thus Mary is the mother of God. And Christ, together with God the Father and the Holy Spirit, is very God from eternity who became man in time. So God the Father does not have a son apart from Mary's, nor does Mary have a son apart from God the Father's. This is the foundation on which our faith rests: that Jesus Christ has two natures even though He is one indivisible Person. There are not two sons and two persons; there is one Son and one Person.[55]

Luther's primary point in this section echoes his interpretation of John 3:35. He argues, essentially, that one may rightly ascribe human predicates (such as spatial movement) to Christ who is God, without thereby suggesting that the divine nature of Christ is thereby

zustehet, und wie kan sich auch die Vernunfft schicken in diese seltzame rede, das sie kondte vernemen, wie sich das zusamen reime: Herab fharen und gleichwohl droben sein, und widerhinauff fharen und doch stets droben gewesen. Das kan in keines menschenhertzen noch gedancken kommen. Es ist unmuglich, sagt die vernunfft, das vom himel herab steigen und gleichwohl droben bleiben kundte bejdes zu gleich war sein. Darumb sind wir Christen aus der massen nerrissche leute, das wir solch unmoglich dieng gleuben, so stracks wider die Vernunfft strebet."

55. LW 22:323–24. WA 47:52: "Aber es ist nur ein Sohn, und doch zwo Naturn, das Mariaalso kan sagen: Dieser Sohn Jhesus, den ich geborn und an meiner brust geseuget hab, ist ewiger Gott und vom Vater in Ewigkeit geborn, Gottes Sohn, und auch mein Sohn. Dergleichen saget Gott auch: Marien Sohn ist mein einiger Sohn. Jst also Maria Gottes Mutter, und Christus warhafftiger Gott von ewigkeit mit gott dem vater und dem Heiligem Geist und zeittlich mensch geborn worden, das Gott der vater nicht einen andern Sohn hat den Maria, noch Maria einen andern Sohn den Gott der vater. Das ist der grund, darauff unser glaub stehet, das Jhesus Christus zwo naturn hab, ob er schon ein einige, unzertrenliche person ist. Es sind nicht zwene sohne noch zwo personen, sondern ein Sohn und eine person."

affected. Christ's deity always remains what it was, according to Luther, and suffers no change when human properties or activities are applied to Christ. In order to make this clear, Luther furnishes his hearers with the analogy of a human person comprised of body and soul, which illustrates how speech can sometimes refer to a whole as if undifferentiated, even when there exists within that whole constituent realities which relate to that particular reference differently. A human stabbed by a knife will not customarily specify that she is stabbed according to her corporeal body, but refers the action to the whole of her person. Nevertheless, this does not mean that a person's soul is somehow also stabbed by a knife as a consequence of the predication![56] Luther recognizes the same semantic patterns of whole-part specification within christological discourse. Of course, it is true that God cannot move spatially, suffer, or die, he reasons, but God and man are truly one person in Christ, and therefore predicates deriving from one nature or the other can rightly be applied to the whole person in which these "parts" together subsist.[57]

> We are told here that Christ, true God and born as true man, descended according to His humanity, that God's Son died, descended into hell, and ascended again into heaven; that at the same time God remained in heaven, for the Godhead does not move about hither and thither but is omnipresent; and that according to His human nature, Christ ascended up above all. One may properly say that since there are two natures in one Being and Person, God's Son came down and entered the Virgin's womb and God's Son descended into hell. Although this really applied only to the human nature, by virtue of the personal union in Christ it is also ascribed to the other nature. "That which applies to one nature, applies to the entire person in the concrete."[58]

56. LW 22:327–28; WA 47:55–56. Of course, there are a number of ways in which this analogy falls short, as Luther himself acknowledges in his explanation.
57. Luther's use of this analogy need not commit him to a whole-parts analogy for the hypostatic union, as Richard Cross argues Aquinas to endorse. He is, of course, far from unique in the history of theology in appropriating the body-soul metaphor for a christological purpose.

In this text we find an additional clue for how Luther intends the statements Ngien isolates, which seem, on a prima facie level, to indicate a two-way communication of attributes. In the penultimate statement of the paragraph, we find another instance in which Luther affirms that human properties are "ascribed to the other nature," a statement that, were it not for its immediate context, could easily count as evidence in favor of a divergence reading. But one need only consult the first half of the same statement to see that Luther cannot intend here an exchange of ontologically conditioning bidirectionality, since he specifically restricts the various human predications directed to Christ as "really" applying to his human nature alone. A divergence interpretation of his explanation would also cut against the grain of the larger textual pericope, since Luther is arguing throughout that, although surely the divine nature cannot experience the things apparently attributed to it christologically in Scripture (a restriction that remains in force even after the incarnation has taken place), such attributions are, in fact, licit, because they refer to the whole (Christ) on account of a specific "part" (the human nature).[59]

58. LW 22:328. WA 47:56: "Dergleichen wird alhier auch gesaget, das Christus, warer Gott und mensch geborn, sej herab gefharen nach seiner menscheit, und ist Gottes sohn gestorben und nidder in die Helle gefharen und wider hinauff in himmel gefharen und dennochs Gott, droben geblieben, den die Gottheit nirgends hin fheret, nicht dort oder da, sondern allenthalben ist, und nach der menscheit ist ehr hinauff uber alles gefharen. Noch sol man also sagen, dieweil in einerperson und in einem wesen zwo naturn sind, das Gottes Sohn herab gestiegen sej in der Jungfrauen Marien leib und in die helle gefharen, wiewol solchs allein der menschlichen natur zustunde, jedoch wirds der andern naturn auch zugeeignet umb der personlichen einigkeit willen in Christo. Nam quae uni naturae conveniunt, toti personae conveniunt in concreto." Luther's invocation here of the medieval distinction between abstract and concrete predication is extremely important, and will be the object of specific focus in the subsequent discussion of Luther's 1540 disputation.

59. Again, the term *part* appears here within quotation marks because a consistent application of this analogy yields implications that Luther, like many medieval authors who also use it, will want to avoid. It could be taken, for instance, to imply a composite doctrine of Christ's personhood as a "fusion" or "mixture" of two previously separate parts. These unwanted consequences are a large reason why the substance-accident model is generally preferred in medieval antecedents, an analogy that Luther also invokes rather prevalently. One example

Prima facie impressions aside, these considerations render it clear that when Luther speaks in terms of human properties being ascribed to "divinity," he is expressing the point that the person of Christ, who is truly divine, is the attributive object to which all predicates are rightly assigned; and that, in this sense, one may rightly say that God descended, receives gifts, suffers, is crucified, dies, and so forth.[60] In any case, the contextual qualifications that surround Luther's apparently novel statements in the John sermons proscribe concluding on their basis that Luther's Christology includes a clear commitment to divine passibility.[61]

The same is true of Luther's 1540 "Disputation on the Divinity and Humanity of Christ," which Ngien similarly appropriates as evidence for a two-way communication between natures. To be sure, here again one finds a number of phrases in Luther's discourse that appear to point in such a direction. For instance, in his opening

appears in the 1540 disputation itself in Luther's examination of how "whiteness" is ordinarily ascribed to a person or object; see below.

60. Without the apparent implication that each "nature" is conditioned thereby.

61. Subsequent sections of Luther's sermons on John from 1537 to 1540 continue to reinforce this argument. For instance, in another text commenting on John 3, Luther reflects upon the fact that the evangelist predicts Christ being lifted up upon the cross. In order to explain how such a thing may be spoken of Christ who is God, Luther says: "This applies properly only to His human nature, since God cannot suffer and be crucified. And yet Christ says here that the Son of God was given into death and was crucified. From this we learn about the 'communication of properties,' the fact that the attributes of both natures pertain to the one person, that the attributes of both natures inhere in the one person" (LW 22:361). In the same section, he also states: "To be sure, Christ was crucified according to His humanity, and He created heaven and earth according to His divinity; but since this one person is God and man, it is proper to say: God's Son is the Creator of heaven and earth, and God's Son was also crucified. One dare not divide the Person, leaving only the human nature; but one must bear in mind that this Person is also God" (LW 22:362). WA 47:86: "Den solches eigenet auch der menschlichen naturn allein zu, den Gott hatt nicht konnen leiden noch ans creutz geschlagen werden. Noch spricht ehr alhier, das der Sohn Gottes sej in den tod gegeben und ans creutz gehenget worden, auff das wir hieraus lernen communicationem idiomatum, das die eigenschafft beider naturn sich zihen auff diese einige person, und also beider naturn eigenschafft zu stehen der einigen person." WA 47:87: "Nach der Menscheit, do ist wohl gecreutziget, und nach der Gottheit allein Himel und Erden geschaffen, aber dieweil diese Person Got und mensch ist, so wird recht gesaget: Gottes Sohn ist Schopffer himmels und der erden und wirdt auch gecreutziget. Man mus die Person nicht zutrennen, als, das alleine die Menscheit da bliebe, sondern sie auch Gott gewesen ist."

preface to the public debate, Luther comments, "what is attributed to one nature is attributed to the other as well, because they are one person."[62] This mode of description clearly lays emphasis upon the personal union of God and man, but seems semantically to suggest that this union enables Christ's two natures to exchange with one another all of their respective properties.[63] In this, Luther's vocabulary is strangely reminiscent of the sermons on John 1–4 from 1537–1540, as well as his earlier explanation in the 1528 "Confession concerning Christ's Supper." The question, which must be addressed, is whether Luther's language in 1540 is accompanied by similar mechanisms of qualification, which explicate his theological intent along similar lines. Locating these scattered statements within the framework of Luther's overarching argument throughout the disputation provides important preliminary clues about what this intent might be.

In some ways, the object of Luther's concern in this text is analogous to what was already found to be the case in his homiletic treatment of John 3:35. The fundamental question he is obliged to address, in both instances, is whether and how "human" properties may be predicated of Christ, even though he is fully divine. In the case of the 1540 disputation, the urgency of the riddle is impressed upon Luther, not by a specific scriptural text (like John 3:35, for instance), but by a series of recent and burgeoning complaints registered by Caspar Schwenckfeld that Lutheran theologians (along with Roman Catholic and Reformed counterparts) are wrong to endorse the statement, "Christ is a creature," on the grounds that

62. Trans. Christopher Brown, http://www.iclnet.org/pub/resources/text/wittenberg/luther/luther-divinity.txthttp. WA 39/II:98: "Non sunt duo filii, non duo iudices, non duae personae, non duo Iesus, sed propter unitam coniunctionem et unitatem duarum naturarum fit communicatio idiomatum, ut, quid uni naturae tribuitur, tribuitur et alteri, quia fit una persona."

63. Similar language shows up in at least two versions of the public debate. WA 39/II:102a: "Crucifigi est unum idioma naturae humanae, sed quia duae naturae sunt in una persona unitae, tribuitur utrique naturae"; and WA 39/II:108b: "Est communicatio idiomatum. Hoc quod proprium est humanae naturae, est commune divinae."

the full divinity of Christ is called into question thereby.[64] Although the focus of Luther's argument naturally rests upon defending the legitimacy of Christ's "creatureliness," the disputation also deals with matters of christological predication in general and the analysis of theological statements. This is because Schwenckfeld's complaint implicitly calls into question any instance in which an unambiguously human attribute is ascribed directly to Christ. Luther's strategy of response is, accordingly, wide-ranging in scope. It enlists the explanatory assistance of multiple predication examples, each of which serves further to devalidate Schwenckfeld's accusation.[65]

Schwenckfeld errs, according to Luther, because he treats internally differentiated objects of reference (in this case, Christ) semantically, as if they were nondifferentiated or uniform. He fails to account for the possibility that Christ's unique ontological status might require an internally differentiated application of predicates.[66]

64. For additional comments on the argument of the 1540 disputation, see the discussion already provided in ch. 2 regarding what it communicates about Luther's view of suppositional carrying.

65. Luther's tendency to clarify a particular matter of predication in light of others is also anticipated in the sermons on John, where, for instance, the question of Christ "receiving" something is elucidated in light of Christ also being said to suffer, die, be lifted up, etc. Luther can adopt this more comprehensive mode of response because the root issue of predication uniting these various examples is the same, namely, May one licitly refer human properties to Christ who is the Son of God?

66. Graham White helpfully condenses Luther's response by isolating the central "fallacies" the disputation exposes within Schwenckfeld's apparent critique of the statement that "Christ is a creature." See Graham White, *Luther as Nominalist: A Study of the Logical Methods Used in Martin Luther's Disputations in the Light of Their Medieval Background* (Helsinki: Luther-Agricola Society, 1994), 239–53. More specifically, White refers to two logical fallacies that Luther finds in Schwenckfeld's reasoning: (1) *simpliciter* and *secundum quid*; and (2) composition and division. See ibid., 239. Luther lays explicit emphasis upon the latter of these fallacies, stating in the preface that Schwenckfeld's use of it is the "hidden tooth of the serpent." WA 39/II:99: "Schwenckfeld scelerate advertit: Ergo Christus simpliciter est creatura. Quare tu nequam non addis: Christus secundum divinitatem est creator? Ergo est creatus. Sed non addit, quia dicit: Ego sino ita debilitari meam conscientiam. Ideo omisi, id est, scelerate feci. Ipse utitur fallacia compositionis et divisionis. Hic est occultus morsus serpentis et verum sacrificium diaboli etiam apud papistas." For more on the fallacy of *secundum quid ad simpliciter*, see Allan T. Bäck, "Aquinas on the Incarnation," *New Scholasticism* 56 (1982): 137.

Christologically, Schwenckfeld mistakenly assumes that the statement "Christ is a creature" applies to Christ *simpliciter*; that is, without restrictive or specificatory qualification. This strange flattening of christological discourse is the source of his confusion. Because of it, he argues in essentially the following way:

1. Christ is divine.
2. Divinity, by its very nature, is *not* created.
3. The term *creature*, however, denotes a being that *is* created.
4. Therefore, it is false to say that "Christ is a creature."

On the basis of this implicit reasoning, Schwenkfeld concludes that the phrase "Christ is a creature" is tantamount to an outright endorsement of Arianism. It appears to consign Christ to a merely "created" status. Luther's response to this line of reasoning seems, first and foremost, to be exasperation. Schwenckfeld evinces, for him, a truly stunning lack of logical-semantic sophistication, for which Luther knows not whether to credit ignorance or malice.[67]

67. Luther expresses this point with characteristic vigor. WA 39/II:97: "Causa huius disputationis est haec, quod volui, vos esse instructos et praemunitos ad futuras insidias diaboli, quia edidit quidam cavillationem quandam contra Ecclesiam. Non me hoc tam movet, quod homo indoctus, imperitus ac ignarus omnium quaerit sibi laudem et nomen aliquod, quam hoc, quod homines inferioris Germaniae moti sunt illius ineptis, stultis, imperitis, incultis ac ridiculis cavillationibus." The reformer's incredulity on this score is a function of two primary observations, both of which are expressed in the theses of the disputation itself. In the first place, he notes that the presupposed meaning upon which Schwenckfeld's repudiation of the statement "Christ is a creature" is based rests entirely upon a rendering that mutilates its unambiguous intent within contemporary sixteenth-century christological discourse and (more prominently) the ancient Christian tradition. Schwenckfeld's inability to discern this fact, Luther speculates, must stem from either his unwillingness or his inability to understand that the statement is ascribed according to Christ's humanity. Thus, without any accompanying denigration of the Son's full and eternal divinity. Luther's frustration with this oversight is apparently compounded by his second observation, namely, that differentiated predications of this sort are by no means the provenance of theology alone, but are also native to ordinary human discourse. The statement, "The Ethiopian is white according to his teeth," for instance, does not entail that the Ethiopian is white in every respect. Neither does it imply that the Ethiopian's "whiteness," applied in a more restricted manner (that is, according to his teeth), essentially conditions the pigmentation of any other dimensions of his corporeal existence. It

Luther's response is not that the divinity of Christ suffers ontological limitation. He does not repudiate Schwenckfeld for his concern to emphasize the "noncreated status" of the divine nature of Christ's divine nature.[68] The ground upon which Luther criticizes Schwenckfeld's christological semantics illustrates an underlying agreement with Schwenckfeld's governing insistence that the divinity of Christ is not ontologically conditioned by the creatureliness of his humanity. Luther's gripe with Schwenckfeld's criticism, then, is not that it wrongly defends the legitimate noncreatureliness of Christ (with respect to his divinity), nor that he expresses reticence to apply human predicates to the divine nature. Luther's fundamental concern is that the statement "Christ is a creature" does not weaken either of these commitments. Christological predication must be nuanced by careful distinctions. It refers to an internally differentiated object of reference. Schwenckfeld's problem is that he insists upon operating within a crude semantic framework in which every predication of the "whole" automatically conditions each of the "parts."

The non sequitur standing at the center of Schwenckfeld's criticism, in other words, is his assumption that the assertion, "*Christ* is a creature," is essentially the same as "Christ's *divinity* is a creature." Luther rejects this semantic equation. For him, "Christ is a creature" is a necessary affirmation, because the divine *Logos* is the subject in which the humanity subsists. With respect to his divine nature, Christ is surely not a creature but, rather, the creator. The basis for such "differentiated speech" is the correspondingly differentiated union

would not preclude, for instance, affirming as equally valid the statement that "the Ethiopian is black according to his hair." The extent to which this analogy is directly applicable to christological speech is somewhat limited for various reasons, a point that both Luther and the medieval Scholastics who enlist it readily acknowledge.

68. In other words, he tacitly accepts the premises reflected in the first two steps of Schwenckfeld's argument, as summarized in the previous paragraph. This mirrors Luther's evident assumption in the John 3 sermon that God cannot really receive anything.

of divinity and humanity in the one person of Christ. This union makes it possible and necessary to affirm Christ's creatureliness and noncreatureliness. Along with the patristic and medieval tradition before him, Luther does not take this to entail any logical contradiction. Schwenckfeld's failure to agree raises serious doubts in Luther's mind whether he grasps the full reality of the incarnation.[69]

Luther uses Schwenckfeld's evident confusion concerning the creatureliness of Christ as an occasion for general reflection upon modes of christological speech. The statements Ngien isolates from the 1540 disputation as evidence of an endorsement of divine passibility emerge from this subsidiary exercise. The larger context, which surrounds these "passibilist comments" mitigates the preliminary impression, upon which Ngien capitalizes, that Luther intends by them to affirm the suffering of Christ's divine nature. If his intent were to endorse this point of view, why would Luther go to such great lengths to demonstrate (contra Schwenckfeld) that property ascriptions referring to the single subject of Christ (such as creatureliness) do not entail any transformation of Christ's divinity? Why doesn't Luther simply attack Schwenckfeld's reticence to acknowledge that divinity is a creature, because the incarnation ontologically conditions the divine nature of Christ by way of two-way, communicative exchange? In other words, if Luther protects the divine nature from the ascription of "creatureliness" or the capacity to "receive" something, why would other human predicates—like the capacity to suffer—be any different?

These plausibility questions would be largely irrelevant, of course, if it could be convincingly shown that Luther simply does ascribe

69. This is why Luther registers his suspicion that Schwenckfeld's unwillingness to refer to Christ as creature harbors latently Eutychian sensibilities, by which he means that the genuine humanity of Christ is potentially compromised by being absorbed into divinity (WA 39/II:95). How exactly this interpretation relates to the actual position of Eutyches in the christological controversies of the early church is a question that needn't detain us here.

suffering and other human predicates to the divinity of Christ within other sections of the disputation. This, however, is not the case. Luther employs clear specificatory qualifications that supervise and restrict the meaning of the *communicatio idiomatum*. This discourse places unambiguous limits on how human *idioma* may be applied to Christ. So, for instance, one transcript of the public debate records the following, which is again strangely reminiscent of Luther's early treatment of John 3:35.

> Argument: If Christ were true God, of the same essence with the Father, the Scripture would not teach that he received all things from the Father. But Scripture so says. Therefore he is not true God.
>
> I respond to the minor premise: This [pertains to] his ministry and humanity. For in divinity he is equal in power with the Father.[70]

Luther's response here that "receiving" pertains exclusively to the humanity of Christ underscores his acquiescence to the presupposition that the divinity of Christ cannot receive, a restriction that clearly retains its force even postincarnation. The biblical statement that "Christ receives" is nevertheless valid, because reference to the one person does not entail a symmetrical characterization of both natures.

This same pattern of differentiating analysis appears in Luther's analysis of the statement that "Christ" or "God suffers" elsewhere within the disputation.

> The Father does not will that the human nature should have to bear divine epithets . . , despite the union, and yet sometimes [Christ] speaks of himself as of God, when he says, "The Son of Man will be crucified." To be crucified is a property of the human nature, but because there are

70. Trans. Christopher Brown. WA 39/II:104a: "Si Christus esset verus Deus, eiusdem essentiae cum patre, non doceret scriptura: Omnia a patre accepit. Sed scriptura ita dicit: Ergo non est verus Deus. Respondeo ad minorem: Quod ad suum ministerium et humanitatem. Nam in divinitate est aequalis potentia cum patre."

> two natures united in one person, it is attributed to both natures. Again, "Whoever believes in the Son has eternal life." There he speaks of the divine nature. Or again, "They crucified the Lord of glory," where he speaks of the property of the humanity.[71]

This text embodies the descriptive tension that lies at the center of the question treated throughout this chapter. On the one hand, Luther seems to endorse a two-way communication of attributes by suggesting that the property of "being crucified" is "attributed to both *natures*."[72] On the other hand, this endorsement is forcefully overturned by restrictive statements, which limit Christ's "being crucified" exclusively to his humanity. What can be made of this internal variegation?

The tension appears again in the second half of the fifth argument, as recorded in the disputation's published transcripts.

> Question: It is asked, whether this proposition is true: The Son of God, the creator of heaven and earth, the eternal Word, cries out from the Cross and is a man?
>
> Response: This is true, because what the man cries, God also cries out, and to crucify the Lord of glory is impossible according to the divinity, but it is possible according to the humanity; but because of the unity of the person, this being crucified is attributed to the divinity as well.[73]

71. Trans. Christopher Brown. WA 39/II:102a: "Pater non vult, ut humana natura debeat gerere dicta divina, etiamsi sit unitas, sed tamen aliquando loquitur de se tamquam Deo, cum dicit: Filius hominis crucifigetur. Crucifigi est unum idioma naturae humanae, sed quia duae naturae sunt in una persona unitae, tribuitur utrique naturae. Item, qui credit in filium habet vitam aeternam. Ibi de divina natura loquitur. Item dominum gloriae crucifixerunt, de idiomate humanitatis loquitur." This passage is excerpted from the third argument, recorded in the published transcripts of the public debate.
72. Emphasis mine.
73. Trans. Christopher Brown. WA 39/II:103a: "Quaestio: Quaeritur, an illa propositio sit vera: Filius Dei, creator coeli et terrae, verbum aeternum, clamat in cruce et est homo? Responsio: Est vera, quia quod clamat homo, clamat etiam Deus, et crucifigi dominum gloriae est impossibile secundum divinitatem, est autem possibile secundum humanitatem, sed quia est unitas personae, illud crucifigi tribuitur etiam divinitati."

A divergence interpretation of this text will, no doubt, call attention to the fact that Luther ascribes "being crucified" to Christ's divinity. The text, however, cannot easily be reduced to this emphasis. One must account for conspicuous use of *secundum quid* qualifiers, which designate the nature according to which a particular predication is valid. If Luther means to expunge the doctrine of divine impassibility, why retain such semantic restrictions at all? Is his point simply to acknowledge that the divine nature can't suffer on its own, but only suffers once united with the humanity of Christ?

Such a "diachronic" rendering fails to comport, though, with the thrust of Luther's rejoinder to Caspar Schwenckfeld. In this rejoinder, the mechanics of semantic specification are enlisted to demonstrate the legitimacy of ascribing human attributes to Christ while retaining the unaltered integrity of the divine nature (that is, God's abiding noncreatureliness). When the same qualificatory pattern is applied to the present context, it becomes clear that it is the divinity *of Christ* which Luther has in mind, when he states that "being crucified" is "*impossible* according to the divinity."[74] He is not simply conceding the point that "preincarnate deity" cannot suffer and die.[75] Luther's use of traditional restrictive qualifications denotes an ongoing commitment to the doctrine of divine impassibility.

The core of the 1540 disputation rests, finally, as in the case of the 1528 "Confession concerning Christ's Supper" and the sermons on John from the late 1530s, upon the ascription of human properties to the single person of Christ.[76] The purpose of Luther's enlisted specificatory discourse is to identify the nature according to which ascriptions are valid. The resultant "partitive analysis" also makes it

74. That is, the referent is not the preincarnate divine Son, but the incarnate Christ. Emphasis mine.
75. After all, Luther's response to Schwenckfeld is not that preincarnate divinity is not a creature. Such an argument would only confirm the semantic suspicions that Luther set out to allay.
76. That is, the tensions that proceed from the juxtaposition of traditional qualificatory discourse beside an apparent endorsement of a two-way exchange between natures.

abundantly clear that descriptive characterizations of Christ do not necessarily apply symmetrically to each of Christ's two natures. Many predicates, which are true of Christ as human, are decidedly not true of Christ as divine.

To this point, the present section has argued in favor of a "nondivergence" reading of Luther's 1540 disputation on the basis of two main factors. In the first place, this interpretation comports with the grain of Luther's response to Caspar Schwenckfeld. His response does not depend upon a diachronic ontological shift within the nature of deity, but focuses instead upon the person of Christ as the one proper recipient of all property ascriptions. Second, a nondivergence interpretation makes clearer sense of Luther's prolific use of *secundum quid* qualifiers. These qualifiers register his ongoing commitment to the unaltered integrity of the divine nature as noncreaturely and impassible, before and after the event of the incarnation.

In addition to these considerations, there is a third compelling source of counterevidence, which has not yet been the direct object of this chapter's examination. It consists in Luther's employment in the disputation of the distinction between abstract and concrete predication, which represents a second means of semantic qualification. The importance of this distinction is highlighted by its conspicuous frequency of appearance in the opening series of theses.[77]

1. This is the catholic faith, that we confess one Lord Jesus Christ, true God and man.
2. From this truth of the double substance and the unity of the person follows the communication of attributes [*communicatio idiomatum*], as it is called.

77. A smaller portion of these theses has already been surveyed in ch. 2.

3. So that those things which pertain to man are rightly said of God, and, on the other hand, those things which pertain to God are said of man.
4. It is true to say: This man created the world, and this God suffered, died, was buried, etc.
5. But these are not correct in the abstract (as it is said) of human nature [*in abstractis humanae naturae*].
6. For it cannot be said, Christ is thirsty, a servant, dead; therefore he is thirst, servitude, death.
7. Wherefore this [statement] too is condemned: Christ is humanity, even though it is said: Christ is divinity.
8. Even though man and humanity are otherwise synonyms, as are God and divinity.
9. In the divine predicates or attributes there is not a difference of this kind between the concrete and the abstract.[78]

Theses 4 and 5 of this series demonstrate the importance of the distinction between abstract and concrete predication for ascertaining Luther's conception of divine passibility, because they insist rather directly that the statement "God suffered" is valid only when spoken in the concrete, and not when spoken in the abstract. What does Luther intend to emphasize by means of this distinction?[79]

78. Trans. Christopher Brown; italics added. WA 39/ II:93: "1. Fides catholica haec est, ut unum dominum Christum confiteamur verum Deum et hominem. 2. Ex hac veritate geminae substantiae et unitate personae sequitur illa, quae dicitur, communicatio idiomatum. 3. Ut ea, quae sunt hominis, recte de Deo et e contra, quae Dei sunt, de homine dicantur. 4. Vere dicitur: Iste homo creavit mundum et Deus iste est passus, mortuus, sepultus etc. 5. Non tamen haec rata sunt in abstractis (ut dicitur) humanae naturae. 6. Non enim dicere licet, Christus est sitiens, servus, mortuus, ergo est sitis, servitus, mors. 7. Unde et illa damnatur: Christus est humanitas, etiamsi dicatur: Christus est divinitas. 8. Licet homo et humanitas sint alias synonyma, sicut Deus et divinitas. 9. In divinis praedicatis seu idiomatibus non est differentia talis inter concreta et abstracta."

79. The distinction itself shows up rather frequently in many of Luther's other written texts. Two of the more conspicuous examples include his already-mentioned sermons on the Gospel of John, and his commentary on Isaiah 53, which he composed in 1544.

Divergence interpreters are accustomed to think that Luther's distinction between "abstract" and "concrete" description reflects the diachronic ontological shift, which conditions postincarnate deity.[80] Suffering is not possible for the divine nature, in other words, until it forms a single "concretion" together with Christ's humanity. Thus, when Luther states that God does not suffer "in the abstract," Ngien takes him to mean that God's being does not (and cannot) suffer prior to the incarnation.[81] Ngien's implicit definition of this distinction is representative, and could be condensed as follows:

> *Abstract Predication:* Predication referring to one of Christ's natures conceived outside of, or prior to its participation within, the reciprocal, ontologically conditioning relationship it shares with its counterpart in the hypostatic union.
>
> *Concrete Predication*: Predication referring to one of Christ's natures as

80. For instance, Kjell Ove Nilsson, *Simul das Miteinander von Göttlichem und Menschlichem in Luthers Theologie*, Forschungen zur Kirchen- und Dogmengeschichte, Bd. 17 (Göttingen: Vandenhoeck & Ruprecht, 1966), 255–57. Nilsson's interpretation of the distinction is clearly expressed in a summary description he provides on 257: "Erst die unauflösliche Personeinheit macht—in concreto—eine Vermittlung zwischen den Naturen möglich. Also: die Vermittlung ist realis, nicht nominalis; sie geschieht im genus idiomaticum sowohl als auch im majestaticum und tapeinoticum." Schneider defines the concretion in terms of a dynamic union of opposites. Florian Schneider, *Christus praedicatus et creditus: die reformatorische Christologie Luthers in den "Operationes in Psalmos" (1519–1521), dargestellt mit beständigem Bezug zu seiner Frühzeitchristologie* (Neukirchen-Vluyn: Neukirchener, 2004), 184. See also Jens Wolff, *Metapher und Kreuz: Studien zu Luthers Christusbild* (Tübingen: Mohr Siebeck, 2005), 440. Schwarz is less clear, perhaps, but also seems to assign a similarly "diachronic" meaning to Luther's use of specificatory discourse. He acknowledges, for instance, that Luther uses the qualification "according to the humanity," but this does not mean, in his judgment, that Luther denies the genuine suffering of the divinity. Instead, he thinks it is intended to denote the nature from whom the attribute in which both now share is properly derived. Reinhard Schwarz, "Gott ist Mensch: zur Lehre von der Person Christi bei den Ockhamisten und bei Luther," *Zeitschrift für Theologie und Kirche* 63 (1966): 311–13. The prominence of this diachronic hermeneutic is expressed by the fact that Paul Fiddes, a contemporary systematic theologian, simply assumes it to represent accurately Luther's rendering of divine suffering. See Paul S. Fiddes, *The Creative Suffering of God* (Oxford: Clarendon, 1988), 29.
81. This is why we are referring to this interpretation as "diachronic." Ngien is aware that a stark emphasis upon this "shift" creates awkward problems for maintaining an agential continuity between God's being and act. This is why he suggests, somewhat in the manner of Jürgen Moltmann, that the divine Son is always proleptically conditioned by the incarnation, even before the decisive ontological shift actually takes place.

ontologically conditioned by its union with its counterpart inside the hypostatic union.[82]

By adopting a version of this interpretation, Ngien sidesteps the implication that Luther's employment of the abstract/concrete distinction attenuates or restricts his apparent endorsement of divine passibility. He is, after all, only acknowledging that the genuine suffering of the divine nature comes as a result of its union with humanity, and not from within its own discrete experience. This strategy mirrors the divergence thesis's diachronic rendering of other partitive analyses, such as *secundum quid* qualifiers.[83]

A "diachronic" interpretation of Luther's differentiated specificatory analysis succeeds, however, only if its medieval provenance is entirely ignored.[84] Luther's use of the abstract/concrete distinction is not, in other words, a semantic device of his own innovation, but a practice he appropriates unambiguously from medieval discursive custom. Qualificatory mechanisms such as those treated within this chapter are employed within the medieval period as a means for testing and articulating the internal consistency of

82. This definition is sometimes used as a means of characterizing Luther's theological epistemology. According to this application, it is precisely knowledge of God in the "abstract" that Luther rejects. The point represented here often carries with it a clear polemical edge. Whereas Scholasticism is content simply to define God and Christ on the basis of detached speculation, Luther allows God to define Godself. He thus allows God to be Godin God's own way, rather than imposing upon God human philosophical projections. There is not space to address this particular extension of the divergence interpretation.

83. That is, Ngien's apparent assumption that God suffers "according to the humanity" really only means that the divine nature suffers "on account of its union with the humanity" (since prior to this union, divinity cannot suffer).

84. By differentiated specificatory analysis, I refer to analysis that identifies and distills the specific reality or entity by virtue of which a given predication is deemed valid or true. Whatever interpretation of Luther's Christology one finally defends, the fact that Luther enlists such specificatory and restrictive discourse must be acknowledged and therefore interpreted. The crucial question is whether this discourse ought to be seen as "*diachronic*, differentiated specificatory analysis" or as "*synchronic*, differentiated specificatory analysis." The following argument will argue in favor of the latter, in light of (1) the late medieval provenance of these distinctions (i.e., Luther obviously has absorbed them from the medieval textbooks perused throughout his education and beyond); and (2) Luther's own explicit reflections upon this discourse, specifically the abstract/concrete distinction.

Christian belief, a project whose very impetus presumes the prima facie dissonance of divine and human predicates (for instance, passibility and impassibility).[85] While the origins and development of the abstract/concrete distinction, in particular, exceed the scope of the present discussion, it behooves us here to reflect briefly upon the christological application of this distinction in representative examples of late medieval discourse.[86]

The salience of such medieval antecedents for the present section consists in the unequivocally nondiachronic significance their use of the abstract/concrete distinction reflects, so far as the analysis of christological predicates is concerned. The primary intent of the distinction's application during this period is to distinguish between those predicates that refer to the single person of Christ (concrete), and those that denote each nature as such (abstract). Thomas Aquinas, for instance, distinguishes concrete terms as predications that refer to natures as they are possessed by subject, whereas abstract terms refer to natures per se.[87] This distinction regulates the grain of

85. For instance, the fact that Christ is both passible and impassible is an ostensible contradiction that medieval theologians seek to avoid by specifying the restricted "respect" according to which each predication is valid. Presumed in all this is the fact that a genuine union between divinity and humanity must preserve all of the essential attributes of the same, and this includes the humanity's intrinsic capacity to suffer, and the divinity's intrinsic incapacity to suffer. In the absence of these commitments, no qualificatory discourse would be necessary, because Christ's "suffering" would not raise the specter of latent contradiction at all. All of this raises the question, If Luther does not share these commitments, then why would he bother so extensively with the same medieval qualificatory discourse that is begotten from them? For more on the role of qualificatory propositions in relation to establishing the noncontradictory consistency of the doctrine of the incarnation, see Bäck, "Aquinas on the Incarnation," 127–45; and idem, "Scotus on the Consistency of the Incarnation and the Trinity," *Vivarium* 36 (1998): 83–107.

86. The distinction traces ultimately to the theory of predication espoused by the philosopher Aristotle, whose work was reintroduced into the Western theological tradition during the early medieval period. Luther expresses his own awareness of the distinction's Aristotelian derivation in argument twelve of the transcribed debate; see WA 39/II:108a. For more on Aristotle's views on predication, see Allan T. Bäck, *Aristotle's Theory of Predication* (Leiden: Brill, 2000). Another important instance of Luther's extended utilization of the distinction between abstract and concrete is to be found in his 1544 commentary on Isaiah 53. See WA 40/3:707–708.

87. *ST* III, q. 16, art. 1. For an English translation, see Thomas Aquinas, *Summa theologiae: Latin text and English translation, introductions, notes, appendices, and glossaries*, 50 (Cambridge: Blackfriars, 1964), 7. The editors provide a useful footnote (note "g"), which summarizes

christological description for Aquinas and other medieval thinkers. Concrete terms may apply to any subject that possesses the "nature" to which a particular abstract term belongs. Human properties may therefore be ascribed to the Son of God (in the concrete) by virtue of the fact that the humanity of Christ is "possessed," so to speak, by a divine subject.[88] The predication may not run in reverse. Concrete terms do not necessarily apply to each of Christ's natures. Hence, the Son of God suffers (abstract to concrete), but divinity does not suffer (concrete to abstract).

William of Ockham adheres to the same basic set of semantic regulations. He stipulates that, while one may licitly say that "Christ is man" (a predication that denotes the concrete person possessing a human nature), it cannot be said that "Christ is humanity," because "humanity" refers to the abstract nature on account of which Christ (the concrete) is rightly characterized as fully human. Christ is no more to be identified with "humanity" on account of his being human than the person of Socrates is to be identified with "whiteness" on account of his being white.[89] Aquinas and Ockham are representative here of medieval Christologies in general. In no instance does the distinction between abstract and concrete predication signal a diachronic, ontological shift, according to which the divinity of Christ undergoes constitutional alteration. The distinction stipulates the sense in which Christ is human, and

Aquinas's deployment of the distinction. ". . . *abstract* and *concrete* forms of a term (e.g. *human nature* and man) both *signify* the same nature, but differently: the abstract term signifies the nature alone, the concrete term signifies the nature as possessed by a subject. As a consequence, in a statement an abstract term *stands for* the nature, while a concrete term *stands for* the subject having the nature." For more on Aquinas's treatment of the communication of attributes, see Borchert, *Der Einfluss des Nominalismus*, 40.

88. See, for instance, the manifestations of this restriction in the writings of Konrad of Soltau, Petrus of Candia, Pierre D'Ailly, Nicholas d'Oresme, and William of Ockham. Ibid., 78, 98, 100, 106, 110.

89. For more on this restriction and Ockham's discussion of it, see Marilyn McCord Adams, "Relations, Inherence, and Subsistence," 68–69.

regulates the application of predicates accordingly. For the medievals, such specificatory analysis is clearly "synchronic" in nature.

Is Luther's appropriation of the abstract/concrete distinction marshaled to an equivalent restrictive purpose? Theses 6 and 7 of the 1540 disputation suggest an affirmative response to this question. Here, the reformer reproduces Ockham's line of argument.[90] Perhaps most explicit in this regard is the published record of argument 12, which one finds in a transcribed version of the public debate.

> Argument: "Man" and "humanity" have the same meaning. Therefore it is rightly said that Christ is humanity.
>
> Response: This is not conceded, but rather that Christ is man, because this is a concrete term with personal signification, whereas an abstract signifies the mode of nature, or naturally, so that therefore it is false that Christ is human nature, that is, humanity, or that Christ is humanity. Aristotle says that abstract terms refer to nature, and concrete terms to a person.[91]

Contra Ngien's interpretation of Luther's qualificatory discourse, this text illustrates Luther's appropriation of a medieval rendering of the abstract/concrete distinction, with its differentiation of person-oriented predicates and nature-oriented predicates. The differentiation expressed by this distinction is clearly not a function of diachronic ontological adjustment. It refers, instead, to the internally differentiated unity of the incarnate Christ, and seeks to reflect the peculiar nature of this unity through a correspondingly differentiated mode of discourse. The distinction between abstract and concrete possesses, for Luther, an explicitly "synchronic" significance. Thus,

90. This is not to suggest that the point originates with Ockham.

91. Trans. Christopher Brown. WA 39/II:108a: "Homo et humanitas significant idem. Ergo recte dicitur: Christus est humanitas. Responsio: Illa non conceditur, sed illa: Ergo Christus est homo, quia est hoc concretum significans personaliter, sed abstractum significat modum naturae vel naturaliter, sicut igitur falsum est: Christus est humana natura, id est, humanitas, sic Christus est humanitas. Aristoteles dicit: Abstracta sonant naturam, concreta personam."

when he denies in thesis 5 that the statement "God suffered" is true in the abstract, the underlying intent is clear. He means by this qualification to ascribe "suffering" to the single person of Christ who is both God and man. By stipulating in this same section that all predicates of the humanity may be applied to Christ only in the concrete, Luther unambiguously proscribes any implication that the "suffering of God" in any way conditions the divinity of Christ as such. Luther's emphasis rests again upon the single personal agency of Christ, who is the rightful recipient of all divine and human predicates. The overarching intent of this emphasis, along with its accompanying qualificatory discourse, is to demonstrate, just like the medieval theologians surveyed in the previous chapter, that one may affirm the mysterious realities of the incarnation without falling into contradiction or violating the integrity of the divine nature by ascribing to it exclusively human attributes.[92]

Is Luther's use of qualificatory discourse sufficient to displace the prima facie evidence, which seems to evince a reciprocal doctrine of the communication of idioms? The qualifications surveyed above certainly furnish significant reason to doubt that a "two-way" understanding is what Luther has in mind. The lingering riddle, however, is why Luther sometimes speaks as if there is a mutual sharing of attributes, even if contextual qualifications ultimately prohibit this view. This section has sought to illuminate Luther's theological intent by attending both to the broader context of his argument and to the specificatory discourse that accompanies its development. So long as the primary "divergence statements" remain

92. This intent is clear from what we have already observed about Luther's primary response to Schwenckfeld's concern that referring to Christ as a creature compromises his divinity. Luther grants the concern, but denies the simplistic semantics that fund Schwenckfeld's criticisms. His task, in other words, is to show how traditional christological speech does not entail that divinity changes, or suffers ontological defect. The traditional speech is necessary, though, for maintaining the doctrine of the incarnation, which he suspects Schwenckfeld implicitly to deny.

unexplained, however, there will be space for the identification of a divergence "strand" within Luther's Christology, be this strand ever so slender in its textual support. Once again, the decisive question hinges upon the recognition of "novelty" in Luther's language. So far as the "two-way" statements are concerned, this novelty consists in Luther's suggestion that human predicates be ascribed not simply to "God," but to "divinity" as well. The preceding section has suggested, in effect, that although this sounds like a predication which ontologically conditions the divine nature, it actually refers to the person of Christ, who is God. Is there historical warrant for such an interpretation? Are there theologians before Luther who sometimes enlist "nature vocabulary" in order to refer to predications that actually apply to Christ *qua* person?[93] The third volume of Gabriel Biel's *Collectorium circa quattuor libros Sententiarium* provides crucial background for addressing this question.[94]

In question 1 of distinction 7, Biel asks whether the properties of Christ's divine and human nature may accurately be predicated of one another within the *communicatio idiomatum*, so long as this predication is conceived of in the concrete.[95] Biel addresses this question in a few stages. In the first place, he reminds his reader that the "communication of idioms" refers to the exchange of properties that takes place within the person of Christ.[96] Biel continues, on the basis of this preliminary definition, to note that this exchange

93. In other words, do others suggest that "suffering is ascribed to divinity," and really mean "Christ who is God suffers—that is, God suffers"?

94. This discussion is to be found in Gabriel Biel, Wilfrid Werbeck, Udo Hofmann, Martin Elze, Renate Steiger, Hanns Rückert, and Volker Sievers, *Gabrielis Biel collectorium circa quattuor libros Sententiarum: Liber tertius*, Gabrielis Biel Collectorium Circa Quattuor Libros Sententiarum (Tübingen: J. C. B. Mohr [Paul Siebeck], 1979), 153f.

95. Ibid., 153: "Utrum per idiomatum communicationem concreta utriusque naturae Christi, divinae scilicet et humanae, praedicantur de seinvicem vere et affirmative."

96. Ibid., 154: "Quantum ad primum notandum circa istum terminum »communicationem idiomatum«, quod 'idioma' graece est 'proprietas' latine; et accipitur hic pro concreto importante proprietatem alicuius. Dicitur ergo 'communicatio idiomatum' communicatio proprietatum."

includes within it a mutual ascription of properties between Christ's two natures, all of which apply to the single *suppositum*, which is Christ himself. The governing proviso, however, which constrains the meaning of this description, is Biel's preliminary insistence that such mutual ascription is valid only "in the concrete." In order to illustrate his point, Biel recalls Nicholas Oresme's influential tractate on the communication of idioms. Along with Oresme, Biel affirms a "concrete" discourse of mutual predicate ascription and furnishes several interesting examples of what such predication looks like:

> A first example: as that which, with respect to the divine nature in the concrete, that is, "God," is predicated "de concreto" of the human nature, that is "man," and vice versa, it is to be said that: "Man is God," "God is man," "man is eternal, infinite, creator," and etc. [It is also to be said that] "God is temporal, corruptible, passible, mortal," and etc. Or the second example: "Christ is God," and "Christ is man," etc. This is spoken of concrete things, because abstract things of the natures are not predicated of one another.[97]

This text from Biel provides a crucial hint for determining why Luther occasionally speaks as if Christ's divine nature were the recipient of communicated human properties.[98] Like Luther, Biel refers in this text to a mutual attribution between the divine and human natures of Christ. He even defends the validity of statements which advance the potentially scandalous notion that, in Christ, God

97. Ibid., 154: "Exemplum primi: Ut quod concretum divinae naturae, scilicet 'Deus', praedicatur de concreto humane naturae, scilicet 'homo', et econverso, dicendo: 'Homo est Deus', 'Deus est homo', 'Homo est aeternus, infinitus creator' etc., 'Deus est temporalis, corruptibilis, passibilis, mortalis' etc.—Exemplum secundi: 'Christus est Deus', 'Christus est homo' etc. Dicitur notanter »concretorum«, quia abstracta naturarum non predicantur de seinuicem."

98. Luther's close familiarity with Biel is reflected in Philipp Melanchthon's anecdotal remark that the reformer was capable of referencing entire sections of Biel's theological and pastoral writings from memory. Although Luther was by no means content with every aspect of Biel's theology, he continued to recommend his works in a number of respects even later in his life. See Heiko A. Oberman, *Luther: Man between God and the Devil*, trans. Eileen Walliser-Schwarzbart (New York: Doubleday, 1992), 138. What is clear from all this is that Luther was deeply influenced by his study of Biel, a fact that may go some way in explaining the characteristically nominalist character of several of his late disputations.

is temporal, corruptible, passible, mortal, and so forth. The key for understanding these descriptions, of course, resides in Biel's supervisory insistence that mutual predications apply only "in the concrete." They really refer, in other words, to the single acting subject (Christ) who is both God and man. What we observe in Biel, however, is the appearance of a crucial nuance in the semantics of "nature." He often refers to the person of Christ either as the divine nature in the concrete, or as the human nature in the concrete. Moreover, Biel evinces no awareness that such linguistic practice is revolutionary, or even remarkable.[99] The salient point, so far as interpreting Luther is concerned, is the implication that "divine nature" can denote either divinity itself, or Christ the divine person, depending upon whether this descriptive phrase is considered in the abstract or in the concrete.

This distinction helps make sense of why Luther will occasionally speak as if there is a two-way exchange of attributes between natures even in a context whose accompanying restrictive discourse effectively proscribes such a view. Speaking in this manner does not, in itself, introduce anything fundamentally new within Luther's treatment of the *communicatio idiomatum* when considered against the background of late medieval discourse.[100] Like Biel, Luther's explicit

99. It would be worthwhile, in a future study, to chart the origins of this descriptive pattern. For present purposes, it suffices to observe that referring to Christ as "divinity in the concrete" appears in the work of a late medieval theologian with whose writings Luther was intimately familiar.

100. Are there any direct indications in Luther's discussion that he accepts such a nuanced distinction? In argument 15 of the public debate, Luther responds to the argument that because Moses asserts God to be one, Christ must therefore not be divine. In order to devalidate this syllogism, Luther reinforces the classical distinction between one divine essence and three divine persons. As a means of illustrating this distinction, however, Luther returns to the question of divine suffering, and asserts the following: "Cum ergo dicitur: Divinitas est mortua, tunc includitur, quod etiam pater et Spiritus sanctus sint mortui. Sed hoc non est verum, quia tantum una persona divinitatis, sed filius est natus, mortuus et passus etc. *Ideo natura divina, quando capitur pro persona*, est nata, passa, mortua etc., hoc est verum. Est ergo distinguendum. Si intelligis divinam naturam pro tota divinitate seu unitate, tunc argumentum est falsum, quia solus Christus non est tota trinitas, sed tantum una persona trinitatis" (WA 39/ II:110a; emphasis

restriction that all ascriptions of human properties to divinity refer to God *in the concrete* makes it clear that the object of reference is always the one person of Christ, and never the divine nature as such. By acknowledging this point, even the previously acknowledged prima facie warrant for a divergence interpretation of Luther's christological language effectively erodes away.[101]

Conclusion

In the course of this chapter, we have argued that the textual evidence adduced in favor of a divergence reading of Luther's doctrine of the *communicatio idiomatum* fails to defend its claim adequately that the reformer endorses a participatory suffering of the divine nature of Christ. Most of the textual evidence directed in support of this claim relies upon a false identification of novelty within Luther's preferred modes of christological description. Because of this mistaken identification, divergence interpreters often attach an inordinate degree of significance to texts whose contents turn out to be rather mundane once situated within the discursive landscape of Luther's intellectual environment. A case in point is Luther's mere ascription of human properties "to God," which is frequently vested with revolutionary theological import. A divergence appraisal of such texts

mine). Although not nearly as clear as the passage translated by Biel, this text furnishes at least one instance in which Luther explicitly admits using the language of "divine nature" when the intended referent is actually "persona."

101. John of Damascus constitutes an additional precursor to this descriptive tendency. In chapter 4 of book 3 of *The Orthodox Faith*, he writes of the *communicatio idiomatum*: "Such, then, is the manner of this exchange by which *each nature communicates its own properties to the other* through the identity of their person and their mutual immanence" (emphasis mine). John of Damascus, *Writings*, trans. Frederic H. Chase (Washington, DC: Catholic University of America Press, 1958), 276. John of Damascus receives ample attention throughout the medieval period, as illustrated by the many citations of his writings that populate Lombard's *Sententiae*. It would be premature to conclude that Luther speaks in these terms because of some direct, historical influence (though that is a worthy question for future study). More modestly, though, we can conclude that such reciprocal turns of phrase needn't *entail* a substantive deviation from traditional christological norms.

egregiously overlooks the fact that such ascriptions had been the well-worn semantic custom of mainstream christological reflection for over a millennium before Luther's birth.

A far smaller assemblage of textual loci do seem to lend prima facie support for a divergence interpretation of Luther's Christology. Upon closer investigation, however, even these texts have been shown specifically to proscribe the suffering of Christ's divine nature as such. In the analysis of these texts, it has been crucial to note that Luther's novel tendency to describe a mutual communication of attributes between Christ's natures actually possesses important precedent in the work of Gabriel Biel, a late medieval Scholastic with whose work Luther was intimately familiar. Luther's prolific use of the distinction between abstract and concrete predication (and *secundum quid* qualifiers) makes it abundantly clear that, despite whatever occasional ambiguities may exist in his descriptive vocabulary, his intent is consistently to affirm the single subjectivity of Christ as the rightful recipient of predicates belonging to the divinity and humanity. In expressing this intent, Luther specifically rejects any notion that the divine nature is directly conditioned by the human properties of Christ. He prohibits this implication by enlisting characteristically medieval qualificatory discourse. God suffers, for Luther, only in the sense that the one person who is both God and man suffers on account of his genuine humanity. In light of all this, the widely accepted divergence interpretation of Luther's doctrine of the communication of idioms must be rejected. So far as the suffering of God is concerned, Luther's writings evince fundamental agreement with the patristic and medieval authors who precede him.

Christological Novelty? A Few Concluding Reflections

The past two chapters of this study have sought to address two very specific questions: (1) Does Luther reject or retain the medieval conception of Christ's divine-human person in terms of suppositional carrying?; and (2) Does Luther endorse or proscribe a two-way doctrine of the communication of attributes between natures in which the divine nature of Christ suffers along with the humanity?[102] Recent literature on Luther's Christology often presupposes an answer to these questions, which points rather decisively in the direction of a divergence reception of his thought. According to this view, Luther loosens the shackles of the classically developed doctrine of God by executing a twofold reconfiguration of traditional Christology. The adjustments are deemed necessary, in retrospect, in order to affirm the passionate involvement of God within the events of salvation history.

In its attempt to assess the allegation of twofold christological reconfiguration, chapters 2 and 3 have capitalized upon the fact that most important proponents of a divergence view readily concede that broad swaths of Luther's writing reproduce decidedly traditional views on the matters in question. Because of this concession, the preceding discussion has occupied itself almost exclusively with specific texts adduced by scholars as sites of unambiguous deviation, either with respect to his conception of the hypostatic union, or as it pertains to the communication of attributes. The last two chapters have demonstrated that even these texts evince a robust continuity with characteristic late medieval christological intent, as expressed in

102. Its intent is not, in other words, to ask whether Luther's theology comports with medieval norms in every respect. Such a task would involve a vast array of concerns, and, as such, falls outside the scope of this chapter. Accordingly, the argument for continuity here is neither comprehensive nor necessarily programmatic. Its focus rests entirely upon the issues distilled above.

the heuristically distilled four *desiderata* provided in chapter 2. Like his medieval predecessors, Luther enlists the doctrine of suppositional carrying in his attempt to speak intelligibly (albeit analogically) about the doctrine of the incarnation in a way that avoids fundamental contradiction, and guards against compromising the integrity of Christ's impassible divinity.

All this being the case, it must be concluded that a divergence interpretation of Luther's Christology lacks substantive evidentiary warrant. On the contrary, it may be affirmed (1) that Luther retains the doctrine of suppositional carrying; and (2) that Luther rejects the attribution of Christ's suffering to the divine nature. This twofold conclusion is significant on its own historical terms. It is also important, however, because it represents a fundamental destabilization of many longstanding appropriations of Luther's Christology within contemporary reflection. An analysis of the implication that attends this destabilization must await discussion in chapter 5. The following chapter turns its attention to the way in which Luther's commitment to divine impassibility fits within the fabric of his soterio-logic.

4

Only the Impassible God Can Help

Luther on the Sufferings of Christ and the Invigoration of Human Frailty

The doctrine of divine impassibility seems an obstruction to Luther's soteriology, in the appraisal of many scholars. His is a theology of redemption saturated with divine immanence. In Christ, God enters into radical solidarity with the vulnerable. He shares in their suffering and forsakenness. He absorbs humanity's death and alienation as his own. This chapter will not minimize the importance of these themes within Luther's soteriology. The question is whether these points of emphasis require, as their condition of possibility, a God capable of ontological vulnerability. On the divergence account, the matter is relatively straightforward. To the extent that salvation depends upon God's radical condescension into the state of human misery, Luther simply must expunge the doctrine of divine impassibility.[1]

1. In this respect, Luther is taken to be a harbinger of modern theological tendencies. For one example of how Luther is interpreted as part of the "prehistory" for these recent developments, see Victor Keding, "Wider das Apathieaxiom: Die theopaschitische Christologie des späten

This is to presuppose a specific sort of coordination between Luther's Christology and soteriology. Salvation requires a passible God, and Luther's renovated doctrine of the *communicatio idiomatum* delivers. In this chapter, we will argue in favor of a contrary mode of alignment: the structure of Luther's soteriology does not eschew, but actually requires, an abiding affirmation of divine impassibility.

Christology and Soteriology in Luther's Thought

Luther's doctrine of the "joyful exchange" is a major site of intersection between his respective doctrines of Christ and redemption.[2] The exchange motif envisions a redemptive sharing of attributes between Christ and the Christian. The resultant transaction is reciprocal in its effects. Christ takes upon himself all of the sin, death, curse, and punishment that belongs to sinful flesh, and imparts to Christians his own righteousness, vitality, and innocence. Creative permutations of this exchange pattern pervade Luther's theological output from its earliest stages and remain to the end of his career.

Elert und ihre Wirkungsgeschichte," in *Mit dem Menschen verhandeln über den Sachgehalt des Evangeliums: die Bedeutung der Theologie Werner Elerts für die Gegenwart*, ed. Rudolf Keller and Michael Roth (Erlangen: Martin-Luther-Verlag, 2004), 83.

2. Among the most important studies are: Uwe Rieske-Braun, *Duellum mirabile: Studien zum Kampfmotiv in Martin Luthers Theologie*, Forschungen zur Kirchen- und Dogmengeschichte, Bd. 73 (Göttingen: Vandenhoeck & Ruprecht, 1999); and Walter Allgaier, *Der "froehliche Wechsel" bei Martin Luther; eine Untersuchung zu Christologie und Soteriologie bei Luther unter besonderer Beruecksichtigung der Schriften bis 1521*, unpub. diss. (Erlangen-Nürnberg, 1966). Another chapter treatment of Luther's use of this theme is available in Raymund Schwager, *Der wunderbare Tausch: zur Geschichte und Deutung der Erlösungslehre* (München: Kösel, 1986). Theobald Beer also provides copious citations that demonstrate the importance of this image throughout Luther's lifetime, although I strongly disagree with the manner in which Beer seeks to interpret Luther's soteriology. Theobald Beer, *Der fröhliche Wechsel und Streit: Grundzüge der Theologie Luthers* (Leipzig: St. Benno-Verlag, 1974). This chapter will assume what each of these books amply demonstrates, namely, that Luther's soteriology is often expressed in terms of a joyful exchange, and that the metaphor itself furnishes something like an organizational nerve center for Luther's understanding of redemption.

Luther's 1520 treatise "On the Freedom of a Christian" contains a representative instance.[3]

In this text, Luther likens the union of Christ and the believing Christian to the nuptial bond that unites an earthly husband with his wife. Just as the material possessions carried into marriage become the shared "property" of both spouses, so the Christian is grafted into the riches of Christ's boundless life and righteousness. Luther explains:

> Accordingly the believing soul can boast of and glory in whatever Christ has as though it were its own, and whatever the soul has Christ claims as his own. Let us compare these and we shall see inestimable benefits. Christ is full of grace, life, and salvation. The soul is full of sins, death, and damnation. Now let faith come between them and sins, death, and damnation will be Christ's, while grace, life, and salvation will be the soul's; for if Christ is a bridegroom, he must take upon himself the things which are his bride's and bestow upon her the things that are his. If he gives her his body and very self, how shall he not give

3. The Latin version of this description is available in WA 7:54–55: "Tertia fidei gratia incomparabilis est haec, Quod animam copulat cum Christo, sicut sponsam cum sponso. Quo sacramento (ut Apostolus docet) Christus et anima efficiuntur una caro. Quod si una caro sunt verumque inter eos matrimonium, immo omnium longe perfectissimum consumatur, cum humana matrimonia huius unici figurae sint tenues, Sequitur, et omnia eorum communia fieri tam bona quam mala, ut, quaecunque Christus habet, de iis tanquam suis praesumere et gloriari possit fidelis anima, Et quaecunque animae sunt, ea sibi arroget Christus tanquam sua. Conferamus ista, et videbimus inaestimabilia. Christus plenus est gratia, vita et salute, Anima plena est peccatis, morte et damnatione. Intercedat iam fides, et fiet, ut Christi sint peccata, mors et infernus, Animae vero gratia, vita et salus: oportet enim eum, si sponsus est, ea simul quae sponsa habet acceptare et ea quae sua sunt sponsae impartire. Qui enim corpus suum et se ipsum illi donat, quomodo non omnia sua donat? Et qui corpus sponsae accipit, quomodo non omnia quae sponsae sunt accipit? Hic iam dulcissimum spectaculum prodit non solum communionis sed salutaris belli et victoriae et salutis et redemptionis. Cum enim Christus sit deus et homo eaque persona, quae nec peccavit nec moritur nec damnatur, sed nec peccare, mori, damnari potest, Eiusque iustitia, vita, salus insuperabilis, aeterna, omnipotens est, Cum, inquam, talis persona peccata, mortem, infernum sponsae et propter annulum fidei sibi communia, immo propria facit et in iis non aliter se habet quam si sua essent ipseque peccasset, laborans, moriens et ad infernum descendens, ut omnia superaret, peccatumque, mors et infernus eum absorbere non possent, necessario in ipso absorpta sunt stupendo duello. Nam iustitia sua omnium peccatis superior, vita sua omni morte potentior, salus sua omni inferno invictior. Ita fit anima fidelis per arram fidei suae in Christo, sponso suo, omnibus peccatis libera, a morte secura et ab inferno tuta, donata aeterna iustitia, vita, salute sponsi sui Christi. Sic exhibet sibi sponsam sine macula et ruga gloriosam, mundans eam lavacro in verbo vitae, id est per fidem verbi, vitae, iustitiae et salutis. Sic sponsat eam sibi in fide, in misericordia et miserationibus, in iustitia et iuditio, ut Oseae 2. dicit." English translation for this passage is available in LW 31:351–52.

> her all that is his? And if he takes the body of the bride, how shall he not take all that is hers?[4]

This text is representative of the motif in Luther's theology, but not exhaustive of the range of applications to which he directs it. Uwe Riesko-Braun rightly cautions against any facile reduction of the metaphor to a single aspect of salvation.[5] Luther's soteriological vocabulary is rich in creative diversity. The exchange motif provides a framework within which a whole range of specific applications can appear.[6]

The christological substructure implicit in the motif is significant. It includes two essential affirmations: (1) a genuine condescension of Christ into the state of sinful humanity; and (2) a genuine exaltation of Christ from this state. In the absence of either affirmation, the redemptive union Luther envisions between God and humanity is a sham. If Christ really is genuinely united with sinners, he must appropriate their drastic situation existentially as his own. The bridegroom must share in all things that belong to the bride. On the one hand, this requires a christological vocabulary that is able to affirm a radical condescension, indeed. On the other hand, condescension is not redemptive in and of itself. Christ cannot remain at the nadir of human abjection. He must emerge victorious

4. LW 31:351.
5. For a sense of the range of emphasis available to Luther through this metaphor, see the following studies: Rieske-Braun, *Duellum mirabile*; Allgaier, *Der "froehliche Wechsel"*; Carl Heinz Ratschow, "Christologie und Rechtfertigung: Luthers Christologie nach seinen Disputationen," in *Iustificatio impii* (Helsinki: Suomalaisen Teologisen Kirjallisuusseura, 1977), 204–226.
6. This semi-nondeterminate malleability is partially the cause of longstanding debates within Luther scholarship over how best to characterize Luther's atonement theology. For a helpful overview of these debates, see Rieske-Braun, *Duellum mirabile*, 23–65; and Hans-Martin Barth, *Der Teufel und Jesus Christus in der Theologie Martin Luthers*, Forschungen zur Kirchen- und Dogmengeschichte, Bd. 19 (Göttingen: Vandenhoeck & Ruprecht, 1967), 50–73. Part of the problem with many aspects of the debates described in these books is the reductive presupposition that many of its participants share, namely, that Luther's soteriology must finally be distilled into a single governing point of emphasis.

from the depths of human suffering, carrying the redeemed in his train.

The shape of Luther's soteriology is thus "parabolic." Becoming like humanity in all things, Christ, the Son of God, descends into the depths of sin's abyss. From this low estate, he emerges triumphant, and ascends into glory along with those who, through faith, live in union with him. Christ conquers sin, death, and hell, as it were, from the inside out. He plunges into the dark recesses of human misery and defeats it. The principalities of oppression are overcome. Christ appropriates the curse of sin, corruption, and death, and rises up in unqualified triumph, crushing them beneath his feet. These descriptive patterns account for the dramatic character of Luther's doctrine of salvation.

The parabolic structure just described enables us to pose a few specific questions that pertain to the divergence thesis. Many of these questions have to do with the theme of radical condescension. What does it mean, for instance, when Luther insists that the Son of God—or even God in Godself—enters fully into the estate of human abjection? In what way does God experience the ontological limitations of finitude in doing so? Would it be appropriate, for instance, to surmise that Christ's divine nature becomes vulnerable? On the other hand, what accounts for the second half of the parabola? Why is Christ victorious over death? What must Luther presuppose christologically in order to affirm that Christ really appropriates human frailty in the most radical sense, yet breaks the shackles of death itself? These questions may be condensed into four central issues:

1. How does the divine nature relate to the "solidarity motif" embedded within the metaphor of exchange?

2. What role does Christ's divinity fulfill in the suffering and death of his passion?
3. What are the precise soteriological "mechanics" through which Luther deems it possible for humanity to be translated from its "low" estate (in suffering and death) to the exalted status bestowed upon it through Christ?
4. What, according to Luther, accounts for this transition *christologically*?

Each of these questions circles in upon a single, synthetic concern: How does Luther's soteriology coordinate and interface with two-nature Christology?

The divergence thesis offers a plausible account of this coordination, which may be summarized as follows. Salvation, for Luther, requires the radical condescension of God, and such a condescension requires the divine nature to share in human suffering. Therefore, an impassible God cannot save. This passibilist account of the condescension motif is compelling as a synthetic construct. The remainder of this chapter will demonstrate, however, that it seriously misunderstands the christological substructure of Luther's soteriology.

Divergence Soteriology

The divergence thesis provides a compelling theological rationale for Luther's alleged rejection of divine impassibility. According to this rationale, the redemptive potency of Christ's suffering solidarity requires that he be capable of suffering not simply as a man, but also as God. This is because a Christ impassible according to his divinity would ostensibly signify a God incapable of real condescension. If the incarnate Son remains somehow "untouched" or "invulnerable" in the midst of his passion, then the downward bend of Luther's redemptive parabola would stop short of genuine intersection with its symptotic baseline. An impassible God cannot genuinely share in the desperate condition of human beings hopelessly entangled in the deleterious effects of corruption and sin.[7] God must become "vulnerable," because that is precisely the estate of those God condescends to redeem.

In this way, the "solidarity of God" motif presupposed by Luther's exchange soteriology functions as a conceptual wedge, urging upon readers the intrasystemic necessity for Luther to reject the doctrine of divine impassibility. It is on the basis of this fundamental rationale that the divergence thesis triangulates its alleged coordination between Christology and soteriology in Luther's theology. A reciprocal doctrine of the *communicatio idiomatum* walks hand in hand with the redemptive exchange Luther envisions between Christ and the Christian. The divinity of Christ shares in human weakness, and only thus is Christ truly united with those he comes to redeem. At the base of the parabola is a God rendered ontologically vulnerable, standing in radical solidarity with the godforsaken.

The exchange motif, as interpreted by the divergence thesis, thus amounts to a kind of redemptively oriented inversion of Christ's divine and human attributes. Divinity is brought low so that humanity might be raised up. Christ suffers and dies according to both natures, and a moribund human race, enmeshed in the suffering,

7. It is fairly common for divergence interpreters to volley the charge of docetism against soteriologies that stop short of a passibilist solidarity. See, for instance, Marc Lienhard, *Luther: Witness to Jesus Christ: Stages and Themes of the Reformer's Christology* (Minneapolis: Augsburg, 1982), 175–76, 335–36. There is irony in this charge, however, since the patristic theologians responsible for identifying "docetism" in the first place were themselves deeply committed to the doctrine of divine impassibility. It seems illegitimate to apply the nomenclature of "docetist" in a way that cuts against its original meaning. For more on the history of the doctrine of divine impassibility in relation to patristic debates over Christology and the doctrine of God, see Paul L. Gavrilyuk, *The Suffering of the Impassible God: The Dialectics of Patristic Thought*, Oxford Early Christian Studies (New York: Oxford University Press, 2004).

death, and corruption of sin, is healed and raised up to life immortal. What are the soteriological mechanics that account for this transition? How is it that Christ does not simply meet human beings in the mire, but also pulls them up from it? If Christ suffers, bleeds, and dies according to his divinity, how is it that he defeats death? In other words, why aren't the left-wing Hegelians right? If God died, they reason, then God does not exist. Luther, of course, has no room for this conclusion. In a representative text from 1544, he insists that Christ did not enter the grave so that he might stay there.[8] If Christ died according to both natures, though, in what sense is Christ victorious over death?

A historical ontology of God's being offers an answer to this question. For many divergence interpreters, God absorbs and overcomes death by means of dialectical mediation. The negations of sin, death, and hell are resolved, according to this view, on the basis of a doctrine of God's ontological historicity.[9] It is therefore not just the event of salvation that is "parabolic," but God's own being (as expressed by and related to this event) as well.[10] The pain and plight of fallen human beings becomes an episode of the divine life. It is assumed as an ontologically conditioning, and thus constitutive, aspect of God's own self-actualization.[11]

8. See WA 40/3:732.
9. For a list of the various scholars and theologians who credit Luther with the historicization of God's being, see the summary provided in ch. 1.
10. Care must be exercised to avoid an overly determinate account of what the historicity of God entails for various modern interpreters of Luther. As in contemporary theology, the term itself may be invoked in a number of different ways. In this context, we are using it to denote any view that includes within it the idea that God's being has a history that is conditioned in some way by the events of salvation history. Whether this is explained entirely in terms of a free, self-electing prolepsis, as some Barthians today argue, or through Pannenberg's idea of eschatological analepsis, is not important to the point we are trying to make here. These and many other views would all fall together within the general trend that divergence interpreters believe Luther to anticipate.
11. This interpretation of the relation between Luther's Christology and soteriology has led a number of scholars to detect conceptual resonances between Luther and G. W. F. Hegel. The question of what counts as "Hegelian" with respect to the doctrine of God is often contested

The fundamental soteriological mechanics operative in a divergence interpretation of Luther's doctrine of redemption could therefore be summarized in the following manner:

> God becomes truly vulnerable in Christ by entering into the depths of human corruption. Christ resolves the defects of sinful existence by subsuming them within the historical process of God's own dialectically mediated self-existence. Those in union with Christ through faith are caught up into the sequential processes of divine becoming. In Christ, God identifies God's own being with sinful humanity. In so doing, God offers them a share in God's eschatological future.

The conceptual progression embedded within this interpretation proceeds as follows:

> *Guiding Principle*: The radical solidarity of God as sympathetic suffering.
>
> *Requisite Conceptual Substructure*: A Christology of divine vulnerability.
>
> *Soteriological Mechanics*: The dialectical historicity of God.

The chief consolation for those bound up in sin, suffering, and death, in other words, consists in the fact that God truly suffers for us and with us. God identifies with the plight of humanity in sympathetic condescension and allows the defects of postlapsarian finitude to condition God's very being. Because God becomes frail or vulnerable as humans are, so also can those who live in union with God hope

in modern theological discourse. Jürgen Moltmann, for instance, emphasizes the historicity of God's being, but has consistently rebuffed the accusation that this emphasis stems from directly Hegelian influences. For our purposes, we can only document the shared trajectory many interpreters of Luther have identified regarding the notion of God's essential *historicity*. There are any number of theological directions in which this basic insight can be, and has been, directed. For more on Hegel's point of view, see the pertinent sections of Peter C. Hodgson, *Hegel and Christian Theology: A Reading of the Lectures on the Philosophy of Religion* (New York: Oxford University Press, 2005); Quentin Lauer, *Hegel's Concept of God* (Albany: State University of New York Press, 1982); and Cyril O'Regan, *The Heterodox Hegel* (Albany: State University of New York Press, 1994).

to share in the final telos of God's own parabolic, transhistorical development.[12]

Advocates of the divergence thesis defend a passibilist coordination of Luther's Christology and soteriology on the basis of a few central texts. The most important appears in Luther's 1539 treatise "On the Councils and the Church":

> We Christians should know that if God is not in the scale to give it weight, we, on our side, sink to the ground. I mean it this way: if it cannot be said that God died for us, but only a man, we are lost; but if God's death and a dead God lie in the balance, his side goes down and ours goes up like a light and empty scale. Yet he can also readily go up again, or leap out of the scale! But he could not sit on the scale unless he had become a man like us, so that it [sic] could be called God's dying, God's martyrdom, God's blood, and God's death. For God in his own nature cannot die; but now that God and man are united in one person, it is called God's death when the man dies who is one substance or one person with God.[13]

Here is an exemplary instance of the solidarity motif, which is so central to the parabolic structure of Luther's soteriology. For Dennis Ngien, this text demonstrates the essential role of divine passibility within this structure. Ngien's comments are representative of many other scholars:

12. This overview is a heuristic survey. Some scholars would arrange the data somewhat differently. The common affirmation, for all advocates of the divergence thesis, is that Luther's soteriology requires divine passibility.
13. LW 41:103–104. WA 50:590: "Denn wir Christen muessen das wissen, wo Gott nicht mit in der woge ist und das gewichte gibt, so sincken wir mit unser schuessel zu grunde, Das meine ich also: Wo es nicht solt heissen, Gott ist fur uns gestorben, sondern allein ein mensch, so sind wir verloren, Aber wenn Gottes tod und Gott gestorben in der wogeschuessel ligt, so sincket er unter und wir faren empor, als eine leichte ledige schuessel, Aber er kan wol auch wider emporfaren oder aus seiner schuessel springen. Er kuendte aber nicht in die schuessel sitzen, Er mueste uns gleich ein mensch werden, das es heissen kuendte, Gott gestorben, Gottes marter, Gottes blut, Gottes tod, Denn Gott in seiner natur kan nicht sterben, Aber nu Gott und Mensch vereinigt ist in einer Person, so heissts recht Gottes tod, wenn der mensch stirbt, der mit Gott ein ding oder eine Person ist."

> [In this text] Luther justifies his remarks on the suffering and death of God in Christ on soteriological grounds. Already in his *Church Postil* (1522), Luther says that if it is true that only the human nature suffers and the divine nature has no part in it, then Christ is of no more use to us than any other saint because his death is merely that of a human being. Christ's achievement would then become a pure model for the faithful, turning Christ simply into an exemplar. In order to redeem human beings from the power of death, God has to co-suffer and co-die in Christ. That is why Luther makes use of the image of the scale, to illustrate that God can go down, can rise and jump out of his pan. God lets himself be overtaken by death in the suffering and dying of Jesus, and yet he remains the victor over death. The divine nature was present throughout the earthly life of Jesus, and was not untouched by the whole affair of the incarnation. With this it becomes clear how closely the two-nature Christology and soteriology are linked in Luther's thinking. It is a theological axiom that Christ be affected by suffering even according to his divine nature, otherwise salvation through Christ's suffering is inconceivable to him.[14]

Ngien's reasoning here presupposes a key semantic equation that has already surfaced in previous chapters. He assumes that the phrase "God suffers" is essentially the same, in Luther's mind, as "divinity suffers." Predicates, which are applied to God, in other words, are taken automatically to apply to Christ's divine nature. This assumption is premature, as chapter 3 demonstrates. Luther's christological semantics are nuanced and complex. Along with a multitude of patristic and medieval antecedents, he often applies attributes to God that belong in the strict sense to Christ's human nature.[15] In any case, the mere appearance of such predications in the 1539 text copied above is hardly sufficient evidence for the revolutionary significance Ngien purports to find.

14. Dennis Ngien, "Chalcedonian Christology and Beyond: Luther's Understanding of the *Communicatio Idiomatum*," *Heythrop Journal* 45 (2004): 59.

15. In other words, the human predicates apply to God in the sense that Christ, the second person of the Trinity, is the acting subject in whom the humanity subsists. The attributes really do belong to God, but only according to the humanity God has assumed.

In fact, Luther specifically clarifies the intended sense of these predications by stipulating that "God cannot die in His nature."[16] What is the function of this qualification? Ngien insists upon a diachronic reading. God was incapable of death prior to the incarnation, but is now capable of ontological deficiency on account of the *communicatio idiomatum*. A major weakness of this approach is that it attaches novel significance to ordinary speech.[17] In any case, the previous chapter has already argued against a diachronic rendering of Luther's christological semantics. A closer analysis of this particular text will yield the same conclusion.

The "God on the scale" passage appears in a section of Luther's 1539 treatise "On the Councils and the Church," in which Luther is engaging the ancient heresy of Nestorianism.[18] The text singles in upon Nestorius's persistent refusal to ascribe human predicates to God. He famously refuses to describe the virgin Mary as the "bearer of God," or Θεοτόκος. For Luther, the denial is pernicious. Christ is a single person and not two agencies thinly stitched together. Unless Christ is truly God, our salvation is a hollow charade. This is the context of the paragraph in question. We must speak boldly of "God's blood" and "God's death." Orthodox Christology and the reality of salvation depend upon our doing so. What is the specific nature of Luther's critique of Nestorius in this text? That is the crucial question, which we must now address.

Ngien assumes that Luther's dissatisfaction has to do with Nestorius's commitment to the doctrine of divine impassibility.[19] Nestorius errs because he imports a philosophically determined

16. Emphasis mine. WA 50:590: "Denn Gott in seiner natur kan nicht sterben."
17. In other words, qualifications of this sort are not alien to late medieval christological discourse. Luther's intent is far from ambiguous once this context is presupposed.
18. Luther, however, deals with Nestorius primarily in relation to the council of Ephesus—a reflection, no doubt, of the insufficient historical resources with which he was working. This portion of Luther's description reflected in this section's discussion is available in WA 50:583–92. An English translation may be found in LW 41:95–106.

concept of God and artificially restricts christological discourse on its basis. He wrongly assumes that "divinity" is incapable of suffering and death. Luther's response, on this account, is to reject Nestorius's philosophical assumptions about deity. This specification of Luther's anti-Nestorian polemic is inaccurate. Luther does not chastise Nestorius because he assumes that divinity is incapable of suffering. He criticizes the fifth-century bishop for rejecting orthodox christological speech on the basis of faulty logic. Nestorius wrongly assumes that an ascription of human predicates to God must entail a coextensive application of the same predicates to Christ's divinity. The entailment does not follow. Nestorius's failure to understand this leads him to speak as if Christ were two distinct persons.

Luther concedes, then, that Nestorius did not intend to divide Christ into two agencies. Yet, he functionally betrays the unity of Christ by rejecting the *communicatio idiomatum*: "Thus Nestorius' error was not that he believed Christ to be a pure man, or that he made two persons of him; on the contrary, he confesses two natures, the divine and the human, in one person—but he will not admit a *communicatio idiomatum*."[20] What Nestorius fails to recognize are

19. Dennis Ngien, *The Suffering of God according to Martin Luther's 'Theologia Crucis'* (Vancouver: Regent College Publishing, 2005), 75. Ngien cites the interpretation of Reiner Jansen as corroboration of this view.

20. LW 41:100–101. The quote continues: "I cannot express that in one word in German. *Idioma* means that which is inherent in a nature or is its attribute, such as dying, suffering, weeping, speaking, laughing, eating, drinking, sleeping, sorrowing, rejoicing, being born, having a mother, suckling the breast, walking, standing, working, sitting, lying down, and other things of that kind, which are called *idiomata naturae humanae*, that is, qualities that belong to man by nature, which he can and must do or even suffer; for *idioma* in Greek, *proprium* in Latin, is a thing—let us, for the time being, call it an attribute. Again, an *idioma deitatis*, 'an attribute of divine nature,' is that it is immortal, omnipotent, infinite, not born, does not eat, drink, sleep, stand, walk, sorrow, weep—and what more can one say? To be God is an immeasurably different thing than to be man; that is why the *idiomata* of the two natures cannot coincide. That is the opinion of Nestorius." WA 50:587: "So ist nu Nestorij jrthum nicht der, das er Christum fur einen puren Menschen helt, auch nicht zwo personen draus macht, Sondern zwo natur, Gott und mensch, in einer person bekennet, Aber Communicationem idiomatum wil er nicht zugeben, das kan ich mit einem wort nicht deudsch reden, Idioma heisst, was einer natur anhangt oder jr eigenschafft ist, Als sterben, leiden, weinen, reden, lachen, essen,

the semantic implications entailed by single-subject Christology. The predicates of Christ's human nature *must* apply to God, otherwise the incarnation is not real. Nestorius's heresy is thus an inadvertent product of logical incompetence, not an intentional perversion of doctrine through malice.[21] Luther writes:

> This crude, unlearned man did not see that he was asserting the impossible when simultaneously he seriously took Christ to be God and man in one person and yet declined to ascribe the *idiomata* of the natures to the same person of Christ. He wants to hold to the truth of the first, but what follows from the first should not be true—he thereby indicates that he himself does not understand what he is denying.[22]

In this respect, Luther's critique of Nestorius anticipates the impending skirmish with Caspar Schwenckfeld, reflected in his christological disputation of 1540.[23] In neither case is divine impassibility the hub of controversy. What Nestorius and Schwenckfeld share in common, albeit for different reasons, is a refusal to ascribe human predicates to God on account of the hypostatic union. Nestorius, in particular, is caught on the horns

trincken, schlaffen, trauren, freuen, geborn werden, mutter haben, brueste saugen, gehen, stehen, erbeiten, sitzen, ligen, und was des mehr ist, heissen idiomata naturae humanae, das ist eigenschafft, die einem menschen von natur anhangen, als die er thun oder leiden kan auch wol mus, Denn Jdioma griechisch, proprium latine, ist ein ding, Lasts uns dieweil ein eigenschafft heissen. Widerumb, Jdioma Deitatis, Goettlicher natur eigenschafft ist, das sie unsterblich, allmechtig, unendlich, nicht geborn, nicht isset, trinckt, schlefft, stehet, gehet, trauret, weinet und was sol man viel sagen? Es ist gar ein unmeslich ander ding, Gott, weder ein mensch ist, darumb koennen die idiomata beider natur nicht ubereinkomen, Dis ist die meinung Nestorij."

21. In this respect, Luther's treatment of Nestorius echoes longstanding appraisals originating in the patristic period. The early church historian Socrates, for instance, felt that Nestorius's error was one of pride and ignorance, not substantive theological disagreement. See Frances Young and Andrew Teal, *From Nicaea to Chalcedon*, 2d ed. (London: SCM Press, 2010), 292.
22. LW 41:102–103. WA 50:589: "Denn der große ungelerte Man sahe das nicht, das er unmueglich ding furgab, das er zugleich Christum ernstlich fur Gott und mensch in einer Person hielt, und doch die Jdiomata der naturn nicht wolt derselben Person Christi zugeben, Das erst wil er fur war halten, und das sol nicht war sein, das doch aus dem ersten folget, damit er anzeigt, das er selbs nicht verstehet, was er verneinet."
23. Luther explicitly lumps Nestorius and Schwenckfeld together in his 1544 commentary on Isaiah 53; see WA 40/3:703. There are also deep resonances with Luther's oft-expressed criticism of Ulrich Zwingli. Luther draws this connection within the 1539 treatise; see WA 50:591.

of an illusory dilemma. He assumes that he must choose either (1) to protect the integrity of deity; or (2) to affirm the application of human predicates to God in Christ. The choice is a false one. The dilemma only exists because Nestorius fails to distinguish between ascriptions that refer to the person of Christ and those that refer to the natures of Christ.[24] Luther's quarrel is not with what Nestorius's semantic proscription denies, but with what it inadvertently fails to affirm.

The besetting problem, in other words, is a clumsy christological semantics. Nestorius imagines that the application of creaturely predicates to God logically demands that Christ's divinity is ontologically conditioned. For him, the term Θεοτόκος entails Arianism. It implies the Son of God derives his divine existence from an act of temporal generation. Luther accepts Nestorius's premise, but rejects his conclusion. He agrees that Christ's divinity is not derived from Mary's womb.[25] And yet, because Christ is a single person, the predicates of both natures must apply to God. It is thus not Nestorius's doctrine of God that misleads him, but his lack of logical sophistication.[26] The phrase "God suffers" does not entail

24. This is the very distinction Luther's qualificatory discourse seeks to express.

25. The problem is that Nestorius denies more than he needs to in order to preserve this belief. Once again, Luther ultimately credits his incompetence for his inadvertent heresy; see WA 50:589.

26. Luther articulates this basic criticism throughout his treatment of Nestorius. Perhaps the most forthright example appears in LW 41:101–102: "Thus his folly is exactly that against which one teaches in the schools, 'One who admits the premise of a good conclusion cannot deny the conclusion.' In German we would say, 'If the one is true, the other must also be true; if the second is not true, then the first is not true either.' Whoever admits that Greta is your wife cannot deny that her child (if she is pious) is your child. If one teaches these things in the schools, no one thinks that there could be such crude people; but ask the regents and jurists whether they are not often confronted by such parties, who admit something and still do not want to grant what follows from it." WA 50:588: "Und ist seine narrheit eben die, dawider man leret in den schulen: Qui concedit antecedens bonae consequentiae, non potest negare consequens, Auff Deudsch reden wir also: Jst eines war, so mus das ander auch war sein, ist das ander nicht war, so ist das erst auch nicht war. Wer das zugibt, das Greta dein ehefrau sey, der kan nicht leugnen, das jr kind (wo sie from ist) dein kind sey. Wenn man solchs in der Schulen leret, so denckt niemand, das solche grobe Leute sein koennen, Aber frage die Regenten und

divine passibility. To reject the phrase "God suffers," however, entails a rejection of the incarnation.

Ngien misconstrues the nature of Luther's criticism of Nestorius. This is why he advances a passibilist interpretation of Luther's scale metaphor, even though the passage strictly states that God cannot suffer in God's own nature. Luther affirms Nestorius's unwillingness to say that Christ suffers according to his divinity. Ironically, Ngien's interpretation presupposes the very semantic equation for which Luther chastises Nestorius—namely, that "God suffers" is basically the same as "*divinity* suffers."[27]

The Deathless Might of Christ

Luther's soteriology presupposes that something is uniquely true of Christ, on account of his being divine, which allows him to enter into death and yet live; to fall under condemnation, and yet attain vindication; to suffer, and yet not be destroyed. In a 1537 sermon preached on John 1, Luther comments: "If Christ is not true and natural God, born of the Father in eternity and Creator of all

Juristen drumb, ob sie nicht haben offt solche Part fur sich gehabt, die ein ding bekennen und doch nicht zulassen wollen, was daraus folget."

27. The "scale metaphor" appears elsewhere in Luther's corpus. In a sermon on John 3, preached in 1538, Luther writes: "Daruber haben die aldten veter sehr gekempfft und es widder die ketzer erhalten, das in Christo zweierlej naturen sind, aber nicht zwo person, sondern nur ein Sohn. Also redet die Schriefft, und wir sollen auch also reden. Nach der Menscheit, do ist wohl gecreutziget, und nach der Gottheit allein Himel und Erden geschaffen, aber dieweil diese Person Got und mensch ist, so wird recht gesaget: Gottes Sohn ist Schopffer himmels und der erden und wirdt auch gecreutziget. Man mus die Person nicht zutrennen, als, das alleine die Menscheit da bliebe, sondern sie auch Gott gewesen ist, wie den S. Hilarius saget: Christus passus est requiescente verbo. Und wen wir auch das nicht erhalten, das diese person sej Gott und mensch, so am creutz gestorben ist, so musten wir ewiglich verdampt und verlorn sein, den wir mussen einen Heiland haben, der mehr sej, dan ein Heilige oder Engel, den wen ehr nicht mehr, grosser und besser were, so wurde uns nicht geholffen. So ehr aber Gott ist, so ist der Schatz so schweer, das ehr nicht allein wegkwieget und auffhebt die Sunde und den todt, sondern auch gibt das ewige leben. Das kondte sonst kein Mensch geben noch thun, oder den Teuffel und tod uberwinden" (WA 47:87). The partitive qualifications, which specify what is true of Christ according to each nature, are even clearer here.

creatures, we are doomed. For what would Christ's suffering and death avail me if Christ were merely a human being like you and me? As such He could not have overcome devil, death, and sin; He would have proved far too weak for them and could never have helped us."[28]

In Christ, God is indeed radically involved. God enters into the condition of sinful humanity. God does not do so, however, in such a way that renders God the helpless victim of powers beyond God's control. Luther portrays the incarnate Christ as vulnerable and invulnerable at the same time. In a sermon preached in 1538, Luther writes: "The incarnate God, who was born of the Virgin Mary, suffered the old serpent's sting and bite, but without being devoured and destroyed."[29] What accounts for the apparent incongruity? Two questions must be posed: (1) How is Christ "stung"? and (2) Why is he not thereby destroyed?

The tension is christologically sourced. Two sets of radically different properties are true of the incarnate Christ at one and the same time. In 1513, Luther writes of Christ that "He is at the same time cursed and blessed, at the same time alive and dead, at the same time grieving and rejoicing."[30] Contrastive litanies like this one

28. LW 22:21. WA 46:554: ". . . denn bleibet Christus nicht warer, natuerlicher GOTT, von Vater in ewigkeit geboren, und Schoepffer aller Creaturn, so sind wir verloren. Denn was were mir mit der HERRN Christi leiden und sterben geholffen, wenn er ein Mensch nur were wie ich und du? so hette er den Teufel, Tod und die Suende nicht uberwinden koennen, er were jnen viel zu schwach gewesen, hette uns auch nicht helffen koennen."

29. LW 22:469. WA 47:180: "Sondern der Gott, der do ist mensch worden, geborn von Maria der Jungfrauen, der leidet den stich und biss der altten schlangen. Aber ehr wirdt drumb nicht gahr auffgefressen und verschlungen." Luther's main point in this section is to illustrate the impotence of all assaults against Christ, of which the rejection of Christ's teaching as heresy is foremost. Luther likens this impotence, however, to the fact that Christ truly dies (thus appearing to be vanquished) and yet rises again in victory.

30. LW 10:364–65. WA 3:426: "Non intellexerunt etiam, quod maledictio ista non potuit totam personam absorbere, sed fuit absorpta, quia deus erat nulli potens maledictione subiacere, sed tantummodo caro eius. Et ideo simul maledictus et benedictus, simul vivus et mortuus, simul dolens et gaudens, ut omnia in se absorberet mala et omnia ex se conferret bona. Benedictus dominus noster Amen." The reader will note, in this broader context, that Luther explains the unconquerability of Christ in light of his divinity, which renders his person incapable of being swallowed up and destroyed. Subsequent discussion will highlight the implications of this point for "aligning" Luther's soteriology and Christology.

are common throughout Luther's writings.[31] The sheer simultaneity of Luther's twofold designation of Christ is striking. The incarnate Christ is not first blessed, and then cursed; first alive, and then dead; first invulnerable, and then vulnerable. No, there is a synchronic concurrence of contrastive attributes, which continues throughout the life of Christ, and reaches the apex of its intensity precisely at the nadir of the parabola's downward swing: the radical solidarity of God with sinners enacted in the crucifixion of Jesus. If the divergence account were true, we would not expect this to be the case. A passibilist Christology could only account for half of the contrastive attributes. If Christ is ontologically vulnerable according to both natures, then one would expect to find *only* grief, death, suffering, and condemnation at the crucifixion. And yet, Luther insists that Christ is blessed even as he is cursed; alive even as he is dead; and rejoicing even as he grieves. This contrast is not easily reconciled with a divergence interpretation of Luther's soteriology.

These predicate oppositions are crucial for Luther's soteriology. The exchange metaphor envisions a massive strife of contraries, which comes to a climax at the nadir of God's condescension in Christ. The low point of this descent is the site of a great redemptive battle—an epic struggle between life and death; sin and righteousness; corruptibility and incorruptibility; God's power and the devil's sting. There is not just an exchange that transpires, but also a duel and

31. A late manifestation of this sharp contrast is to be found in Luther's 1544 commentary on Isaiah 53; see WA 40/3:700–706. In this section, Luther is addressing the criticism that Christ cannot be the Messiah, or God, because he is described as deformed and unsightly. Luther's fundamental response is that Christ is both true man and true God at one and the same time.

conflict.[32] Luther's 1520 treatise "On the Freedom of a Christian" is representative of this *Kampfmotiv* ("battle motif").

> Here we have a most pleasing vision not only of communion but of a blessed struggle and victory and salvation and redemption. Christ is God and man in one person. He has neither sinned nor died, and is not condemned, and he cannot sin, die, or be condemned; his righteousness, life, and salvation are unconquerable, eternal, omnipotent. By the wedding ring of faith he shares in the sins, death, and pains of hell which are his bride's. As a matter of fact, he makes them his own and acts as if they were his own and as if he himself had sinned; he suffered, died, and descended into hell that he might overcome them all. Now since it was such a one who did all this, and death and hell could not swallow him up, these were necessarily swallowed up by him in a mighty duel; for his righteousness is greater than the sins of all men, his life stronger than death, his salvation more invincible than hell.[33]

A poetic description of the same, redemptive confrontation appears in the fourth stanza of Luther's 1524 Easter hymn, "Christ Lay in the Bonds of Death."

> That was a right wondrous strife
> When Death in Life's grip wallowed:
> Off victorious came Life,

32. The centrality of the so-called *Kampfmotiv* in Luther's soteriology of exchange has been well documented, especially by Uwe Rieske-Braun in his book *Duellum mirabile*. Space precludes establishing here what Rieske-Braun's work amply demonstrates, namely, that the "battle motif" pervades Luther's theology from its earliest stages of development until the works published during the year of his death. This pervasive quality is a major assumption of this chapter, albeit one for whose legitimacy we must rely upon the labors of other secondary studies. One late manifestation of the "battle motif" is to be found in Luther's 1544 commentary on Isaiah 53, where Christ is likened to the "strong man" who defeats all the enemies fighting against humanity by overpowering them; see WA 40/3:733, 741–42.
33. LW 31:351–52. WA 7:55: "Hic iam dulcissimum spectaculum prodit non solum communionis sed salutaris belli et victoriae et salutis et redemptionis. Cum enim Christus sit deus et homo eaque persona, quae nec peccavit nec moritur nec damnatur, sed nec peccare, mori, damnari potest, Eiusque iustitia, vita, salus insuperabilis, aeterna, omnipotens est, Cum, inquam, talis persona peccata, mortem, infernum sponsae et propter annulum fidei sibi communia, immo propria facit et in iis non aliter se habet quam si sua essent ipseque peccasset, laborans, moriens et ad infernum descendens, ut omnia superaret, peccatumque, mors et infernus eum absorbere non possent, necessario in ipso absorpta sunt stupendo duello. Nam iustitia sua omnium peccatis superior, vita sua omni morte potentior, salus sua omni inferno invictior."

Death he has quite upswallowed.
The Scripture has published that—
How one Death the other ate.
Thus Death is become a laughter. Alleluia![34]

These descriptions exhibit positively no interest in the permanent reification of antithesis for its own sake.[35] The "strife of contraries" that attends Christ's radical solidarity with sinners possesses, rather, a clear redemptive terminus. The life of Christ is stronger than his death, and thus overcomes it. The battle yields a victor.

The *Kampfmotiv* provides an important clue for how Luther coordinates soteriology and two-nature Christology. The divine and human natures of Christ fulfill complementary soteriological functions within Luther's parabolic economy of strife and exchange.[36] Many of the contrastive predicates surveyed above reflect this determinate christo-soteriological coordination.[37] Such an alignment is rendered explicit, for instance, in Luther's 1537 sermon on Luke 1, where he states: "Therefore, [Christ] dies as a human, and lives as God. Death is swallowed up in life, and the immortality of God devours the mortality of human beings."[38] Christ's vulnerability is

34. LW 53:257. WA 35:444: "Es war eyn wunderlich krieg, da todt und leben rungen, Das leben behielt den sieg, es hat den tod verschlungen. Die schrifft hat verkundet das, wie eyn tod den andern fras, Eyn spott aus dem tod ist worden."

35. Contra Beer.

36. Beer's attempt to suggest that Christ's natures are entirely *reducible* to combative functions for Luther is one that I find rather strange, indeed. It simply does not follow that because Christ's natures *have* soteriological functions that they simply *are* soteriological functions. If so, then the same accusation would apply to much of the patristic and medieval tradition as well. For Beer's claim that Luther "functionalizes" nature language, see, for example, Beer, *Der fröliche Wechsel*, 382.

37. This is not true of *every* contrastive pair. Christ, for instance, is not righteous as God but sinful as a human. Luther believes that Christ is perfect in obedience to the law according to both natures. He is like us in our humanity in all things *except* for sin. Luther affirms the innocence of Christ's humanity, for instance, in his 1544 commentary on Isaiah 53; see WA 40/3:696. Our particular focus here rests upon attributes, which reflect the invulnerability and vulnerability of Christ. In this more specific set of contrasts, there is a clear christological alignment.

38. WA 45:436: "Moritur igitur ut homo, Et vivit ut Deus, Et mors absorbetur in vita, et immortalitas Dei devorat mortalitatem hominis." In the broader context of this text, Luther

associated here with his mortal humanity, and Christ's invulnerability with his immortal deity. Christ is "dead and alive," in short, because he is human and divine. Here we see how it is, for Luther, that Christ can enter into human abjection, yet transcend its limitations in triumphant victory. The person of Christ cannot die, nor his human flesh molder in the grave, because the divine nature with which this flesh is personally united is invincible.[39] The invulnerability of Christ's divinity is crucial here. Without it, the logic of Luther's soteriological description cannot get off the ground.

Luther reinforces the same "christological alignment" in a wide range of colorful metaphors enlisted to explain how Christ is victorious over corruption, death, and the devil. In an Easter sermon, from 1526, Luther likens the person of Christ to the burning bush depicted in Exodus 3. Just as fire is unable to burn or consume the

is fashioning an apologetic for the legitimacy of two-nature Christology. On the basis of the passage from Luke 1, Luther isolates aspects of Christ's identity that point either to his divinity or humanity. For instance, because Christ is declared to be the Son of David, he must be genuinely human and thus mortal as other humans are. On the other hand, because the messianic kingdom promised to him is without end, Christ must also be immortal and therefore fully divine. Luther's reflection upon the death of Christ seeks to filter this broader insight concerning the intrinsic duality of Christ's existence and apply it to the death of Christ.

39. The following excerpt from a 1533 sermon of Luther's furnishes a similar instance of this logic at work. The devil kills Christ's humanity, but the person lives on account of the divine nature. Because the *person* of Christ lives, however, his humanity cannot really die either, and thus Christ attains victory. WA 37:28–29: "Die humanitatem hellt er ihm fur, lest ihn drauff stechen, wueten &c. ubi hoc effecit et occidit, occidit quidem humanitatem, sed persona vivit, quae est Got et homo zu samen, ut symbolum, cum igitur persona non mortalis, ergo nec humanitas. Er hieb nur der person ein wunden i.e. Er schlug auff die menscheit, die Gottheit kund er nicht treffen, schrecken, gesetz &c. et angriffen person, quam non &c. Ibi cogitur mors nidderliegen und Teufel unter fus, quia hat all sein gifft und zorn &c. et tamen non die recht person troffen. Hactenus die rechten getroffen. Sed quia non ius zu ihm, ideo zerreist im Christus ventrem, os &c. Non solum, quod non debuit mori, sed quod non potuit. Es hat mors, infernus &c. an der person verlorn, quia accusaverunt ut peccatorem, ut ubeltheter &c. ut purum hominem, ist nicht war. Ideo quare, peccatum, mors, diabole schendlicher, accusas me? Ibi nihil possunt dicere. Ideo iam dicimus non solum, quod verus deus, sed unschuldig secundum humanitatem. Ideo facienda persona magna. Si hoc, tum etiam historia resurrectionis auch gros. Est deus et verus deus in humanitate, verus dei filius et virginis, Maior caelo et terra. unschuldig. Non peccatum fecit. Ideo maius hoc quam omnes diaboli, peccata &c. wigt tausent mal mher. Si Christianus hanc magnitudinem personae fasset, agnoscit fructus magnitudinem, quam gering diabolus gegen ihm. Si maior caelo et terra, peccato, morte &c. Ideo quicquid facit, patitur &c. mus seer gros sein."

branches of the bush, Christ's humanity likewise cannot be destroyed in death, but is raised up immortal. This is so, because Christ's divinity inhabits its assumed humanity in bodily form and renders it impossible for death to overcome it. Under ordinary circumstances, Luther notes, fire ought to be stronger than a bush's combustible branches. In the same way, Christ the human being should be devoured by the sheer depth of his sufferings and death, and thus utterly annihilated by them. Nevertheless, on account of the deathless might of divinity united with Christ's frail humanity, the incarnate Son is *morte fortior*.[40] In the midst of death, he yet lives. The essential invulnerability of Christ's divine nature is, for Luther, an intrinsic presupposition of resurrection.

There is perhaps no metaphor more frequently enlisted by Luther to express this theme than mythological image of the "baited Leviathan."[41] In this image, Luther likens death and the devil to a great and ferocious beast. Like a fish lured in by the angler's worm, the devil is deceived by the ostensible weakness of Christ's humanity and thus tricked into devouring him. The devil does not recognize, however, that Christ is also fully divine and thus incapable of destruction. The divine nature of Christ is, to death and the

40. WA 20:354–55: "Rubus est Christus, in quo habitat deus et est viridis, quia est innocens homo absque omni culpa. Sicut rubus crevit in deserto absque ulla hominis opera, sic ipse natus absque virili &c. Deus est in rubo, ideo non potest comburi i. e. rubus i. e. humanitas Christi steckt mitten im leiden, stirbt et tamen non moritur, certe mirum. Sic hic Christus non solum purus homo, alias Satan eum het hin gefurt, aber da die deitas corporaliter in eo homine habitabat, erat ergo impossibile, ut comburatur, sed in media morte oportet ista persona vivat. *Es sol ja das feuer sterckher quam busch, sed contrarium. Sic mors debebat Christum vorare, sed Christus morte fortior est &c.*" (emphasis mine).

41. For a survey of the various patristic and medieval theologians through whose work Luther likely came into contact with this image, see Rieske-Braun, *Duellum mirabile*, 115–226, esp. 171–78. See also Theobald Beer, *Der fröliche Wechsel*, 328, 346–47. Beer, of course, must try to argue that although Luther closely echoes many of these antecedents, he actually warps their thought in a way that disfigures Chalcedonian Christology. I am not convinced that the essential features of Luther's use of this theme differ in any dramatic way from what one finds in the patristics and medievals that Beer and Rieske-Braun cite. Luther conducts the metaphor's emphasis in his own way, to be sure, but the governing soteriological mechanics are the same so far as the functional alignment of Christ's two natures is concerned.

devil, very much like a clandestine fishing hook concealed beneath its "bait" (in this case, the frail vulnerability of the humanity). Once "swallowed" (a metaphorical concept that closely approximates what we have so far referred to as the "solidarity motif" in Luther's exchange soteriology), Christ shreds death, the devil, and hell from the inside out.[42] An emblematic occurrence of this motif appears in a 1538 sermon on John 3:16 that Luther delivered on the third week after Trinity Sunday.

> Christ died; death devoured the Son of God. But in doing so death swallowed a thorn and had to get rid of it. It was impossible for death to hold Him. For this Person is God; and since both God and man in one indivisible Person entered into the belly of death and the devil, death ate a morsel that ripped his stomach open.
>
> It was the counsel of God the Father from eternity to destroy death, ruin the kingdom of the devil, and give the devil a little pill which he would gleefully devour, but which would create a great rumpus in his belly and in the world. Now the Lord wants to say: "Dear Nicodemus, it is miraculous, as you see, that God should spend such a great and precious

42. One especially clear example of this sequence appears in an Easter sermon delivered on March 31, 1521. See WA 9:661, where Luther states: "Der Todt schlecht den rachen daher und will die Person fressen, wie er allen menschsen fressen hatt, trifft aber ein sulch person, die do ist got und mensch. Got kan nicht sterben und styrbt dennoch nach der menscheyt. Darumb gibt die schrifft der gantzen person, was einem widerfert. Alß wen ainer an kopff verwundt wirt, Szo ist nur der leyb vorwundt, dennoch sagt man, der menschs sey vorwund. Drumb wie leyb und seel ein mensch ist, Szo ist Christus ein person auß einem menschsen und gotth. Was der menscheyt widerfert, Ist Christo widerfaren, und was Christus thut, das hat Gotth than. Szo ist der Todt in dem leben erseufft, wie Paulus sagt. Drumb wirt in Christo alle sundt und boeß gewissen erseufft, Szo dw in yn glawbst, das es dir nichs thuen kan. Das wirt anzeygt Iob 40, Do er sagt vom Behemoth 'In oculis eius quasi hamo capiet eum' &c. 'An extrahere poteris Leviathan hamo' &c. Eben wie der vischer den hamen sencket ins basser, das man in nicht siecht, mitt einem regenwurm, und kummet der visch, meinett, er woll in fressen, Schlecht mit dem rachen in hamen und wirt alßo gefangen. Szo auch hie mit Christo. Die angelschnur ist das geschlecht Jesu Christi von Abraham her, ist gebunden an die menschlich natur. Der angel ist die gotlich natur, die hat er anzcogen mit der Menschlich, die hat muessen leyden und ist voracht gewest wie ein regenworm. Do kam der todt und gedacht: har, ich wil in vorschlinden. Nymant sach, das er got waß: Szo meinett er, er woll den menschen fressen, Szo trifft er gotth. Do wirt er gefangen, und Christus zceucht in her fuer und macht in zcu schanden fur aller weltt." For an extensive record of the many occurrences of this metaphor within Luther's corpus, see Beer, *Der fröliche Wechsel*, 339–44. See also Barth, *Der Teufel und Jesus Christus*, 77, esp. n.496.

> treasure for our rebirth. For is it a miracle that I, the Son of man and the Son of God in one Person, am sacrificed to death and enter the jaws of death and the devil? But I shall not remain there. Not only will I come forth again, but I will also rip open deaths [sic] belly; for the poison is too potent, and death itself must die."[43]

The invulnerability of Christ's divinity is once again the pivotal affirmation. The solidarity of God in Christ, for Luther, does not mean that the divine nature comes to share in frailty and weakness. To align Luther's soteriology and Christology in this way is to invert its fundamental logic. It is precisely because Christ cannot be harmed or destroyed according to his divine nature that he can plunge into the abyss of human affliction and emerge victorious.[44]

Why, then, is Christ described by Luther as simultaneously vulnerable and invulnerable? It is because both ascriptions belong properly to him as one who is both fully human and fully divine. Both are deemed by Luther to be soteriologically necessary in the following way. The frailty of humanity is essential in order for Christ truly to enter into solidarity with sinners in their abject condition of affliction and weakness. Like other human beings, Christ suffers, experiences fear, and bears the sting of corruption at its fullest extent.

43. LW 22:355. WA 47:80: "Christus ist gestorben und hatt der Tod den Sohn Gottes verschlungen, aber der tod hatt an ihme einen angel geschlungen, das er ihnen hat mussen widergeben, den es wahr unmuglich, das ehr im tode bleiben soltte. Den die person ist gott, und do Gott und Mensch in einer person, unzertrennet, in des todes und Teuffels bauch gefharen ist, so hatt der todt ein bisslein an ime gessen das ihme den Bauch zureist. Das ist auch Gottes des vaters rath von ewigkeit gewesen, das ehr also den tod verschlingen und des Teuffels reich zerstoren woltte und dem Teuffel ein kleine pillen geben, die ehr mitt lust fressen soltt, aber darmit in seinem bauche und in der welt ein solch gerumpel anrichten. Nun will der herr sagen: Lieber Nicodeme, du sihest recht ein Mirackel, das Gott einen solchen grossen, theuern schatz an unser Widergeburtt wendet. Den ist es nicht ein wunderwerck, das ich des menschen Sohn und Gottes Sohn bin, in einer person, und in den todt dahin gegeben, das ich dem Teuffel und tode in rachen fhare? Aber ich werde nicht drinnen bleiben und nicht allein wider heraus fharen, sondern ime auch den bauch zerreissen, den die gifft ist zu starck, das der tod mus dran sterben."

44. To remove this affirmation from Luther's vocabulary is to collapse his soteriology, at least so far as it touches upon the redeeming work of Christ in freeing human beings from suffering and death.

But, for all this, he is not destroyed. This is because Christ, for Luther, is no mere man. He remains fully divine even at the nadir of his condescension and retains all the properties pertaining thereunto. This retention of unaltered divine properties is necessary for Luther's soterio-logic to function properly. If Christ's divine nature were diminished by condescension and made to be weak even as the humanity is weak, then Christ would be utterly devoured in the abyss.[45]

Luther does not believe that Christ's divinity and its attendant properties are "conditioned" by his human weakness but rather "clothed" by it. He expresses as much in a 1540 sermon on John 4:

> Therefore since we could not bear to hear God in His majesty, He humbly adopted flesh and blood, assuming not only our nature, that is, flesh and blood, but also all the frailties with which body and soul are afflicted, as, for example, fear, sadness, anger, and hatred. This is really burying and concealing His divine majesty! Now this is preached to us. We are told that He was weak, that He was like any other man in body and soul, that He made Himself subject to all human infirmities, that He hungered and thirsted, that He experienced all the wants of flesh and blood. In this weakness the true and eternal God shows Himself. For me He humbles Himself; and for me He is finally crucified, although He is at the same time very God, who redeems me from sin and death.[46]

45. This is the point that lies behind Luther's statement, which divergence interpreters often quote, that a Christ who suffers only as a human being would need his own savior. The point is not that the divine nature must also suffer, as many conclude it to be. Luther insists, rather, that a nondivine suffering Christ will be just as helpless in the face of death and corruptions as all other mortal flesh. He would be consumed and annihilated by the principalities of this world.
46. LW 22:507. WA 47:212: "Darumb so durffen wir Gott nicht hoeren in seiner Maiestet, do ehr dan untreglich ist, sondern ehr hat sich gesenckt auffs tieffste ins fleisch und bluth, das ehr nicht allein unser natur annimpt, das ist: leib und seel, Sondern auch alle gebrechen, die leib und seel anhangen, als furcht, traurigkeit, zorn, Hass &c. Das heist ja tieff beschorren die gottliche Maiestet, und dasselbige wirdt uns geprediget, das ehr schwach sej und gleich sej als ein ander mensch an leib und Seel und alle gebrechen an sich genommen hab als ein anderer mensch, der do durstet und hungert und alles, was fleisch und bluth anhenget. Jn dieser schwacheit lest sich der ewige, warhafftige Gott finden und fur mich demuttiget ehr sich also bis ans creutz und ist gleichwohl warhafftiger Gott, der mich von sunden und todt erloset."In a 1534 sermon, Luther also comments how the earthly appearance of Christ could often be an obstacle for faith to those who saw him. Who could believe that such a weak person could be God, the king of kings? See WA 37:655.

In the incarnation, God genuinely reveals Godself to human beings. At the same time, however, and precisely in so doing, God also shields or "covers" God's true majesty from their sight.[47] God presents Godself to the world in the form of frail humanity.[48] God perpetrates no docetic masquerade in doing so, for Christ truly is human on account of the hypostatic union of divinity and humanity in Christ.[49] Nevertheless, despite this frail appearance and the underlying doctrinal reality it expresses, Christ's divinity is not weak, nor can it ever become so. He remains "unconquerable life" even in the midst of death, just as he remains "infinite righteousness" even in the likeness of sinful flesh. If the divergence reception of Luther's Christology were correct to conclude that the suffering and death of Christ is truly constitutive of the divine life, then why would this dialectic of revealing and covering be necessary? If God simply is what we see in the passion, death, and resurrection of Jesus, then Luther's characterization of these events as a "covering," and, in some cases, as the revelation of God "under the form of His opposite," makes no sense.

That Christ is vulnerable in humanity and invulnerable in divinity is an abiding presupposition of Luther's theology of redemption. He invites this conclusion in the 1540 sermon's next statement:

> Thus the evangelist has a twofold message regarding Christ: first of all, he proclaims His glory and informs us that He comes to us in splendor

47. Luther reflects upon the hiddenness of God in Christ's abject weakness in his 1544 commentary on Isaiah 53. It is because of this "covering" that many in Jesus' lifetime found it impossible to acknowledge his true identity; see WA 40/3:711. This exposes another weakness of the divergence interpretation. If Christ reveals to human beings that God really suffers (i.e., displaces classical notions of God as immutable and impassible), then why is the self-revelation of God in Christ characterized by Luther as a veiling? If God *suffers*, why is the suffering of Christ described as a covering of God's true majesty; in some cases, as a revelation of God's very *opposite*?
48. The interplay between appearance and reality is accentuated in Luther's metaphorical description of death and Satan being "tricked" by Christ's ostensible weakness.
49. Christ, moreover, *really dies* in his humanity, according to Luther. See his comments from 1544 in WA 40/3:743.

> and divine majesty that we might know that He is truly God; then he tells us that He also comes to us clad in weakness and in the greatest humility. When He died, he tore hell to shreds and removed sin, which is a divine work and reflects sheer deity. Then He also demonstrates that He is true man, when He decides to leave Judea and takes flight before those great prelates, the Pharisees, whom He, of course, could have felled with a breath.[50]

The divinity of Christ is therefore not altered or conditioned by the frailty of its assumed humanity. This much is clear from the passages surveyed throughout this section. At the same time, the humanity of Christ is altered and conditioned by its union with incorruptible divinity. The deathless might of God inhabits the humanity of Christ, and enlivens his mortal flesh as fire radiates through glowing iron.[51]

50. LW 22:507. WA 47:212–13 "Also prediget der Euangelist zweierlej von Christo, Erstlich, das ehr hehrlich sej und in pracht und Gottlicher maiestet zu uns komme. Darnach, das ehr auch in schwacheit und hochster demuth kompt, auff das wir wissen, ehr sej warhafftiger Gott. Dan ehr ist gestorben und hat die helle zurissen, die sunde wegkgenommen, das ist eittel gottheit und eittel gottliche werck. Darnach beweist ehr, das ehr warhafftiger mensch sej, dan ehr fleucht und wil nicht in Judea bleiben fur den hehrlichen Prelaten, den Phariseern, die ehr doch kondte mit einem odem umblasen." The reader will note, in passing, how many of the citations provided in this section are derived from Luther's sermons on John from the late 1530s and early 1540s. This pattern is by my design, because it provides further corroboration of the point argued against Ngien in a previous chapter that these texts represent no exception to the rule in Luther's other writings that Christ does not suffer according to his divinity.
51. Luther reflects upon the divinization of Christ's flesh in relation to the eucharist in a sermon on John 6 from the early 1530s. WA 33:190–91: "Darumb spricht Christus: 'das brott, das ich gebe, ist mein fleisch'. Was meinstu vor fleisch? nicht kalbfleisch oder riendtfleisch, so in stellen ist, das ist auch wohl sein fleisch, aber ehr saget: 'das ich geben werde fur das leben der welt', Es ist ein lebendig fleisch undt todt fleisch, so gestorben ist, das dardurch die gantze welt lebe. Do gehöret kein Iohannes Baptista noch Maria zu oder einiger Engel, Sondern diese einige person Christus, doran wil uns gott haben gefasset undt gebunden. Ausser der person, so von Maria geboren ist, undt hat warhafftig fleisch undt blutt undt ist gecreutziget worden, sol man gott nicht suchen noch finden, den gott sol man allein durch den glauben ergreiffen undt kriegenn im fleisch undt blutt, undt das das fleisch undt blutt nicht fleischert noch bluttert undt doch fleisch undt blutt sei, Sondern beides vergöttert sei, wie ich den vom Zuckerwasser gesagt habe. Jtem Eisen, wen es ohne feur ist, so ists auch Eisen, wen es aber gluendt gemacht wirdt undt feuer oder hitze drein kompt, so kan ich den sagen: dis eisen das eisert itzt nicht mehr, sondern es fewert gahr, Es ist wohl Eisen, aber es ist so gahr durchfeuert, das, wen du es sihest oder angreiffest, das dein auge nicht sagen kan: Es ist Eisen, Sondern du fhulest eitel feur, so gahr ist eitel feur fur augen. Wen du nun wilt ein loch darmit durch ein fas bohren oder ein zeichen auff etwas brennen oder machen, do thuts das Eisen nicht, Sondern das feur thuts, dan wen ich ein ander eisen neme, das nicht gluendt were, so wurde ich noch lange nicht ein Zeichen brennen, Sondern Jch mus das Eisen nemen, dorinnen das feur ist, undt widerumb wil das feur

This is why it is not only the person of Christ that survives death; the humanity is restored and invigorated as well. Because Christ's humanity is united with God through an inseparable, though irreducibly distinct, union, it, too, cannot finally be destroyed but rises up in radiant immortality.[52] The glorification of Christ's flesh is thus a reality perceived in its fullness only in the resurrection, where the form of human weakness gives way to deathless vitality.[53] In all this, we see clearly that the logic of Luther's soteriology rests upon a christological substructure, which admits only a "monodirectional" doctrine of exchange between Christ's natures. The humanity is conditioned on account of its union with deathless, invulnerable

seine arbeit nirgendts thun dan in dem Eisen. Also ist hie gott in Christo auch leibhafftig undt thut, wie ein gott thun sol, oder thut, wie das feur im eisen thut, man sihet wohl nur fleisch undt blutt, aber der glaube sihet einen solchen menschen, ein solch fleisch undt blutt, das do sei wie ein feurig eisen, den es ist durchgöttertt." Despite the abject humility of its appearance, Christ's humanity genuinely mediates the fullness of divinity, and comes through union with it also to share in its majesty. The effect is likened metaphorically by Luther to golden coins enclosed within a purse; WA 47:636. This christological pattern is the basis for Luther's reflection upon other, secondary media of God's presence such as Holy Scripture and the sacraments. The believer is tempted, by virtue of the lowly earthliness of God's chosen vessels, to doubt their legitimacy. For one example of this conceptual extension, see Luther's continuing discussion in the 1540 sermon on John 4 in WA 47:212f.

52. According to Luther, only passing glimpses of this transformative union peek through the Gospel narratives of Jesus' life, as in the evident power operative in his miraculous works or in the apocalyptic splendor of the transfiguration. See, for instance, the description in Barth, *Der Teufel und Jesus Christus*,46; and Sammeli Juntunen, "The Christological Background of Luther's Understanding of Justification," *Seminary Ridge Review* 5, no. 2 (2003): 29.

53. For an example of this contrast, see Rieske-Braun, *Duellum mirabile*, 205. This does *not* mean for Luther that Christ ceases to be human. His is, however, a "divinized" humanity, different in some important respects from the corruptible flesh of other human beings wholly conquered by the grave. See, for instance, the following comments from a 1527 controversial text on the sacrament, WA 23:243: "Es mangelt den schwermern alles daran, das sie Christus leib 'nicht unterscheiden' (wie S. Paulus sagt .1. Cor. xi.) von anderm fleisch und reden nicht anders davon denn als were es ein vergenglich verdewlich verzerlich fleisch, das man ynn denn scherren keufft und ynn der kuchen kocht. So grobe hempel sind sie, das sie nicht sehen, wie dis fleisch ist ein unvergenglich unsterblich unverweselich fleisch, wie der .xv. Psalm singet von yhm: 'Du wirst deinen heiligen nicht lassen verwesen, Und mein fleisch wird rugen ynn hoffnunge'. Der tod hat sich wol ein mal dran versucht und wolts verzeren und verdawen, Aber er kund nicht, sondern es zureis yhm den bauch und hals mehr denn ynn hundert tausent stuck, das dem tod die zeene zu stoben und zu flogen sind, und bleib lebendig. Denn die speise war dem tod zu starck und hat den fresser verzeret und verdawet. Es ist Gott ynn diesem fleisch, Ein Gotts fleisch, Ein geistfleisch ists, Es ist ynn Gott und Gott."

divinity, but the latter suffers none of the defects that apply to Christ on account of his human nature.

Why is it, then, on the basis of all these considerations, that Luther is so adamant that the suffering Christ be fully God? Why must God plunge to the low point of the scale, and how is the "divinity" of the suffering Christ soteriologically necessary? The answer to all these questions hinges upon Luther's abiding insistence upon the invulnerability of Christ's divine nature. The suffering Christ must be fully God because only a person invulnerable in divinity can withstand the awful power of death and hell and tear it to shreds. It is on account of this deathless might that Luther confesses Christ to be *dominus mortis*, the "Lord over death."[54] All that afflicts weary sinners in body and soul genuinely collapses upon him in the weakness of his humanity. These powers, however, cannot finally destroy him. They expend themselves against him, and break apart upon his deathless might.[55] Thus, Christ taunts the devil, saying: "Oh Devil, all evil has fallen upon me, and yet I live!"[56] The "passibilist symmetry" advanced by the divergence interpretation fails in its apprehension of Luther's insistence upon the suffering of God, because it overlooks the critical function of divine invulnerability within the soterio-logic that accompanies this insistence. Earlier, the resultant construal was represented as follows:

54. Luther refers to Christ as the Lord over life and death in a sermon preached in 1525; see WA 17/1:79. He also refers to him as the Lord over death and Satan in a sermon of 1529; see WA 29:290b.
55. A crucial instance of this motif appears in Luther 1544 commentary on Isaiah 53; see WA 40/3:721: "Deus posuerat illum, ut ferret impetum Satanae, mortis, legis, totius mundi et omnium hominum peccata; peccatum occidit eum, sed eum, qui occidi non potuit; occisus secundum nativitatem carnis, et tamen dicitur vere occisus filius Dei. Non potuit occidi propter illum aculeum in Euangelio, quod ipse Deus vivus, ut dicit: 'Ego vivo, et vos vivetis'; Ego quidem morior pro vobis, sed tamen moriendo vivam, quia Deus sum et homo. Mors potest me mordere et occidere, sed retinere non poterit in morte." For another text that refers to all evil being expended upon Christ, see ibid., 731. Luther expresses Christ's destruction of death in a more visceral way by dubbing him *Todfresser* in a sermon of 1537; WA 45:43b.
56. WA 15:518. This statement is taken from a sermon on the resurrection delivered in 1524.

Guiding Principle: The radical solidarity of God as sympathetic suffering.

Requisite Conceptual Substructure: A Christology of divine vulnerability.

Soteriological Mechanics: The dialectical historicity of God.

In the light of the argument just developed, however, the following structural summary seems preferable.

Guiding Principle: The radical solidarity of God as site of eschatological battle.

Requisite Conceptual Substructure: A Christology of divine invulnerability.

Soteriological Mechanics: The deathless might of God victorious over the powers of corruption.

Conclusion

In the course of this chapter, no attempt has been made to furnish a comprehensive treatment of Luther's theology of salvation. Neither has it been suggested or implied that the relation of impassible divinity to the suffering solidarity of Christ constitutes a central focal point of Luther's soteriological vision. It has sought merely to evaluate the "passibilist symmetry" postulated by proponents of the divergence thesis and assess its widespread claim to legitimacy. In order thoroughly to refute the accuracy of the "passibilist symmetry," the present chapter has proceeded in three stages. The first stage examined aspects of Luther's larger theological framework that together serve to situate the narrower question of divine suffering within the landscape of his soteriology. The second section demonstrated that the textual evidence adduced in defense of a passibilist interpretation of Luther's soteriology is deeply problematic.

A careful examination of the pertinent texts shows that Luther unambiguously affirms the doctrine of divine impassibility. The third major section cemented this criticism by furnishing a synthetic re-presentation of Luther's reflection upon the immanence of God in the sufferings of Christ. This alternative highlighted the extent to which a divergence understanding of these matters inverts the conceptual mechanics of Luther's soteriology. A Christ vulnerable according to his divinity would be, for Luther, a Christ who simply could not redeem. Only if Christ's divinity remains wholly incorruptible in the jaws of death can Christ plunge into humanity's low estate and rise up victorious from it.

This chapter concludes the historical portion of this study. As such, it is worthwhile briefly to take inventory of what has so far been argued. The first chapter of this study suggested that a divergence reception of Luther's Christology relies for its historically traced legitimacy upon three sequentially organized assumptions:

1. That Luther recalibrates the traditional theology of the hypostatic union in order to accommodate an insistence upon suffering divinity.
2. That Luther espouses a soteriological vision that both requires and openly affirms the sympathetic sufferings of Christ's divine nature.
3. That these two basic doctrinal modifications effect as their consequence an implication-laden adjustment to the doctrine of God, which consists primarily in the intrinsic historicization of divine being.

Chapters 2 and 3 demonstrated that stages one and two of this logical progression are historically unjustified. Because of this demonstration, it naturally follows that the divergence reception of Luther's theology reflected in the third stage of this summary rests upon a highly tenuous understanding of Luther's theology. Theologians and historians may continue, of course, to insist upon theological or philosophical grounds that Luther ought to have pursued these various conceptual adjustments. They could even make the case that adjustments of this sort would have comported well with many of Luther's most basic theological insights; at least as these insights are perceived from the retrospective vantage point of contemporary concerns.[57] So far as Luther's actual views are concerned, however, the evidence points decidedly elsewhere.

57. An interesting argument to this effect, though not specifically concerned with Luther, is outlined in Bruce McCormack, "The Only Mediator: The Person and Work of Christ in Evangelical Perspective," in *Renewing the Evangelical Mission*, ed. Richard Lints (Grand Rapids: Eerdmans, 2013), 250–69. McCormack's claim runs parallel with the argument of Ian Kingston Siggins, *Martin Luther's Doctrine of Christ*, Yale Publications in Religion 14 (New Haven: Yale University Press, 1970), which is surveyed in ch. 1.

5

Deathless Might in the Form of Mortal Weakness

Toward a Renovated Appropriation of Luther's Christology

In light of all that has been argued to this point in this study, we turn now to a question of constructive theological import: How is Luther's Christology significant for modern reflection upon the immanence of God in Christ? Taken as a whole, the divergence thesis represents an attempt to provide a substantive response to this question. Despite its widespread appeal, this proposal fails because it builds a constructive edifice upon an illusory historical foundation. The passibilist symmetry, which stands at the base of a divergence reception, represents a mistaken specification of Luther's christological views. In its association of Luther with modern reconfigurations of the doctrine of God, the divergence thesis does not extend, but contradicts, the reformer's Christology. This counterverdict consolidates, *in nuce*, what the preceding chapters of this study have sought, from a variety of critical angles, to demonstrate. The salient consequence of this argument, as it pertains to the question addressed in this chapter, is that constructive appraisals of Luther's ongoing significance ought no longer to proceed under the assumption that the reformer's Christology advances a recalibration of the *communicatio idiomatum* for the sake of a soteriologically ordered, participatory suffering of Christ's divine nature. Trajectories that begin the complicated process of appropriating Luther's Christology with this assumption set out upon a wayward heading.[1]

This critical verdict, however, does not represent progress in the attempt to reconsider the nature of Luther's ongoing significance. It does not yet provide any indication of how contemporary appropriations of Luther's Christology ought to proceed in the wake of the divergence thesis's refutation. In its attempt to address these subsidiary concerns, this chapter presupposes that the problem with the divergence thesis is not the mere fact that it tries to retrieve Luther's insights for modern consideration. If Luther had executed a passibilist reconfiguration of two-nature Christology, then the divergence reception would represent a fairly noncontroversial appraisal of the reformer's significance in the history of dogma. The presupposed reconfiguration, however, is not valid. What are the implications of this verdict for the reception of Luther's theology? More to the point: How ought Luther's contemporary significance be recalibrated in accordance with a nondivergence interpretation of his Christology?

This chapter, then, extends beyond the circumscribed confines of historical inquiry as such. In its attempt to remap the contours of Luther's contemporary significance within the light of a

1. This point is binding only to the extent that such trajectories purport to extend historically legitimate aspects of Luther's theology.

nondivergence presentation of his Christology, the forthcoming investigation is obliged to engage intellectual currents, questions, and concerns, many of which are inescapably foreign to Luther's sixteenth-century frame of reference. This does not mean, however, that the gleaned insights of historical exegesis are left behind, or somehow bracketed in the interest of securing contemporary relevance. The goal of this chapter is to reflect, in a historically responsible manner, upon legitimate ways in which Luther's christological ideas may "transition forward" and engage constructively with major currents of modern theological reflection.

Setting the Stage for Constructive Engagement

It is characteristic of a great deal of recent theology to suppose that the doctrine of divine impassibility simply cannot be reconciled with a robust acknowledgment of God's immanence in Christ. These commitments are presumed to signify conceptual affirmations that stand unavoidably at odds with one another. A major reason for the widespread perception of this antinomy is the conceptual specification of "impassibility," which its alleged incompatibility with God's immanence presupposes. Impassibility, this antinomy suggests, is essentially a conceptual byproduct of divine transcendence poorly understood. It denotes an aloof deity, differentiated from finite reality by the insertion of quantitative ontological distance.[2] To be "impassible," according to this construal, is to be "remote and detached"; to be essentially removed from any substantive involvement in events that include change or defect.[3] This rendering

2. That is, God is distinguished from the sphere of finite existents by the insistence that God is entirely removed from any involvement in its malleabilities.

3. Books within contemporary theology that take issue with the doctrine of divine impassibility are legion. One example of its equation with "remoteness" is to be found in Heribert Mühlen, *Die Veränderlichkeit Gottes als Horizont einer zukünftigen Christologie* (Münster: Aschendorff,

of God's otherness falters because it creates insurmountable obstacles for affirming biblical portrayals of God as intimately involved in the events of human history. In other words, it forecloses a robust affirmation of divine immanence. Immanence, after all, denotes the very opposite of unsullied abstraction. It suggests a radical and meaningful proximity, a relation of intimate presence or closeness. An agent who is "immanent," in short, is one who draws near and enters into the circumstances of another.

Thus specified, divine impassibility and divine immanence appear for many contemporary theologians to represent two extremes of a univocally polarized spectrum. By specifying the "otherness" of God in terms of ontological remoteness, divine impassibility appears to describe divine transcendence quantitatively, and thus intrinsically to proscribe any affirmation of God's immanence whatsoever.[4] The

1969), 8–9. A helpful overview of reasons for the widespread contemporary rejection of this doctrine is available in Paul S. Fiddes, *The Creative Suffering of God* (Oxford: Clarendon, 1988), 16–45. A sampling of the myriad recent publications that address the debate over divine suffering include Thomas G. Weinandy, *Does God Suffer?* (Notre Dame, IN: University of Notre Dame, 2000); D. Stephen Long, *Speaking of God: Theology, Language, and Truth* (Grand Rapids: Eerdmans, 2009); David Bentley Hart, *The Beauty of the Infinite: The Aesthetics of Christian Truth* (Grand Rapids: Eerdmans, 2003); idem, "No Shadow of Turning: On Divine Impassibility," *Pro Ecclesia* 11, no. 2 (March 1, 2002): 184–206; James Keating and Thomas Joseph White, *Divine Impassibility and the Mystery of Human Suffering* (Grand Rapids: Eerdmans, 2009); Daniel Castelo, *The Apathetic God: Exploring the Contemporary Relevance of Divine Impassibility* (Milton Keynes, UK: Paternoster, 2009); Richard E. Creel, *Divine Impassibility: An Essay in Philosophical Theology* (Cambridge: Cambridge University Press, 1986); Kevin J. Vanhoozer, *Remythologizing Theology: Divine Action, Passion, and Authorship* (Cambridge: Cambridge University Press, 2010); Paul L. Gavrilyuk, *The Suffering of the Impassible God: The Dialectics of Patristic Thought*, Oxford Early Christian Studies (New York: Oxford University Press, 2004); and Robert W. Jenson, *Systematic Theology* (New York: Oxford University Press, 1997). A fuller bibliographical overview of its scope and origins may be found in the citations contained within these materials.

4. By "quantitative," I refer to a mode of negotiating the God–world relation, which locates God upon the same plane of being or existence as finite existents. Within such a framework, the only way to express God's transcendence is to abstract God's being from all proximate contact with creation. Accordingly, impassibility manifests an underlying zero-sum ontological game in which God and the world exist under the same metaphysical umbrella and must therefore, in a sense, compete for space. The distinction is quantitative, because God's being is charted on the same "plane," as it were, simply ontologically enlarged in order to highlight God's otherness. For many theologians, as the following discussion will demonstrate, this mode of

attempt to maintain both simultaneously terminates in descriptive incoherence. A conceptual integration of these commitments would require one to suggest, absurdly, that God is involved, yet uninvolved; intimately close, yet infinitely remote—a being who is immanent, and yet not immanent at one and the same time. To define God as immanent and impassible is to embrace contradiction in principle. Those who do so tear open a fissure of meaning that runs through the heart of premodern conceptualizations of deity. Many contemporary theologians presume the mutual exclusivity of immanence and impassibility on the basis of this argument. They insist, in effect, that impassibility must give way to Immanuel—the God who truly is with us (immanence).[5]

For some, impassibility is a symptom of a larger problem. It is representative of a much deeper conceptual polarity that afflicts traditional reflection on the doctrine of God.[6] The putative source of this polarity is presumed widely to be an early philosophical corruption within the process of dogmatic development. Patristic theologians engaged their Hellenistic interlocutors with noble intentions, but inadvertently opened the door for the influence of pagan conceptualities. The problem enters when such conceptualities are allowed to supervise and constrain the codification of church

locating divine otherness (or transcendence) gets at the heart of the problem. This particular vocabulary is taken from Reinhard Hauber, "Christologie und metaphysicher Gottesbegriff bei Werner Elert," *Kerygma und Dogma* 35 (1989): 136, although the same theme shows up in the work of theologians other than Werner Elert, whom Hauber is describing.

5. Jürgen Moltmann suggests, for instance, that a God who is deemed impassible would need to be "evacuated" away from any involvement with the man Jesus, who hangs upon the cross. Jürgen Moltmann, *The Crucified God: The Cross of Christ as the Foundation and Criticism of Christian Theology*, trans. R. A. Wilson and John Bowden (Minneapolis: Fortress Press, 1993 [1974/German ed. 1973]), 214.
6. They are indicative, for Werner Elert, of an underlying bad metaphysics. See Volker Keding, "Wider das Apathieaxiom: Die theopaschitische Christologie des späten Elert und ihre Wirkungsgeschichte," in *Mit dem Menschen verhandeln über den Sachgehalt des Evangeliums: die Bedeutung der Theologie Werner Elerts für die Gegenwart*, ed. Rudolf Keller and Michael Roth (Erlangen: Martin-Luther-Verlag, 2004), 97.

dogma.[7] The result is an admixture of theology and philosophy, and a hybridized concept of God. Despite an impressive façade of critical synthesis, the two systems can never progress beyond mere juxtaposition. As the doctrines of divine immanence and divine impassibility illustrate, they presuppose two mutually exclusive conceptualizations of God's being. The result of the philosophical corruption is incoherence: two doctrines of God masquerading under the illusion of higher synthesis.[8]

To be sure, patristic and medieval theologians labor extensively to reconcile the competing strands of their conceptual patrimony. Some contemporary theologians acknowledge a measure of progress within this struggle for dogmatic integrity. Wolfhart Pannenberg insists, for instance, that early Christian thinkers subtly modify pagan philosophical commitments as these commitments are enlisted in the service of theological inquiry. The result is a modest "christianization of Hellenism."[9] The underlying polarity of concepts is softened, though never quite resolved. Despite this concession, however, Pannenberg persists in the fundamentally critical verdict shared by so many others. The assimilating progress of early Christian development expires well short of an ultimately satisfying doctrinal

7. The polarity, in other words, is built into the classic statements of Christian orthodoxy, even if most contemporary theologians who accept a version of this view go on to insist that the problematic elements may be shorn away without forfeiting orthodoxy's doctrinal essence.

8. So, Pannenberg comments: "Die Gedanken von Gott als Weltprinzip und als freim Herrn der Geschichte bleiben weithin unausgeglichen nebeneinander stehen. Die unterschiedliche Herkunft der Elemente des altkirchlichen Gottesbegriffs blieb daher aufdringlich sichtbar. Die großen, umfassenden Konzeptionen verknüpften die heterogenen Elemente doch nur oberflächlich." Wolfhart Pannenberg, "Die Aufnahme des philosophischen Gottesbegriffs als dogmatisches Problem der frühchristlichen Theologie," *Zeitschrift Für Kirchengeschichte* 70, nos. 1-2 (January 1, 1959): 43.

9. Pannenberg affirms the task of theology's engagement with pagan thought forms, and is therefore less harsh in his evaluation of the apologists, for instance, than either Adolf von Harnack or Friedrich Loofs. Nevertheless, he still believes there is legitimacy to the charge of "Hellenization," even once the severity of the charge is somewhat softened. See, for instance, ibid., 15–16. This is roughly akin to Johann Ansem Steiger's view that the patristics were well on their way to historicizing God's being, but never quite finished the task.

integrity. The prolonged attempt doctrinally to integrate the necessary, metaphysical *Weltprinzip* ("world principle") of Hellenistic thought, with the free triune God revealed through Christ, thus proves finally to be unsuccessful.[10] The polarity lingers because the disparate conceptual commitments of theology's past fundamentally resist harmonization.[11]

Classical formulations of two-nature Christology do not heal but, rather, ossify the underlying polarity on this account. The conceptual fissure coalesces, as it were, into an authorized theological grammar. Chalcedonian Christology masks the incoherence. It legitimates the juxtaposition of statements, which would otherwise appear contradictory, beneath the misleading appearance of some higher metaphysical unity. The traditional doctrine of the *communicatio idiomatum* is the locus where the insidious polarity manifests itself most blatantly. It not only permits, but actually encourages, the application of mutually exclusive predicates to the Son of God by way of empty, logical-semantic distinctions. One is licensed to assert, for instance, that the Son of God suffers and yet does not suffer; that he changes and yet remains the same; that he is all-powerful and yet frail; that he is radically immanent with human beings and yet never ceases to be the simple, immutable, impassible, and radically transcendent God. By justifying such bifurcations christologically, this discourse

10. So, although Pannenberg acknowledges the importance of early Christianity's sustained interaction with pagan thought (thus softening the verdict advanced by Loofs and von Harnack), he ultimately concludes: "Diese Aufgabe kritischer Umschmelzung des philosophischen Gottesgedankens ist in der frühchristlichen Theologie nicht von Grund auf gestellt und nicht allseitig durchführt worden." Ibid., 45.

11. That is, it is logically impossible for theology and Greek philosophy to share the same criteriological air space without one implicitly displacing the other. See Hauber, "Christologie und metaphysicher Gottesbegriff," 141, 143. Hauber also suggests on 145 that a retention of divine immutability (part of this philosophical inheritance) requires theology to create two "sectors" of God's existence. See also Mühlen, *Die Veränderlichkeit Gottes*, 19–20. Eberhard Jüngel speaks in terms of an "aporia"; see *God As the Mystery of the World: On the Foundation of the Theology of the Crucified One in the Dispute between Theism and Atheism* (Grand Rapids: Eerdmans, 1983), 39–42, 203.

appears to reconcile the underlying incoherence. In reality, however, the *communicatio idiomatum* only explicates and widens the preexisting fissure.[12] Christology in the tradition of Chalcedon is not a solution, but an exacerbation of the problem. Its conceptually bifurcating grammar serves to justify and perpetuate the fateful juxtaposition of theology and pagan philosophy. It allows subsequent reflection to retain and promulgate an immiscible conceptual polarity. The culprit in all this is an exaggerated and wrongly specified polarity between divine transcendence and divine immanence, of which the doctrine of impassibility is but one, especially blatant, manifestation. The classically developed doctrine of God originates and terminates in incoherence. Meanwhile, the casualty is nothing less than a doctrine of God that is transparent to the gospel itself.

12. Heribert Mühlen therefore denigrates two-nature theology as a docetic façade; ee *Die Veränderlichkeit Gottes*, 16–17. Moltmann is similarly critical in *Crucified God*, 227–35. He states: "But theological reflection was not in a position to identify God himself with the suffering and death of Jesus. As a result of this, traditional Christology came very near to docetism, according to which Jesus only appeared to suffer and only appeared to die abandoned by God: this did not happen in reality. The intellectual bar to this came from the philosophical concept of God, according to which God's being is incorruptible, unchangeable, indivisible, incapable of suffering and immortal; human nature, on the other hand, is transitory, changeable, divisible, capable of suffering and mortal. The doctrine of the two natures in Christ began from this fundamental distinction, in order to be able to conceive of the personal union of the two natures in Christ in the light of this difference" (227–28). See also Keding, "Wider das Apathieaxiom," 92. Keding demonstrates how Elert believed the fundamental problem with classical Christology is that it ironically did not allow the incarnation to determine what is true about God, but allowed a predetermined doctrine of God to stipulate what is true of Christ. This is why Elert refers to Chalcedon as a "fall" of sorts, as Keding describes on 94. Reinhard Hauber reinforces this verdict when he surmises (in a manner reminiscent of Schwarz) that classical Christology presumes, a priori, that God and humanity *cannot* be united. Thus, he insists, the problems of classical Christology only emerge if one operates with a nonchristologically determined doctrine of God. Chalcedon tries, of course, to resolve this tension, but ends up with two subjects. See Hauber, "Christologie und metaphysicher Gottesbegriff," 135, 155–57. For similar conclusions, see Wolfhart Pannenberg, "Christologie und Theologie," *Kerygma Und Dogma* 21, no. 3 (July 1, 1975): 164; idem, "Die Aufnahme des philosophischen Gottesbegriffs," 31; and Eberhard Jüngel, "Vom Tod des lebendigen Gottes: ein Plakat." *Zeitschrift Für Theologie Und Kirche* 65, no. 1 (January 1, 1968): 100.

Healing the Polarity with Wittenberg Balm?

According to the divergence reception, Luther's theological contribution to contemporary theology is that he heals the fatal polarity christologically by eliminating impassibility as a legitimate designation of the incarnate Son of God in his divine nature. From this preliminary entry point, Luther inaugurates an implicit reconfiguration of God's transcendent otherness, which is no longer constrained by philosophical assumptions that tend in the direction of "detached remoteness." Luther's Christology purifies the immiscible mixture of philosophy and theology precisely where the absurd juxtaposition reaches its dogmatic climax. In other words, Luther is supposed to reverse what classical reflection upon Christ gets exactly backward. The latter begins with a set doctrine of God and then squeezes christological reflection within its parameters. Luther's procedure is precisely the opposite. It allows the incarnation itself to inform and dictate the doctrine of God, rather than vice versa. In this way, Luther's contribution is an enormous privileging of theology over philosophy.[13]

In this way, Luther burns off the Hellenistic dross of traditional reflection and resolves its latent polarity by driving away the "pseudo-god"—the abstract *Weltgrund* ("ground for the world") of pagan philosophical projection.[14] By doing so, Luther appears to anticipate and point the way forward to a whole host of modern theological trajectories that seek likewise to heal the fateful polarity afflicting classical accounts of the divine being.[15] Many practitioners

13. See, for instance, Keding, "Wider das Apathieaxiom," 92–93. A similar reflection upon the importance of Luther's Christology is to be found in Moltmann, *Crucified God*, 232–35.
14. Eberhard Jüngel suggests, for instance, that Luther's debate with Zwingli is significant because it specifies: "von woher sich der *Gottesbegriff* theologisch zu konstituieren hat." Jüngel, "Vom Tod des lebendigen Gottes," 103.
15. Another prominent permutation of this trajectory is the tendency within contemporary trinitarian theologies to eschew any distinction between the immanent and economic Trinity, or at least to deny that this distinction somehow protects the impassible integrity of the divine

of this restorative venture explicitly single out Luther among its earliest progenitors, but this is by no means universally the case. The trend here in mind extends well beyond the circumscribed reaches of Luther's personal reception-history.[16]

How do recent theologians propose the polarity ought to be mended? A cursory survey of modern discourse in this area unveils a degree of variety that makes any comprehensive response to this question infeasible. Most proposals share in common, however, a generic attempt to reconfigure the relation between divine transcendence and divine immanence in such a way that the two are no longer situated upon a univocally polarized spectrum, which precludes their peaceful coexistence. Permutations of this proposal tend to insist, in particular, that conceptualizations of God's transcendence must be recalibrated, since a corruption in this area is supposed to be primarily culpable for the fatal polarity's development in the first place. The goal, as Werner Elert helpfully expresses it, is to formulate a "qualitative" rather than "quantitative" specification of God's ontological otherness; an account that avoids artificially driving transcendence and immanence apart onto two antithetical poles of a univocal spectrum, which therefore can never be joined somewhere in the middle.[17] The most sophisticated permutations of this approach do not wish to overcome the distinction altogether (as if God were

essence. Most who adopt this approach claim to follow in the footsteps of Karl Rahner. For a helpful analysis of the range of perspective included within this trend, see Fred Sanders, *The Image of the Immanent Trinity: Rahner's Rule and the Theological Interpretation of Scripture* (New York: Peter Lang, 2005).

16. In other words, although a divergence reception of Luther's theology has often provided impetus and support to these trajectories, it is important to note that their contemporary emergence is the result of multiple factors beyond mere Luther interpretation. The theologians surveyed in this section do tend to cite Luther, but the themes their work represents are shared by many who do not. Again, the point in this section is not to focus upon the merits of these trajectories as an extension of Luther, but to see how Luther (as reinterpreted in nondivergence fashion) might make a contribution within contemporary discourse. The fact that a wayward interpretation of Luther happens to have funded major aspects of this discourse is, for the purposes of this chapter, only incidentally significant.

somehow only immanent), but seek, rather, to complicate it in such a way that God's transcendence does not restrict God's capacity for immanence, but actually enables it.[18] Eberhard Jüngel helpfully represents this goal when he explains: "The God who is in heaven *because* he cannot be on earth is replaced by the Father who is in heaven in such a way that his heavenly kingdom can come *into the world*, that is, a God who is in heaven in *such a way* that he can *identify himself* with the poverty of the man Jesus, with the existence of a man brought from life to death on the cross."[19]

Perhaps the most prominent constructive avenue enlisted to secure this "polarity complication" without loss to either transcendence or immanence is the widespread suggestion that God sovereignly chooses, or elects (in freedom), to exist in co-suffering immanence with God's creation. In this way, divine sympathetic involvement does not come at the cost of God's transcendence. It is not the result of external constraint or coercion (as if God's being were simply tangled up in the same exigencies experienced by finite creatures), but emerges from an internal movement of God's free will. God is ontologically conditioned by God's interactions with creatures, in short, because God determines that it should be so.[20] The ostensible dogmatic gain in specifying transcendence in this way is the fact

17. Hauber, "Christologie und metaphysicher Gottesbegriff," 136. I am using Elert's rendering of the distinction as a useful description for what many other theologians propose, albeit sometimes with a different vocabulary.

18. Paul Fiddes helpfully demonstrates the extent to which this prescriptive problematic echoes through the halls of contemporary theology in various varieties and forms. See *Creative Suffering of God*, 110–43. The final paragraph of this section represents Fiddes's constructive proposal, which nicely expresses the polarity complication that I am here trying to describe: "The transcendence of a suffering God can only be understood as a transcendent suffering, not a transcendence beyond suffering. Only the thought of God as Trinity can make sense of transcendent suffering, for only a God who happens as an event of relationships can be both other than and yet inclusive of the world. He can include all suffering in himself as he includes all human relationships, yet he is other than the world in his unique suffering, taking our suffering into himself out of the depths of the more profound and terrible suffering which remains his own."

19. Jüngel, *God as the Mystery of the World*, 209.

that God's otherness is no longer bound by a restrictive philosophical framework, which ironically limits divine freedom precisely where it seeks most ardently to protect it.

It avoids stipulating a priori what God can and cannot do. It deflects the imposition of philosophical conceptualities that specify, on the basis of speculative reasoning, which properties ought to apply abstractly to "divinity." In short, this approach no longer commences its discourse by identifying God as the metaphysical foundation of all that exists.[21] Classical doctrines of God's being, which take this approach, grossly underestimate the extent of God's otherness.[22] At best, they can deliver only a quantitative account of divine transcendence. God is taken to be the highest instance of being, the archetypal foundation of an ontologically closed system. God is identified as the world's metaphysical base—a philosophically abstracted plane of stability hovering undisturbed above or beneath the pervasive malleability of all else that exists. This quantitative account of divine otherness comes at a cost. It places intrinsic and unavoidable limitations upon God's ability to act, and thus

20. See Fiddes's discussion of this view in *Creative Suffering of God*, 66–71. How exactly God's self-election for suffering is explained varies somewhat dramatically from theologian to theologian. The strategy itself represents an important aspect of Karl Barth's ongoing legacy, although it remains a point of somewhat rancorous contention whether Barth *himself* espoused a version of this view, and if he did, what exactly he meant by it.

21. This characterization of Greek philosophy is extremely prominent, as is the assumption that early Christian theology's attempt to reason about God in a similar way has hamstrung its ability to speak clearly about the God revealed in Christ. See, for instance, Pannenberg, "Die Aufnahme des philosophischen Gottesbegriffs, 5, 28, 43. Note also Hauber, "Christologie und metaphysicher Gottesbegriff," 128, 161–62; Mühlen, *Die Veränderlichkeit Gottes*, 7, 15; and Moltmann, *Crucified God*, 214. Eberhard Jüngel also develops the thesis that the defect in classical, metaphysical determinations of God's being, which is intensified with the advent of modernity, is that God's being is defined in terms of "necessity"—a kind of ontological prop designed to secure the stability of the world or human security. This, however, is inescapably at odds with what Jüngel considers to be faithful reflection upon God through God's own self-revelation. In theology's attempt to do both, there tears open an aporia in the tradition. See, for instance, Jüngel, *God As the Mystery of the World*, 249.

22. Pannenberg insists that theology needs a more *radical* account of God's otherness—an otherness beyond the scope of the world's intelligibility. See his essay "Die Aufnahme des philosophischen Gottesbegriffs," 44.

hamstrings God's capacity for genuine immanence.[23] Divine transcendence comes at the expense of divine mercy.

Eberhard Jüngel articulates an especially rich permutation of this iconoclastic narrative. In order to rectify the problem, he insists that God exists *beyond* the sphere of causal necessity altogether. As such, the nature of deity cannot be defined on the basis of a purely abstractive reasoning.[24] In making this case, Jüngel seeks to enlarge divine transcendence (qualitatively), precisely to make space for a robust doctrine of divine immanence.[25] The death of Christ no longer contradicts the transcendent being of God, as classical theism has presupposed to the detriment of its own coherence. Jüngel hopes to overcome the "aporias" of metaphysical polarities by suggesting that the divine essence can be thought together with death, and, indeed, that it ought to be.[26] In doing so, a theology of the cross deconstructs the doctrine of God forged on philosophical grounds, and allows God's own self-revelation in Christ to unveil the true nature of God's deity.[27] In this way, the fatal polarity is healed. Dogmatic integrity

23. Note Pannenberg's emphasis upon divine freedom in ibid., 2, 14, 29–30, 36–39.
24. By abstractive reasoning, I mean reflection, which proceeds upward from the observation of worldly realities to God on the basis of causal reasoning. A very clear articulation of this point is to be found in Jüngel, *God as the Mystery of the World*, 33.
25. It is the common mistake of both modern and premodern conceptions of God, according to Jüngel, to conceive of divinity in such a way that God becomes a prop for the intelligibility of the world or the security of the human subject. See, for instance, ibid., 181, 197. This shared perspective is ultimately a midwife to atheism, since it ironically makes the existence of God dependent upon our need of God. This diagnosis of modern atheism, and the identification of classical theism's complicity in its genesis, accounts for a major section of Jüngel's study.
26. See ibid., 231–34, 100, 188. For Jüngel, there is really no choice but to speak in this way of God, since modern atheism demonstrates that the metaphysical God of absolute nature has now run its course, and is no longer plausible. He argues, for instance: "Christian theology today must make a decision. It must decide whether it will follow Fichte and his theological heirs and renounce the thinkability of God. Or it must (as the only possible alternative, in actuality) be prepared to destroy the presupposed understanding of the divine being 'superior to us' (*supra nos*) in order to think God in the way that he has revealed himself in his identity with the man Jesus" (187).
27. Ibid., 13, 159–69. See also Jüngel's essay, "Vom Tod des lebendigen Gottes," 105–106, 112.

is restored by expunging inadequate conceptualizations of divine transcendence.

The rejection of divine impassibility is but one subsidiary facet of the larger counterproposal, but represents, nevertheless, the crucial point at which Luther's Christology is presumed to align with contemporary sensibilities. Impassibility functions in modern theology somewhat like a shibboleth of conceptual commitments. That Luther apparently rejects impassibility for the sake of a more robust doctrine of divine immanence is the necessary linchpin for his contemporary recruitment. It pilots accounts of his significance that identify him as a resource for the constructive proposal sketched throughout this section. The passibilist Luther appears to reinforce not only the intent, but also the reconstructive means, adopted by modern "theologians of the cross" in their attempt to codify a qualitative account of God's otherness.

But if Luther doesn't reconfigure two-nature dogma in the manner suggested by the divergence thesis (as demonstrated in chapters 2 through 4), and therefore does not pit divine impassibility against divine immanence, how ought the engagement between his Christology and recent trajectories be recast? Must his ideas, thus reinterpreted, simply fade back into the already well-populated mélange of thinkers before and after him who appear wrongfully to propagate a fatal polarity within the doctrine of God? Is contemporary theology left with the same deconstructive agenda, even if it must recruit alternative historical resources for its advance? In various ways, each of these questions seeks to ascertain whether Luther's Christology can still possess anything other than a merely passing antiquarian interest, now that his ideas are shown no longer to reinforce contemporary preoccupations. The following section will address this "receptive" question by providing a few programmatic gestures of how Luther can constructively inform ongoing theological discourse.

Luther's Contemporary Significance

Luther understands immanence and impassibility not as mutually exclusive, but mutually reinforcing, commitments. His Christology directly challenges the validity of the widely presumed antithesis between these doctrines, which occupies a central position in the theological trajectories surveyed in the past section. It could be the case, of course, that Luther is simply inconsistent. He is, after all, by no means the only premodern theologian to speak emphatically about the doctrine of divine immanence. Perhaps he articulates an incoherent admixture of immiscible conceptual elements without realizing it.[28] If divine impassibility is accurately defined in the terms specified by the previous section (that is, aloof remoteness), such a conclusion would be largely inescapable. This, however, is precisely the point where Luther's Christology makes its initial contribution. It suggests an alternative specification of divine impassibility that disrupts the contemporary tendency to interpret this doctrine as an obstructive impediment to an adequate recognition of God's intimate involvement with human history in Christ.

Divine impassibility, for Luther, does not signify an abstract, ontological remoteness that somehow denudes all affirmations of divine immanence of their substantive meaning (that is, God is involved and yet uninvolved). Impassibility refers, for him, to the "mode" of God's radical immanence: a maximally radiant nearness of incorruptible divinity in the midst of abject human weakness; the triumph of deathless might in the very jaws of mortal defeat.

28. Hence, the view of Ian Kingston Siggins.

An impassible mode of presence specifies, for him, what God's involvement in human suffering must be like in order for such involvement to count as redemptive. Only a God, who is incorruptibly divine, can be the Lord over sin, death, and the devil. Only such a one may irradiate human weakness with deathless might and break the power of death and Hades. For God to be present in a mode other than this would stipulate, for Luther, that Christ requires a savior of his own. Luther's soterio-logic also presupposes, more seriously, that a god rendered vulnerable by the incarnation would not actually be God at all. Impassibility, in other words, is not an abstract means of protecting some predetermined notion of divine transcendence in spite of God's presence in Christ. It is not an ascriptive counterbalance that restricts affirmations of divine immanence by heaping qualificatory weight on the opposite side of a univocal, ontological ledger. God is present impassibly because only a God thus present can redeem—and only a God who can redeem is truly God.[29]

Luther's Christology disrupts the polarity narrative's governing equation of "impassibility" with "detached remoteness," and thus calls into question the accuracy of its critical diagnosis in the first place. Divine impassibility does not assert something to be true of God that the reality of divine immanence intrinsically contradicts. It is not a philosophically polarized abstraction from the ephemera of finitude. It specifies a modality of presence appropriate to Christ's divinity, a form of involvement characterized by uncircumscribed, and unassailable, deathless vitality. In this sense, impassibility denotes not a "lack," but a plenitude of sorts. Contemporary defenders of divine impassibility have sometimes expressed a similar point in relation to the question of how an immutable God can act. Luther's emphasis is complementary, but somewhat different. His rendering of

29. For textual corroboration of this summary, see the appropriate portions of ch. 4.

impassibility in the terms of an incorruptible fullness of life describes why it is that the incarnate Christ can enter death and yet save.

Christ enters death, but never ceases in so doing to be the living God. Immanence and impassibility do not compete for space along a univocal, descriptive spectrum of attributes. To pit them as necessarily opposed to one another is, in effect, to commit a category mistake. Luther's Christology presumes the compatibility of the conceptualities in question.[30] The divergence reception is quite right to regard Luther as a champion of divine immanence. It errs, however, in presupposing that this emphasis is irreconcilable with impassibility doctrine. In fact, Luther affirms both. More significant, he enlists the latter as a means of specifying the former. Impassibility characterizes an intrinsic aspect of God's redemptive nearness. The operative complementarity of these two concepts in Luther's soteriology represents an important facet of his contemporary significance.

The efforts of contemporary theology to avoid a quantitative polarization of divine attributes nevertheless reflects constructive values that Luther's Christology genuinely embodies. Like many contemporary theologians, Luther treasures a rich affirmation of divine immanence and regards the transcendence of God as no obstacle to it. This means that Luther remains an interesting conversation partner, even though the divergence thesis locates the nature of his contribution in the wrong place. Insofar as transcendence and immanence meet in Luther's doctrine of Christ, his theology qualifies as a legitimate proposal of the very sort of "qualitative complication" contemporary authors seek to articulate.

30. Of course, this is only true if "impassibility" is shown not to be equivalent with "detached remoteness." In contexts where the operative definition of impassibility directly proscribes God's substantive involvement with created realities, the polarity narrative would be valid, even if its proposed solution is not the only one.

His Christology enacts an understanding of God's transcendence that does not compete with, but actually enables, robust immanence.[31]

In this qualified sense, Luther and his contemporary interlocutors pursue a common dogmatic end. His significance need not be interpreted as purely subversive. His ideas do not simply wag a disapproving finger in judgment of modern improprieties. Luther and modern theology can engage with one another constructively and collaboratively in the pursuit of a shared goal—namely, a profound and conceptually viable emphasis upon God's radical involvement within human history.[32] The crucial question is whether divine impassibility represents a "help" or "hindrance" in the pursuit of this end. Is impassibility an impediment to divine immanence? Is it a marker of transcendence wrongly construed (that is, "remoteness")? Or is impassibility a necessary affirmation for formulating an adequate conceptualization of God's immanence in Christ?

Divine impassibility functions within Luther's Christology to specify the nature of God's immanence. He does not regard it to be a conceptual obstacle that detracts from the affirmation of divine nearness. On the contrary, it expresses for him the important fact that the "god" who *is* radically present in Christ is none other than the one true God. This emphasis has its origin in Luther's soteriology, as specified in chapter 4. Only the God who is incorruptible in the midst of sufferings, and immortal in the midst of death, can enter the depths

31. The divergence reception understandably assumes that the overlap of intent represented here constitutes a major reason why Luther *jettisons* divine impassibility in the first place. This is because contemporary assessments of the doctrine assume it inescapably to reproduce the bad, quantitative polarity, which Luther's strident emphasis upon divine immanence seems unavoidably to deconstruct. This line of receptive reasoning, however, confuses substantive overlap of theological intent with an alignment of instrumental means. The fact that Luther retains divine impassibility *as a critical component of his theology of divine immanence* raises the constructive question whether a theology of divine suffering actually represents substantive progress in the attempt to specify a qualitative account of divine otherness, as its contemporary advocates are wont to insist.

32. I do not mean to imply, of course, that Luther is the only premodern theologian who shares this goal.

of the human condition and emerge victorious. Situated in this way, Luther's soteriology presupposes precisely what modern passibilist accounts intrinsically deny, namely, that the relation between God and the world is ontologically noncompetitive. At first glance, this may seem an outrageous claim. It is the self-avowed intent of modern theologies of divine suffering to suggest that God really intersects with created reality, and does so without ceasing to be God. The critical question, however, is whether divine passibility is consistent with such a claim. There is reason to suppose, on the basis of Luther's Christology, that divine impassibility maintains the fundamental emphasis more transparently than does its denial.

Luther's point of view presupposes an abiding complementarity between the radical transcendence of the divine being and God's equally radical immanent involvement in the events of human history. The abiding impassibility of Christ's divinity means that immanence does not require any sympathetic "adjustment" of God's being. Beneath such an emphasis resides a decidedly qualitative rendering of God's otherness. God is not distinct from creation as a matter of extended degree. On the contrary, God and the world simply do not compete for space within Luther's Christology. Can the same be said for passibilist renderings of divine immanence?

To insist that God "suffers" presupposes (minimally, at least) that immanence requires ontological displacement. God's involvement with creation elicits, perhaps even requires, a conditioning of the divine being. The intersection of deity with sin-warped, creaturely reality entails, in other words, an ontological "yielding" of sorts. God is affected. God experiences pain, suffering, loss, weakness, and defect—all as the result of God's "collision" with postlapsarian finitude. To speak in this way is to presuppose that God's being and the world are the sorts of entities that can compete for space. Why should this be so if God and the world exist on qualitatively distinct planes of being? The oft-purported necessity of divine suffering inadvertently implies that a zero-sum ontological game is still being played. Creator and creature are nudging about for space upon a univocal playing field of causal interaction.

If the outward conditioning of God's being is treated tacitly as a prerequisite of authentic immanence, then divine suffering appears merely to be the ontological cost exacted by God's genuine interaction with finite existents.[33] One finds a dramatic manifestation of this view in the theology of Jürgen Moltmann. He insists that the act of creation itself requires a self-contraction of God's being, in order to make space for the integrity of the other.[34] There is an irony here. Moltmann presupposes the very quantitative relation between God and the world that so many modern passibilist theologians have labored to overcome. His view erects a competitive ontological relation between transcendence and immanence. Eberhard Jüngel's suggestion that God's being must be conceptualized beyond the limits of necessity is far more satisfying. And yet, Jüngel also proffers the notion that God's relation to creation is, from the first instance, a matter of a struggle with nothingness.[35] To what extent do Moltmann and Jüngel actually presuppose the quantitative (and thus competitive) ontological relation they want to avoid?

Why should the prerequisite of divine suffering exist in the first place, if the distinction between transcendence and immanence is qualitative rather than quantitative? The underlying metaphysical assumption would need to be that God and creation cannot converge

33. This applies, whether or not God's decision to suffer is constrained or free. The point is that suffering is treated as a requirement of God's immanence.

34. See, for instance: Jürgen Moltmann, *The Trinity and the Kingdom: The Doctrine of God*, trans. Margaret Kohl (Minneapolis: Fortress Press, 1993 [1981/German ed. 1980]), 108–111; Ron Highfield, "Divine Self-Limitation in the Theology of Jürgen Moltmann: A Critical Appraisal," *Christian Scholars Review* 32 (2002): 47–71; and Siu-Kwong Tang, *God's History in the Theology of Jürgen Moltmann* (Bern: Peter Lang, 1996), 161–72.

35. See Jüngel, *God as the Mystery of the World*, 217–22.

upon the same existential space without ontological displacement.[36] A univocal polarity is at work here, albeit now manifest in an inverted form. The governing presupposition is identical: substantive involvement within the realm of finitude requires a change on God's part. The only real difference is that a passibilist account deems the reality of immanence worth the steep theological cost of admission. In its attempt to heal the fatal, conceptual polarities of premodern dogma, it presupposes a polarity all its own. Despite its best efforts to the contrary, a passibilist reconfiguration of the doctrine of God forces an artificial choice between transcendence and immanence. Ironically, this is precisely the dilemma that much contemporary theology has labored to overcome.

Luther's Christology forces us to consider whether it is possible truly to affirm immanence or impassibility without simultaneously affirming its counterpart. The ontological transmutation of God's being is not necessary in order to secure the genuine immanence of God in Christ. Such a transmutation would actually undermine immanence, because it suggests that the agent with whom humanity deals is someone or something other than the one true God.[37] In this case, God is, ironically, neither transcendent nor immanent.[38] From the perspective of Luther's Christology, then, contemporary

36. Divine being, in other words, would not exist above the laws of Newtonian physics.

37. Does this same criticism apply to passibilist proposals, which retain divine immutability by way of either protological prolepsis or eschatological analepsis? Such models are relatively more successful and promising than other accounts of God's suffering, because they avoid the implication that God must become something other than Godself in order to draw near in the person of Christ. These proposals are still problematic, however, because they presuppose the same ontologically competitive playing field. Whether or not God decides from the beginning to be a certain way, the fact that proximity requires suffering signals that the same framework is operative.

38. Is this alternative conceptually coherent? It may seem not, on the grounds that immanence and impassibility cannot plausibly describe the same agent at the same time. Such an objection merely begs the qualitative question, however, and curiously reproduces the very univocally charged polarity that so much recent theology has labored to heal, namely, the a priori assumption that the nearness of God comes only at the expense of ontologically competitive loss.

theologies of divine suffering legitimately seek to avoid a potential, conceptual pathology that threatens to endanger a robust affirmation of divine immanence. The lingering risk, to which these perspectives bear witness, is so to construe the nature of divine transcendence that the equally necessary affirmation of divine immanence consequently withers to little more than a husk—an exercise in naked assent without genuine content.

A substantive engagement with Luther's Christology demonstrates, however, that recent theology has applied this diagnosis with insufficient discretion. It has assumed that divine impassibility per se signals an artificial polarization of divine transcendence at the expense of divine immanence. But divine impassibility, in and of itself, is not a reliable indicator.[39] The attempt to protect divine immanence by rejecting divine impassibility represents, at minimum, a vast oversimplification of the crucial issue. More seriously, the renunciation of divine impassibility seems to harm more than it heals.[40] Theologies of divine suffering do not overcome the polarity, but reproduce it by inverting it. Luther's Christology, on the other hand, insists with the help of impassibility that God is truly present, and present truly as God. In this, he reinforces contemporary theological intent but subverts its commonly elected instrumental means. Luther points a more fruitful way forward, which, ironically, is, at the same time, also a way back. The reformer whose theology has so often been identified as a fault line in the developmental history of dogma, actually provides the

39. The church father Tertullian chastises the Marcionites for their anemic account of divine immanence, all the while affirming the doctrine of divine impassibility. See, for instance, Richard A. Norris, trans. and ed., with Robert C. Saler, *The Christological Controversy*, Sources of Early Christian Thought (Minneapolis: Fortress Press, 2012), 68.

40. So far as securing an affirmation of divine immanence is concerned, the logic of Luther's Christology suggests that God's natural suffering is perhaps sweet to the taste (it seems to denote radical involvement), but burns like fire in the belly (it undercuts the reality of redemption).

path for a constructive retrieval of premodern conceptualities in a contemporary theological setting.

Conclusion

Luther's Christology is significant for modern reflection upon the immanence of God in Christ on account of the following observations:

1. It disrupts widely held assumptions about the doctrine of divine impassibility as a marker of transcendence wrongly identified.
2. It challenges an influential narrative of dogmatic development, which supposes classical reflection quantitatively to pit divine transcendence over against divine immanence.
3. It provides an alternative account of God's qualitative otherness, which is more consistent in the pursuit of this task than theologies of divine suffering geared toward the same.
4. It clarifies that the point of Christology is not that God is capable of ontological self-limitation, but that God is free intimately to engage with creaturely existents—even entering into union with sinful human beings—without changing "who" or "what" God is.

On a proscriptive level, these observations foreclose the suggestion, which this study may provoke, that the "husk" of Luther's demonstrated adherence to divine impassibility can easily be winnowed apart from the genuine "kernel" of his robust commitment to God's radical immanence. The intent of such an argument would be to urge that Luther's bequeathal to contemporary theology should remain, nevertheless, much as specified by the divergence reception, albeit perhaps now qualified with the passing historical caveat that Luther never quite articulated his own best insights with full integrity.[41] The legitimacy of this proposal would depend, however, upon the assumption that divine impassibility is, at best, an ancillary idiosyncrasy within Luther's theology; a nonessential conceptual pith that can be shorn away without substantive loss. The soteriological integration of divine impassibility and divine immanence within Luther's theology effectively obstructs this receptive avenue.[42] The divergence reception does not extend the logic of Luther's Christology, but cuts against it.

More constructively, Luther's Christology furnishes an opportunity for a theologically fruitful reflection upon the modality of God's immanence in the redemptive sufferings of Christ. In this respect, the content of his theology remains remarkably pertinent to widespread modern concerns, though not in the manner often supposed to be the case. In contrast with the majority of crucicentric theologies developed in recent decades, Luther retains the doctrine of divine impassibility precisely in order to speak adequately about the nature of God's radical immanence in Christ. The mutual complementarity of these affirmations within Luther's theology therefore represents a multiply significant aspect of his contemporary importance.

41. Some already endorse a version of this view, as outlined in ch. 1.

42. Those who hesitantly acknowledge Luther's occasional endorsement of divine impassibility have tended to see this doctrine as a tumor that can and ought to be removed. They have assumed, in other words, that divine impassibility does not intrinsically *belong* to the governing commitments of Luther's theology. If, however, impassibility is a major aspect of Luther's soteriological logic, then it cannot be surgically removed without severely altering Luther's animating theological presuppositions. It is impossible to say, along with Albrecht Ritschl, that Luther must be pitted against Luther in order thus to guide his thought to a deeper level of internal consistency.

Conclusion

The preceding chapters of this study defend a thesis that possesses far-reaching implications for the analysis and contemporary appraisal of Luther's Christology. This conclusion will provide a retrospective overview of the main argument, and suggest a few lingering questions that warrant future inquiry.

Reprise

This study has focused upon a prevalent reception of Luther's theology, to which it has referred generically as the "divergence thesis." The distinguishing feature of this reception is its consistent tendency to identify in Luther's Christology the seeds of a far-reaching conceptual reconfiguration of the classically developed doctrine of God. It supposes Luther, above all, to bequeath unto modern theology the disruptive premise that God suffers in the incarnate person of Christ. In this, Luther departs from the views of previous thinkers of the tradition, for whom the impassibility of God represents something of an axiomatic, supervisory commitment. Luther's rejection of impassibility is alleged to reside specifically in a critical adjustment of two-nature Christology, specifically as it pertains to the *communicatio idiomatum*. The result is an unprecedented insistence that Christ's divine nature shares equally in the sufferings of his humanity.

Luther's apparent affirmation of a reciprocal communication of attributes is perceived by many theologians to mark a major turning point in the history of dogmatic reflection. Above all, it is supposed to create the space necessary for a new and better conceptualization of God's immanence. For Luther, God is present among God's people not as an aloof bystander, somehow shielded from the contaminating defects of postlapsarian corruption. Instead, God shares in human suffering, and takes up death into God's own divine life. The divergence reception, in other words, supposes that Luther's Christology makes it possible for theology to acknowledge the mystery of a God who truly gives of Godself and allows the sufferings of humanity to condition God's very being—a God immanent in the form of passionate and costly solidarity. For many systematic theologians, these insights constitute the marrow of Luther's dogmatic significance.

The divergence reception of Luther's theology has garnered widespread appeal, in part because it provides a historical point of departure from which to address pressing contemporary concerns. For nearly a century, the doctrine of divine impassibility has been widely perceived to represent a serious obstacle to the doctrine of divine immanence. The notion that God cannot suffer has appeared increasingly difficult to reconcile with the biblical attestation of a God substantively involved in the events of human history.[1] The residual trauma engendered by twentieth-century atrocities has only intensified the impression, palpable in the writings of many recent theologians, that a God incapable of suffering is a God who can neither love nor help.

1. This is especially true as it pertains to the revelation of God in the history of Jesus.

The divergence interpretation of Luther's Christology possesses explanatory power, in part because it directly intersects with these theological concerns. It facilitates a constructive recruitment of Luther's Christology within contemporary spheres of discourse. Luther's passibilist adjustment of two-nature Christology is deemed significant, in many instances, because it appears to forge a path beyond the opaque conceptualities of premodern dogma and onward to a more transparent rendering of God's immanence in the person and work of Christ.[2] The divergence thesis has garnered widespread influence, therefore, because it functions so effectively as a midwife to transhistorical relevance. It construes Luther's Christology in a way that underscores his importance for theological questions now hanging in the balance. The contentious status of divine impassibility within modern discourse is especially important in this respect. It represents a major reason why a divergence rendering of Luther's Christology has attracted the amount of attention that it has. This is as true of those who applaud Luther's dogmatic deviation as necessary and salutary as it is of theologians who evaluate the alleged rejection of divine impassibility as grave doctrinal error. In either case, Luther's Christology is supposed, by virtue of the divergence interpretation, to possess a latent constructive potential for informing the labors of contemporary reflection. The narrative of a seminal dogmatic divergence effectively culls this formative potential to the foreground.

2. In this sense, the divergence reception embodies Jürgen Moltmann's programmatic claim, enunciated in the opening paragraphs of *The Crucified God*, that the theologian's goal of contemporary relevance ineluctably makes it difficult to maintain a degree of continuity with the past that is sufficient to preserve the integrity of Christian identity. See Jürgen Moltmann, *The Crucified God: The Cross of Christ as the Foundation and Criticism of Christian Theology*, trans. R. A. Wilson and John Bowden (Minneapolis: Fortress Press, 1993 [1974/German ed. 1973]), 7–31. In the case of the divergence reception's implicit appraisal of impassibility, the cost of continuity weighed against relevance is evidently deemed too steep.

In its attempt to assess this widespread appraisal of Luther's significance, this study has emphasized the fact that the divergence reception is based upon a specific and largely stable analysis of Luther's theological texts. Whether or not this analysis is historically accurate thus represents the rather urgent question, which the majority of the preceding chapters have sought to address. The test of historical accuracy is a criteriological hinge upon which the reception's constructive legitimacy may be evaluated. The interpretation of Luther's Christology, which the divergence reception presupposes, includes essentially three constitutive elements.

1. Luther rejects the doctrine of suppositional carrying, and substitutes for it a composite doctrine of Christ, capable of expressing a more intimate union between divinity and humanity.
2. Within this more intimate union, Luther reconfigures the traditional doctrine of the *communicatio idiomatum* in order especially to affirm the participatory suffering of Christ's divinity.
3. The suffering of divinity is an essential part of Luther's soteriology, and thus central to the fabric of his thought.

These claims represent the three pillars upon which the divergence reception rests. Its status as a viable appraisal of Luther's theological significance remains intact only if each assertion is shown to be valid.[3]

The primary goal of this study has been to demonstrate the historical inaccuracy of these three claims. Chapters 2 through 4 expose the exegetical deficiencies associated with the defense of each.

3. It must demonstrate, in other words, that the structure of Luther's theology *secures* (claims one and two) and *requires* (claim three) the affirmation of divine passibility.

These chapters also outline an alternative specification of Luther's Christology, which is based upon the careful analysis of pertinent texts. Chapter 2 illustrates Luther's continuing employment of the doctrine of suppositional carrying as an analogical description of the hypostatic union. Chapter 3 treats the communication of attributes and demonstrates that Luther retains the doctrine of divine impassibility as a controlling commitment of his analysis. Chapter 4 shows how the invulnerability of God in the midst of human suffering represents a crucial aspect of Luther's soterio-logic. Besides its documentation of the divergence thesis's historical inaccuracy, this sequential refutation also entails a proscriptive conclusion for the constructive appropriation of Luther's theology. Appraisals of Luther's significance, which rely upon a divergence specification of his Christology, must come to terms with the fact that Luther retains the doctrine of divine impassibility. Appraisals that assert otherwise may secure for Luther an appealing degree of "relevance," but do so at the cost of historical accuracy. This, in any case, is the central thesis, which the preceding chapters have sought, at length, to defend and develop.

A devalidation of the divergence reception does not, however, render Luther mute in the face of modern concerns. The central argument of this study intends neither to obfuscate nor eschew the reality of Luther's ongoing theological importance. It should therefore not be perceived as an attempt to discourage the appropriation of Luther as a resource within contemporary reflection. The goal is not to place an opprobrium upon constructive retrievals of Luther's Christology altogether but, rather, to redirect the nature of Luther's constructive potential in the light of a "nondivergence" specification of his ideas. Such "redirection" creates the conditions necessary for an alternative appropriation of Luther's theology that is based upon a more stable historical foundation.

The fifth chapter of this study represents a preliminary gesture of how the constructive potential of Luther's "nondivergence" Christology might be realized. It returns to the question, treated so often within divergence appropriations of Luther's theology, of how Luther's Christology is significant for ongoing attempts to rethink the dogmatic conceptualization of divine immanence. Luther makes an interesting contribution in this area, not because he urges the rejection of outmoded conceptualities, which are already the object of contemporary suspicions. He insists, rather, upon a modality of God's immanence that disrupts and reconfigures the ordinary terms of the discussion itself. The inability of God to suffer, for Luther, is no sign of ontological remoteness, but a marker of the fact that God is present in the midst of death always as the immortal and living God.[4] In this way, he tacitly contends that it is really only the nonsuffering God who can truly help. This insight appears provocative, indeed, when counterposed against the predominant theological sentiments of the contemporary milieu.

Prospect

The bulk of this study has been occupied with the elaboration and defense of a fairly straightforward historical thesis. It has argued that the divergence thesis misrepresents the character of Luther's Christology when it detects in his writing a fundamental swerve regarding the capacity of God to suffer. This relatively

4. We catch a glimpse of this radical simultaneity in a comment Luther makes about the transfiguration, which is cited by Ian D. Kingston Siggins, *Martin Luther's Doctrine of Christ*, Yale Publications in Religion 14 (New Haven: Yale University Press, 1970), 218: "In the transfiguration, for example, God revealed 'the future splendor and glory of our bodies. For it was a thing of wonder that Christ should be glorified while still in His mortal and passible body. By it, He showed the splendor of immortality in the very midst of mortality. What will it be, when mortality is at the last taken completely away and there is nothing but immortality and splendor?!'"

uncomplicated thesis, however, is pregnant with any number of far-reaching implications for the study, evaluation, and appropriation of Luther's theology. Some of these implications have been explored with a necessarily partial brevity within the context of preceding chapters.[5] This brevity signifies to the reader that the sequential refutation of the divergence thesis advanced throughout this study is less a determinate conclusion than it is a point of departure. It represents a programmatic verdict that raises far more questions than it definitively settles. The most portentous of these questions warrant cursory recognition in the remaining pages of this conclusion. By reflecting upon them, it will also be possible to indicate a few significant areas for future research that sprout up from the soil of this study's main argument.

Luther and Late Medieval Scholasticism

The refutation of the divergence thesis encourages a renovated appraisal of the relation between Luther's Christology and the views of late medieval Scholasticism. The present study secures only two relatively modest historical claims that inform this relation. Like his medieval forebears, Luther (1) enlists the doctrine of suppositional carrying as a descriptive model for making sense of the incarnation, and (2) rejects the idea that Christ's divinity experiences a participatory suffering along with the humanity that Christ assumes.[6] This is a very minimal claim. It does not preclude the possibility that Luther dramatically changes or rejects other aspects of late medieval

5. Even ch. 5, above, which addresses the matter of implications more directly, is little more than a preliminary "gesture" when it comes to the subsequent task of elaborating upon the variegated importance of the divergence thesis's refutation.
6. Chapter 4, above, demonstrates the way in which especially the latter affirmation materializes within Luther's soteriology. It does not provide any extensive specification of the extent to which Luther's application of divine impassibility represents a continuity with preexisting tradition.

Christology. Surely, it seems to be the case that Luther emphasizes the "unity" of Christ as a single acting subject in ways that are more forceful than many of his theological forebears. To what extent this emphasis is a matter of style or substance is a legitimate question for future inquiry. In other words, a "nondivergence" interpretation does not mean that Luther's Christology aligns seamlessly with that of his Scholastic predecessors. It is merely an attempt to demonstrate that Luther does not deviate from late medieval Christology in the particular ways modern interpreters so often assume. Taken on its own merits, this study's "nondivergence interpretation" represents merely a slight contribution to a far more complex task that awaits future study, namely, that of specifying the precise nature of Luther's relation to late medieval Christology in general terms.

The divergence thesis has cast a long shadow across generic characterizations of this relation within recent theological literature. Luther's "reformational Christology" is often counterposed diametrically over against preexisting reflection, thus reinforcing the overarching perception of a sheer discontinuity within the reformer's theological development. In some cases, it is implied that Luther differs from his medieval interlocutors at the level of theological first principles. His reflection upon Christ embodies values that are entirely different from the traditions that precede him.[7] For all intents and purposes, the Scholastics were speaking a different language.

Sites of discontinuity between Luther and the Scholastics surely exist. Precisely where these differences lie, however, is a question that emerges with a renewed degree of explanatory urgency in the wake of this study.[8] This is because the previous chapters have refuted

7. In many cases, it is Luther's soteriological focus that is singled out as the point of departure from medieval reflection, which is derided as merely speculative. For more on this trend, see the pertinent discussion in ch. 4.

8. In this sense, a nondivergence interpretation of Luther calls for the same reevaluation of Luther's relation to late medieval Scholasticism that other facets of his thought have received in

the principal interpretive claims that have perennially mediated the perceptions of Luther's christological distinctiveness. In the absence of these orienting claims, it is necessary to reassess the nature of Luther's constructive appropriation of prior tradition. The natural place to begin in addressing this task would be the execution of a critical comparative analysis between Luther's late christological texts and major Scholastic treatises on the person and work of Christ. Of particular significance for such a comparison would be Gabriel Biel's *Collectorium circa quattuor libros Sententiarum*, which chapter 3, above, briefly accessed.[9] Luther was familiar with this work. A record of his early, critical interactions with it survives in the form of marginal notations published in the Weimar edition of his writings.[10] Reinhard Schwarz interacts with these notations extensively, but regards them to be only a point of departure. In his view, they represent doctrinal judgments from which Luther would later swerve in his theological rejection of late Scholastic dogma. Schwarz draws this conclusion, however, because he believes it is clear that Luther defines the person of Christ in his christological disputations in compositional terms.[11] Now that the divergence interpretation of Luther's later works has been set aside, it is time to return to Schwarz's original task with new and better questions.[12]

the past several decades as the result of the work of scholars such as Heiko Obermann, Dennis Janz, and Steven Ozment. The goal in such reevaluation is never to mute difference, but rightly locate it.

9. This text is available in critical edition. See Gabriel Biel, Hanns Rückert, Wilfrid Werbeck, Udo Hofmann, and Vendelinus Steinbach, *Collectorium circa quattuor libros Sententiarum* (Tübingen: Mohr, 1973).
10. See WA 59:29f.
11. The only important remaining question, for Schwarz, is precisely *when* Luther shed the nominalist Christology of his early development.
12. This is precisely the strength of Graham White's book *Luther as Nominalist: A Study of the Logical Methods Used in Martin Luther's Disputations in the Light of Their Medieval Background* (Helsinki: Luther-Agricola Society, 1994). It seeks to interpret Luther's disputations within the context of late medieval logic. The future study that I have in mind in this section would be similar in approach to White, but would focus even more directly than he does upon matters

The comparative analysis between Luther and Biel could easily be multiplied by interacting with other commentaries on Lombard's *Sentences* from the late medieval period. Luther was himself acquainted with this tradition of reflection, and interacted with Lombard's text directly in 1510–1511.[13] It is interesting to note that Luther's intense debates with Zwingli over a decade later are often perceived by contemporary interpreters to be indicative of a fundamental break with conceptual commonplaces of Scholastic Christology (of which Zwingli is assumed to be representative). Luther's own subsequent recollection of these debates tells a different story. For him, it was precisely his familiarity with Lombard's *Sentences* that led him to criticize Zwingli in the first place.[14] Neither this observation nor the larger findings of this study may be taken as evidence that a comprehensive theological uniformity unites Luther and the late medieval Scholastics. Surely, this is far from the case. It will be important, however, for future research into Luther's Christology to map sites of continuity and discontinuity more carefully. Only then will an accurate understanding of Luther's relation to the dogmatic vocabulary of late Scholasticism emerge. The refutation of the divergence thesis merely suggests that longstanding perceptions of this relation are ripe for critical reassessment.[15]

of technical Christology. Also important for this task would be Luther's 1544 commentary on Isaiah 53, which treats these matters at considerable length.

13. See WA 9:28–94.
14. Eberhard Jüngel detects a swerve in Luther away from Scholasticism in Luther's treatise against Zwingli, published in 1528. See Eberhard Jüngel, "Vom Tod des lebendigen Gottes: ein Plakat," *Zeitschrift Für Theologie Und Kirche* 65, no. 1 (January 1, 1968): 102–104. For Luther's recollection, see WA 50:591. English translation is available in LW 41:105.
15. Future study could also seek to identify which of the many strands of medieval reflection upon which Luther is most dependent for his understanding of the hypostatic union. In chs. 2 and 3, the medieval point of view is treated in a way that reflects points of general consensus. This should not obscure the fact that many important differences that distinguish between the thinkers and various schools of the medieval period. It would be interesting to chart where Luther's christological views seem best to fit in relation to this wide diversity.

Luther's Christology and Confessionalization

The divergence interpretation of Luther's Christology has also influenced recent descriptions of Lutheran confessionalization. This influence materializes in at least two major evaluative renderings of the period. A great deal of literature characterizes confessional development as a betrayal of Luther's legacy, because this period purportedly reinserts the doctrine of divine impassibility as a controlling commitment of christological reflection.[16] Others, however, detect in the very same process (alternatively interpreted) the substantive extension of Luther's legacy. On this account, many of the later Lutheran theologians retain Luther's revolutionary redefinition of Christ's person not as a suppositional carrier of humanity, but in compositional terms.[17] Each of these "narratives" presupposes some version of the divergence thesis and leverages this presupposition as a measuring reed for how subsequent theological developments within Lutheranism ought to be characterized.[18] If the

16. A few examples of this common interpretation include Sibylle Rolf, "'Christum und nichts anders': die Kommunikation von Gott und Mensch und die Predigt des Evangeliums," *Luther* 80, no. 3 (January 1, 2009): 158n.26; and Marc Lienhard, *Luther: Witness to Jesus Christ: Stages and Themes of the Reformer's Christology* (Minneapolis: Augsburg, 1982), 340–41. Werner Elert, who holds that Luther clearly affirms divine suffering, admits that neither Martin Chemnitz nor Johannes Brenz reject divine impassibility. See Werner Elert, *The Structure of Lutheranism* (St. Louis: Concordia, 1962), 228.
17. The most extensive articulation of this view appears in Johannes Hund, *Das Wort ward Fleisch: eine systematisch-theologische Untersuchung zur Debatte um die Wittenberger Christologie und Abendmahlslehre in den Jahren 1567 und 1574*, Forschungen zur systematischen und ökumenischen Theologie, Bd. 114 (Göttingen: Vandenhoeck & Ruprecht, 2006). Hund is not alone in defending the "extension" reading, however. A similar view is articulated in Hans Christian Brandy, *Die späte Christologie des Johannes Brenz*, Beiträge zur historischen Theologie 80 (Tübingen: J. C. B. Mohr [Paul Siebeck], 1991); and Johann Anselm Steiger, *Fünf Zentralthemen der Theologie Luthers und seiner Erben: Communicatio, Figura, Imago, Maria, Exempla* (Leiden: Brill, 2002), among others.
18. A variation of the first appraisal is found in the work of Theobald Beer, who highlights the dramatic christological difference between Luther and Melanchthon. Beer suggests that confessionalization is actually the *correction* of Luther's divergence legacy, because he views Luther's apparent redefinition of Christ to be theologically disastrous. See Theobald Beer, *Der fröhliche Wechsel und Streit: Grundzüge der Theologie Luthers* (Leipzig: St. Benno-Verlag, 1974), 513–20.

divergence interpretation of Luther is historically inaccurate, then it follows that a reappraisal of the confessional period is necessary, at least so far as it pertains to the description of Lutheran christological developments in the latter half of the sixteenth century.

Such reappraisal could begin with applying the same diagnostic questions that have directed the present study to various influential theologians of the confessional period, such as Martin Chemnitz, Johannes Brenz, Jakob Andreae, and so forth. That is, do these theologians (1) reject the general concept of suppositional carrying in unambiguous terms?; (2) embrace divine passibility?; and (3) envision redemption in terms of suffering solidarity? Johannes Hund and Hans Christian Brandy engage some of these questions, but do so with the assumption that Luther initiates a prior christological divergence, upon which the confessional writers rely. Since this assumption is incorrect, might it be the case that the theologians of Lutheran confessional development have been similarly mischaracterized?

I suspect that a careful investigation of these matters will yield a combination of the two descriptions outlined above as accurate. The "betrayal description" is correct in its interpretation of Luther's confessional heirs (that is, they maintain divine impassibility), but wrong in its assumption that this represents a departure from Luther. The "extension description" is wrong in its interpretation of Luther and the confessional writers, but right in its identification of an abiding continuity between them. Martin Chemnitz, for instance, who was a major architect of confessional formulation in the late 1570s, explicitly proscribes the suffering of Christ's divinity in his 1561 treatise *De Duabus Naturis in Christo*. Perhaps most significant in this respect is his application of the abstract/concrete distinction, which mirrors its appropriation of Luther as described in chapter 3, above:

> . . . the words which denote the united yet distinct natures we call abstract. And those which indicate the person are called concrete. Therefore, one nature is not predicated of the other in the abstract. The deity is not called the humanity. The rule of the Scholastics is that the substantial attributes of the one nature are not attributed to the other when we consider it in the abstract, but they are communicated to the person in the concrete, that is, by a term which indicates the hypostasis. For it is not correct to say that the humanity is an essence generated from the Father from eternity, or that the deity is pierced with nails or wounded with a spear; but it is perfectly correct to say concretely that the Son of Man ascended where He was before, that the Lord of glory is crucified.[19]

In an earlier section of the same text, Chemnitz specifies a parallel judgment, and makes it quite clear that the divinity of Christ does not undergo any ontological change as the result of the incarnation: ". . . the human nature did not assume the divine but the divine assumed the human. Thus, to the essence of the divine nature, which is completely simple and perfect, nothing is added or subtracted as a result of the union. But the human nature because of the union with the assuming deity is augmented and exalted above every name with many excellent and surpassing prerogatives."[20]

19. Martin Chemnitz, *The Two Natures in Christ*, trans. J. A. O. Preus (St. Louis: Concordia, 1971), 175.
20. Ibid., 102. Here we find a rather straightforward endorsement of the "one-way communication" view defended in chs. 3 and 4, above. Another key synopsis of Chemnitz's view appears in ibid., 70–71: "Since only the divine nature of itself is perfect and immutable, nothing is added to or subtracted from it by this union. But because the human nature of itself and of its own natural constitution is not sufficient and suitable for all the functions of the kingship, the priesthood, and the lordship of Christ, for which it was assumed, it received from the union with the Logos incomprehensible and ineffable gifts and ornaments both created and finite which formally inhere in it. And because the whole fullness of the deity of the Son of God dwelt personally in the assumed nature, this fullness shines forth in it completely, so that the flesh is kindled by this light, as it were, and even shines and is so enriched by divine powers and workings through the dispensation of the union but not through physical effusion or an essential inherence that the Logos in keeping with His kindness exercises and accomplishes the works of His omnipotence in, with, and through the assumed nature, just as the soul communicates to the body and as fire to heated iron their powers and activities."

Chemnitz assumes, in other words, that the person of Christ suffers even as the divine nature remains impassible. This distinction is taken up and deployed in article 8 of the *Solid Declaration*, which states: "Because of this personal union, without which this kind of true communion of the natures is unthinkable and impossible, not only the bare human nature (which possesses the characteristics of suffering and dying) suffered for the sins of the entire world, but the Son of God himself suffered (according to the human nature) and, according to our simple Christian creed, truly died—although the divine nature can neither suffer nor die."[21] One searches these texts in vain for any recognition of a departure or correction of Luther's christological views. In many cases, the impassibilist restriction is based upon Luther's writings themselves.[22]

Of course, neither the *Solid Declaration* nor Chemnitz's treatise are representative of the diversity of opinion, which circulated within Lutheranism especially during the latter half of the sixteenth century.[23] Future study would need to attend to this diversity and specify whatever subtle differences of opinion distinguish the various authors of the period.[24] Even if some theologians were found to

21. *The Solid Declaration*, in Robert Kolb, Timothy J. Wengert, and Charles P. Arand, eds., *The Book of Concord: The Confessions of the Evangelical Lutheran Church* (Minneapolis: Fortress Press, 2000), 619.
22. See ibid., 619f. It is ironic that the so-called scale passage from Luther's 1539 treatise "On the Councils and the Church" is so often recruited as evidence of passibilist divergence. The very same section of text appears in the *Solid Declaration*, where the doctrine of divine impassibility is presupposed; see ibid., 624. For Chemnitz's direct treatment of Luther in relation to these questions, see *Two Natures in Christ*, 190–94. Also helpful is Bengt Hägglund, "Majestas hominis Christi: Wie hat Martin Chemnitz die Christologie Luthers gedeutet?" *Luther Jahrbuch* 47 (1980): 71–88. Hägglund brackets, however, the question of whether Chemnitz faithfully represents Luther's points of view.
23. Another important study in these sources is Joar Haga, *Was There a Lutheran Metaphysics? The Interpretation of Communicatio Idiomatum in Early Modern Lutheranism* (Göttingen: Vandenhoeck & Ruprecht, 2012).
24. Johannes Hund admits, for instance, that the Braunschweig branch of Lutheranism (to which Chemnitz belongs) agrees with the Melanchthonians in Wittenberg concerning how to conceive of the hypostatic union, even though the former group also insists upon real eucharistic presence. In doing so, however, Hund believes that theologians like Chemnitz

embrace divine passibility, however, the confessional norms of late sixteenth-century Lutheranism appear unambiguously to reject such a view.[25] This fact, accompanied by the refutation of the divergence thesis, provides sufficient reason to reassess appraisals of Luther's heirs, which construe confessionalization either in the terms of a passibilist extension or impassibilist betrayal of Luther's legacy.

Rezeptionsgeschichte

If the divergence thesis originates neither in Luther, nor in the writings of his confessional heirs (a point that would, of course, first need to be proved), where does it first originate and why? Why is it that Luther's Christology has come so widely to be associated with contemporary theological trajectories that emphasize the passibility of deity, despite the lack of evidence within Luther's corpus to support this association? In order to address these questions, future study will need to examine the "reception history" of Luther's Christology, specifically as it pertains to developing perceptions of the reformer's interpretation of Christ's suffering. Such an investigation would help to illuminate which contextual factors are operative in the development of the divergence thesis in the first place.

A promising place to begin such a survey would be the religious writings of G. W. F. Hegel, whose unique appropriation of Luther's

depart from Luther's conceptualization of the person of Christ, which he thinks is better expressed by the theologians from Württemberg, including Brenz. The point here is not to suggest that writers like Hund are entirely wrong in their interpretive judgments. His magisterial work provides a tremendously helpful point of entry into the pertinent debates. I am merely raising the question whether certain of Hund's claims ought to be reassessed, since he presupposes the validity of the divergence thesis as the point of departure for Lutheran confessional debates. See his interpretation of Luther in Hund, *Das Wort ward Fleisch*, 45–65.

25. That is, if there are Lutheran divine passibilists, they seem to have constituted a minority of opinion.

"death of God" language has been widely influential within contemporary theology. An identification of the first interpreter to defend the claim that, for Luther, Christ suffers in his divinity would enable a clearer understanding of the divergence thesis, by locating its genesis within a particular setting. A thorough reception history could also help to explain why a "passibilist Luther" has proven to be so appealing for such a wide range of twentieth-century theologians.

Ecumenical Significance

Luther's Christology has often been identified as an interconfessional line of sharp demarcation. It represents the decisive point at which irreconcilable tensions threaten to preclude the development of any meaningful rapprochement between Lutheranism and its various ecumenical conversation partners. The purported source of the insoluble disparity is variably defined. Risto Saarinen, for instance, calls attention to a prominent rendering of this fissure that percolates with some regularity within modern Luther scholarship. This view insists that Luther's theology (expressed in his doctrine of Christ) inhabits and relies upon an alternative set of philosophical first principles, and these principles cannot be made to interact intelligibly with the traditionally presupposed categories of "substance-thought" embraced by other traditions.[26] In another vein, Althina Lexutt suggests that the difference resides in Luther's intense coordination of Christology with soteriology—an observation on whose basis she regards recent ecumenical progress on the doctrine of justification as ultimately hollow.[27]

26. Risto Saarinen, *Gottes Wirken auf uns: die transzendentale Deutung des Gegenwart-Christi-Motivs in der Lutherforschung* (Stuttgart: Steiner Vlg Wiesbaden, 1989), 1–4.
27. Athina Lexutt, "Christologie als Soteriologie: ein Blick in die späten Disputationen Martin Luthers." in *Relationen* (Münster: LIT, 2000) 201–216. Lexutt could easily reinforce her proposal on the basis of the study by Florian Schneider, *Christus praedicatus et creditus: die*

Some recent literature has adapted the fundamental claim of interconfessional demarcation on the basis of the divergence thesis. Luther's christological adjustment helps further to explain the widely presupposed interconfessional *Grunddifferenz* ("fundamental point of difference"), which many perceive to exist in this area. Johannes Hund, for instance, erects a rather sharp barrier between Lutheran theologians who reject suppositional carrying as an adequate rendering of Christ's person, and the Reformed and Roman Catholic theologians (along with a handful of Melanchthon's students) who retain the late medieval view, along with the rest of its conceptual baggage.[28] The ecumenical result of this historical narrative is the identification of an interconfessional fork in the road, beyond which never the twain shall meet.

Theobald Beer's earlier study corroborates the basic trajectory of Hund's assessment, a fact from which Beer draws a sobering ecumenical conclusion.[29] Despite the optimism circulating at the time when Beer's book was first published, Beer raises the question whether the "progress" responsible for this optimism is entirely superficial. If Luther presupposes a conceptualization of Christ that deviates from established dogmatic norms, then such "progress" only conceals underlying incongruities that impair and actually emasculate the artificially drafted points of apparent interconfessional agreement.[30] Beer's solution, of course, is to criticize severely Luther's

reformatorische Christologie Luthers in den "Operationes in Psalmos" (1519–1521), dargestellt mit beständigem Bezug zu seiner Frühzeitchristologie (Neukirchen-Vluyn: Neukirchener, 2004), which argues that Luther develops a distinctly "reformational" Christology—that is, tailor-made to correspond with his entirely "new" soteriology.

28. The source of the bifurcation, for Hund, is a fundamental difference of christological opinion between Melanchthon and Luther, which later Lutheran writers were forced to reconcile. See his description of these two poles in Hund, *Das Wort ward Fleisch*, 45–96.

29. We have already noted the bifurcation that Beer identifies between Luther and Melanchthon regarding the conceptualization of the hypostatic union. See Beer, *Der fröhliche Wechsel*, 513–20.

30. Ibid., 13–15.

rejection of medieval Christology. Luther's modern apologists respond in kind. They insist, in effect, that Luther's adjustment was necessary in order to overcome the detached speculations of Scholastic reflection. Although the resultant crossfire has not yet spilled over into the official documents of ecumenical dialogue, much of the scholarship surveyed in this study gives legitimate reason to wonder whether even marginal agreement on questions of Christology between Lutherans on the one hand, and Roman Catholics and Reformed on the other, is even possible.[31]

The refutation of the divergence thesis does not warrant the reduction of all interconfessional christological differences to indistinguishable shades of ecumenical gray. It does, however, lend an important reminder of an underlying dogmatic commonality, which some recent scholarship has been wont to overlook. It manifests the fact that Lutheranism, Roman Catholicism, and each of the Reformed churches conceive of the hypostatic union in remarkably similar ways, despite whatever neuralgic points of difference may linger beyond the broader, foundational consensus.[32] The elevation of lingering difference to the threshold of architectonic demarcation is neither historically accurate nor ecumenically useful. Further examination of Luther's relation to late medieval Scholasticism may reveal that much of the discourse promulgated on

31. Of course, one could plausibly ask whether Beer's work is influential enough to warrant any real concern. In addition to what has already been said to address this objection, it should also be noted that the Swiss Roman Catholic theologian Hans Urs von Balthasar, whose writings are justifiably the object of extensive study within contemporary theology, relies almost *entirely* upon Beer's characterization of Luther's theology. To be sure, this fact possesses little significance for Luther scholarship per se, but portends much for the popular perception of Luther's theology among systematic theologians today. For Balthasar's use of Beer, see Hans Urs von Balthasar, *The Action*, trans. Graham Harrison (San Francisco: Ignatius, 1994), 284. For a creative engagement between Luther and Balthasar, see Steffen Lösel, *Kreuzwege: ein ökumenisches Gespräch mit Hans Urs von Balthasar* (Paderborn: Schöningh, 2001).

32. There are important differences, for instance, regarding whether the humanity of Christ participates in divine predicates via the *communicatio idiomatum*.

all sides of the confessional divide has been nothing more than an assault upon polemical windmills.[33]

Theological Significance

This study has focused upon the theological significance of Luther's impassibilist soteriology, especially for ongoing conceptualizations of divine immanence. This constructive trajectory focus was adopted because the formulation of an adequate rendering of God's immanence represents a central preoccupation of contemporary theology, and a major reason for its widespread rejection of divine impassibility. Besides the desideratum of dogmatic transparency, however, the rejection of this doctrine has also been impelled, perhaps even more conspicuously, by the pervasive belief that only a God who suffers can offer human beings any real consolation. Dennis Ngien summarizes the salient point with lapidary concision: "Of what help to wounded people is a God who knows nothing of pain himself? 'Only the suffering God can help,' Dietrich Bonhoeffer wrote from his death cell. God helps not through supernatural miracles, but through his own wounds—his suffering with victims and sufferers."[34] Later in the same essay, Ngien elaborates upon the main point: "If it were not the very God himself who became sin and suffered for us, what hope of life is left? What God cannot participate in, he cannot redeem. If God has not entered into our suffering and death, then there is no hope for redemption of our pain."[35]

33. That is, it may be the case that Protestant dismissals of the late medieval tradition as quasi-docetic, and Roman Catholic denigrations of Luther as a christological deviant both aim at illusory targets. Like Don Quixote and Sancho Panza, they trot out to war against attacking giants, which turn out to be the hallucinations of historical misinterpretation.
34. Dennis Ngien, "The God Who Suffers: If God Does Not Grieve, Then Can He Love at All? An Argument for God's Emotions," *Christianity Today* 41 (1997): 40.
35. Ibid., 41.

The rhetorical force of Ngien's appeal is drawn from the nerve center of everyday Christian piety. What hope do the sufferings of Christ lend the believer when confronted by existential distress and difficulty? For many, the fact that God suffers offers an assurance and consolation that easily surpasses the well-worn paths of traditional theodicy. The doctrine of divine passibility is necessary, this perception urges, lest Christianity be forced to fall silent in the face of a resurgent atheism, impelled by an intense recognition of human history's undeniable atrocities.[36] What does the refutation of the divergence thesis mean, then, for Luther's pastoral consolation? If God cannot suffer, what hope can the doctrine of Christ really provide? More pointedly, What comfort is the recognition of Christ's suffering to the believing Christian when she is overcome by the shadow of death?[37]

The divergence thesis is surely right to suppose that Luther cares about these questions. The reformer's sermons often draw direct connections from reflection upon Christ to the consolation of Christian despair. In a sermon preached in the year 1537, Luther provides an instance of this orientation.

> Thus the most precious treasure and the strongest consolation we Christians have is this: that the Word, the true and natural Son of God, became man, with flesh and blood like that of any other human; that He became incarnate for our sakes in order that we might enter into great glory, that our flesh and blood, skin and hair, hands and feet, stomach and back might reside in heaven as God does, and in order that we might boldly defy the devil and whatever else assails us.[38]

36. The depth of this indignance has its roots especially in the immediate awareness of twentieth-century events of mass violence.
37. The future study of this question could also make a contribution to the examination of Luther's cross piety in comparison with late medieval antecedents. For some literature on this topic, see, for instance, Martin Elze, "Das Verständnis der Passion Jesu im ausgehenden Mittelalter und bei Luther," in *Geist und Geschichte der Reformation* (Berlin: de Gruyter, 1966), 127–51; and Robert Guy Erwin, *The Passion and Death of Christ in the Piety and Theology of the Later Middle Ages and Martin Luther*, unpub. PhD diss. (New Haven: Yale University, 1999).

The refutation of the divergence thesis raises the following question for future research: What comfort does Luther believe that the sufferings of Christ furnish the Christian, if it is true that he explicitly rules out the existentially resonant claim that God is sympathetically conditioned by human weakness? In the space that remains, we can provide only a sketch of how Luther's Christology addresses this question.

The determinative frame of reference for this matter consists again in the redemptive union that Luther envisions between Christ and the believing Christian. The hope and consolation of the believer rests in her belief that, just as Christ was raised up victorious over death on account of the deathless might of his divinity, she, too, will pass through the jaws of death and hell unharmed because she participates in the unconquerable Christ. Here one rightly detects the echo of an operative parallelism or analogy between Christ and the Christian that courses throughout Luther's theological writings. Like Christ, the Christian is susceptible to a decidedly "partitive" analysis. Though weak in the flesh and apparently powerless in the face of death and the devil, the believer is actually mightier than death on account of Christ. This "parallelism" is at work in a sermon on John 3 from the late 1530s: "In Acts 2:24 St. Peter says that death was not able to hold Christ, since deity and humanity were united in one person. In the same way we, too, shall not remain in death; we shall destroy death, but only if we remain steadfast in faith and cling to death's Destroyer."[39]

38. LW 22:110. WA 46:631: "So ist nu der edelste schatz und hoehester Trost, den wir Christen haben, das das Wort, der ware, natuerliche Son Gottes, ist Mensch worden, der allerding fleisch und blut hat wie ein ander Mensch und umb unsern willen mensch worden, das wir zu der grossen herrligkeit komen, damit unser fleisch und blut, haut und har, hende und fuesse, bauch und ruecken oben im Himel Gott gleich sitzen."

39. LW 22:356.

Commenting on the same chapter of John, Luther later observes, "In this way you also become heavenly and will ascend to heaven, and the devil with all hell will not be able to restrain you. We will ascend from the midst of sin and death, and from the jaws of the devil; for a Christian has become a heavenly man."[40] The consolation that Luther extends to the Christian in these texts is not that God experiences human vulnerability as a conditioning impingement upon God's very being. It is, rather, that Christ truly became man, and by doing so overcame death from the inside out. The Christian may hope, in other words, because even though she, too, descends in her abject frailty into the abyss, she is united with the One who will bear her up in eschatological victory.

An especially rich exposition of this theme appears in Luther's treatment of John 6:56, which belongs to a series of sermons composed beginning in the year 1530. In this text, Luther considers what it really means to "abide" in Christ, and addresses how the Christian may rightly meditate upon and receive consolation from Christ even in the midst of present struggles. Not all forms of reflective piety are adequate to the task. Luther comments:

> Now there are those who hold with us and declare that Christ abides in them. But when trials confront them and they are faced with loss of life, honor, or goods, and particularly with death, when it is a question of sacrificing their life, then Christ is not found dwelling in them. Then mere thoughts are inadequate, for these are nothing but your work, power, natural reason, and a feeble creature. But if the terrors of a bad conscience are to be subdued, if the devil is to be frightened away and repelled, if death is to be overcome, then a divine force and not a mere thought is required. Something else must reside in you, so that your enemies will have to cope with a power which will prove too strong for them, a power which they fear, from which they flee, and which will permit you to carry off the victory.[41]

40. LW 22:460–61.
41. LW 23:145. WA 33:226: "Also seindt ihr auch wohl, die es mit uns halten, die do furgeben, das

The necessary power of which Luther speaks exhibits itself, for him, in the lives of Christian martyrs who do not waver in their faith, even in the face of intense suffering and death. He continues:

> Something must be found in you which will prove too strong for [Satan]. This was apparent in the martyrs. How bold they were, what spirit and courage they displayed when they confronted the judges, fully aware that life and limb, honor and goods were at stake! Such conduct calls for consolation, not for a mere thought. It must be a matter of the heart that a person can face death and every trial cheerfully and say: "Honor, goods, life and limb, and all that is earthly, begone! I am determined to remain here, right here!" Then it will become manifest whether or not a person is a Christian and remains constant by means of his thoughts.[42]

What is it, then, that furnishes such consolation and imbibes such confidence for Luther? It is not the knowledge that Christ's deity shares in human weakness, but that by faith in the Word made flesh, human beings who are weak participate in his divine strength: "Now this is a precious dwelling place and something to glory in, that through faith in Christ and through our eating we poor sinners have Him abiding in us with His might, power, strength, righteousness, and wisdom."[43] Luther later summarizes:

Christus in ihnen sei undt sie in Christo, aber wen es kompt zur Anfechtung, das sie schaden sollen leiden am leibe, ehre oder gutt undt sonderlich, wen man sterben sol oder verbrennet werden, do ist Christus nicht doheim, da werden es die gedancken nicht thun. Dan was seindt deine gedancken anders dan deine werck, krafft undt naturliche vernunfft undt eine Creatur? solle aber ein schrecken des gewissens untergedruckt werden, der teuffel verjagt, der todt uberwunden werden, da wirdt eine göttliche gewalt zugehören undt nicht ein gedancken, es mus ein anders in dir sein, das ehr finde eine krafft in dir, die ihm zu starck sei, darfur ehr sich scheue, fliege undt du ihm obsiegest."

42. LW 23:145. WA 33:226: "ehr mus etwas in dir finden, das ihm zu starck sei. Solches sihet man an den lieben Merterern, wie kecke sie gewesen sindt, undt einen muth undt hertz darzu gehabt, wen sie fur den Richtern gestanden sindt undt gesehen, das es ihnen geltte leib undt leben, Ehre undt gutt. Da gehörtt ein muth zu undt nicht ein gedancken, es mus im hertzen stecken, das einer das hertz frölich mache wider den todt undt alle anfechtung undt sagen könne: fahre hin, Ehre undt gutt, leib undt leben undt alles, was auff erden ist, hie wil ich bleiben. Do sindet sichs dan wohl, ob einer mit gedancken ein Christ wirdt undt bestendig bleibet oder nicht."

> Christ is serious when He says that you will abide in Him and He in you if you believe in Him. He says: "It matters not if you are still somewhat weak, for I am in you. If you lack anything, I have an abundance of righteousness, holiness, and wisdom; I have no weaknesses. But if you are weak, your weakness is in Me, and I will see to it that I help you, that I drown your weakness in My strength and power, that I delete your sin in My righteousness, that I devour your death in My life." This is the true meaning and significance, the sum and substance, of this text, that He abides in him who believes in Him.[44]

The point emphasized in this final section must not be misunderstood. It does not mean to suggest that the history of Christ is no longer genuinely "parabolic," as if Christ does not experience frailty in his humanity. The incarnate Son truly enters into the condition of suffering human beings. This "condescension motif" of Luther's soteriology is not altogether devoid of consolatory significance. The consolation it provides, however, is not that the divinity of Christ tastes human vulnerability, and thus joins us in our helplessness. It is, rather, that, by participation in Christ through faith, the believer shares in the deathless might that is manifest in the Son's glorious resurrection.[45] A closer examination of these matters

43. LW 23:146. WA 33:228: "So ist nun das eine kostliche wonung undt ruhm, das wir arme Sunder durch den glauben an Christum ihnen haben in uns mit seiner macht, krafft, stercke und gerechtigckeit undt weisheit."
44. LW 23:147–48. WA 33:230: "Darumb so ists dem herrn Christo ein ernst, das ehr saget, wen du an ihnen gleubest, so soltu bei ihm bleiben, ob du schon noch etwas gebrechlich bist, das schadet nicht, den ich bin in dir, undt mangelt dir etwas, so habe ich gerechtigckeit, heiligckeit undt weisheit die fulle. Jch habe keine gebrechen, hastu aber schwacheit, so ist sie in mir undt ich wil sehen, das ich ihr rathe undt deine schwacheit in meiner krafft undt stercke erseuffe undt deine Sunde in meiner gerechtigckeit untergehe undt dein todt in meinem leben verschlungen werde. Diess ist die rechte meinung undt verstandt dieses Textes, das, wer an ihn gleubet, bei dem ist ehr."
45. Another text, which develops similar themes is Luther's commentary on the book of Hebrews, composed in 1517–1518. So, for instance, Luther states: "Sicut enim Christus per unionem immortalis divinitatis moriendo mortem superavit, ita Christianus per unionem immortalis Christi (que fit per fidem in illum) eciam moriendo mortem superat ac sic Deus diabolum per ipsummet diabolum destruit et alieno opere suum perficit" (WA 57:129). Also significant are many of Luther's Easter sermons, preached over the course of his career. For a helpful overview of these sermons, see Uwe Rieske-Braun, *Duellum mirabile: Studien zum Kampfmotiv in Martin Luthers Theologie*, Forschungen zur Kirchen- und Dogmengeschichte, Bd. 73 (Göttingen:

would be significant for tracing the history of Christian piety during the Reformation era. More important for the purposes of the present study, their further exposition would continue to fill out the constructive potential of a nondivergence specification of Luther's Christology.

Vandenhoeck & Ruprecht, 1999), 201–226. See especially the material that Rieske-Braun treats on 204–205.

Bibliography

Adams, Marilyn McCord. "What's Metaphysically Special about Supposits? Some Medieval Variations on Aristotelian Substance." *Aristotelian Society Supplementary Volume* 79 (2005): 15–52.

_________. *Christ and Horrors: The Coherence of Christology*. Current Issues in Theology. Cambridge: Cambridge University Press, 2006.

_________. "Relations, Inherence, and Subsistence; or, Was Ockham a Nestorian in Christology?" *Nous* 16 (1982): 62–75.

_________. "The Metaphysics of the Incarnation in some Fourteenth-Century Franciscans." In *Essays Honoring Allan B. Wolter*, eds. Kenny Kretzmann and Pinborg, 21–57. St. Bonaventure, NY: Franciscan Institute, 1985.

_________. *What Sort of Human Nature? Medieval Philosophy and the Systematics of Christology*. The Aquinas lecture, 1999. Milwaukee: Marquette University Press, 1999.

_________. *William Ockham*. Notre Dame, IN: University of Notre Dame Press, 1987.

Allgaier, Walter. *Der "froehliche Wechsel" bei Martin Luther; eine Untersuchung zu Christologie und Soteriologie bei Luther unter besonderer Beruecksichtigung der Schriften bis 1521*. Unpublished dissertation. Erlangen-Nürnberg, 1966.

Althaus, Paul. *The Theology of Martin Luther*, trans. Robert C. Schultz. Philadelphia: Fortress Press, 1966.

Angelelli, Ignacio. "The Techniques of Disputation in the History of Logic." *The Journal of Philosophy* 67 (1970): 800–815.

Asendorf, Ulrich. *Gekreuzigt und Auferstanden; Luthers Herausforderung an die moderne Christologie*. Hamburg: Lutherisches Verlagshaus, 1971.

_________. *Luther und Hegel: Untersuchungen zur Grundlegung einer neuen systematischen Theologie*. Wiesbaden: Steiner, 1982.

_________. *Die Theologie Martin Luthers nach seinen Predigten*. Göttingen: Vandenhoeck & Ruprecht, 1988.

Assel, Heinrich. *Der andere Aufbruch: die Lutherrenaissance-Ursprünge, Aporien und Wege: Karl Holl, Emanuel Hirsch, Rudolf Hermann (1910–1935)*. Göttingen: Vandenhoeck & Ruprecht, 1994.

Ayres, Lewis. *Nicaea and Its Legacy: An Approach to Fourth-Century Trinitarian Theology*. New York: Oxford University Press, 2004.

Bäck, Allan. "Aquinas on the Incarnation," *New Scholasticism* 56 (1982): 127–45.

_________. *Aristotle's Theory of Predication*. Leiden: Brill, 2000.

_________. *On Reduplication: Logical Theories of Qualification*. Leiden: Brill, 1996.

_________. "Scotus on the Consistency of the Incarnation and the Trinity." *Vivarium* 36 (1998): 83–107.

Barth, Hans-Martin. *Der Teufel und Jesus Christus in der Theologie Martin Luthers*. Forschungen zur Kirchen- und Dogmengeschichte, Bd. 19. Göttingen: Vandenhoeck & Ruprecht, 1967.

Baur, Jörg. *Luther und seine klassischen Erben: theologische Aufsätze und Forschungen*. Tübingen: J. C. B. Mohr, 1993.

_________ . "Lutherische Christologie im Streit um die neue Bestimmung von Gott und Mensch." *Evangelische Theologie* 41, no. 5 (September 1, 1981): 423–39.

Bayer, Oswald. "Das Sein Jesu Christi im Glauben." *Lutheran Quarterly* 10 (1996): 135–50.

_________ ."Das Wort ward Fleisch: Luthers Christologie als Lehre von der Idiomenkommunikation." In *Creator est Creatura*, 5–34. Berlin: Walter de Gruyter, 2007.

_________. *Martin Luther's Theology: A Contemporary Interpretation*. Grand Rapids: Eerdmans, 2008.

_________, and Benjamin Gleede. *Creator est creatura: Luthers Christologie als Lehre von der Idiomenkommunikation*. Berlin: Walter de Gruyter, 2007.

Beer, Theobald. *Der fröhliche Wechsel und Streit: Grundzüge der Theologie Luthers*. Leipzig: St. Benno-Verlag, 1974.

Behr, John. *The Nicene Faith*. The Formation of Christian Theology, v. 2. Crestwood, NY: St. Vladimir's Seminary Press, 2004.

Bell, Theo. *Divus Bernhardus: Bernhard von Clairvaux in Martin Luthers Schriften*. Veröffentlichungen des Instituts für Europäische Geschichte Mainz, Bd. 148. Abteilung Religionsgeschichte. Mainz: P. von Zabern, 1993.

Bielfeldt, Dennis D., Mickey Leland Mattox, and Paul R. Hinlicky. *The Substance of the Faith: Luther's Doctrinal Theology for Today*. Minneapolis: Fortress Press, 2008.

Blaumeiser, Hubertus. *Martin Luthers Kreuzestheologie: Schlüssel zu seiner Deutung von Mensch und Wirklichkeit: eine Untersuchung anhand der Operationes in Psalmos, 1519–1521*. Paderborn: Bonifatius, 1995.

Borchert, E., *Der Einfluss des Nominalismus auf die Christologie der Spätscholastik nach dem Traktat "de communicatione idiomatum" des Nicolaus Oresme*, in: *Beiträge zur Geschichte der Philosophie des Mittelalters* 35, 4/5, Münster i. W. 1940.

Braaten, Carl E., and Robert W. Jenson. *Union with Christ: The New Finnish Interpretation of Luther*. Grand Rapids: Eerdmans, 1998.

Brandy, Hans Christian. *Die späte Christologie des Johannes Brenz*. Beiträge zur historischen Theologie 80. Tübingen: J. C. B. Mohr (Paul Siebeck), 1991.

Brecht, Martin. *Martin Luther*. Tr. James L. Schaef. 3 Volumes. Philadelphia: Fortress Press, 1985-1993.

Burba, Klaus. *Die Christologie in Luthers Liedern*. Gütersloh: C. Bertelsmann Verlag, 1956.

Cameron, Euan. *The European Reformation*. Oxford: Clarendon, 1991.

Castelo, Daniel. *The Apathetic God: Exploring the Contemporary Relevance of Divine Impassibility*. Milton Keynes, UK: Paternoster, 2009.

Chemnitz, Martin. *The Two Natures in Christ*, trans. J. A. O. Preus. St. Louis: Concordia, 1971.

Coates, Thomas. "Luther's Picture of Christ on the Basis of the Church Postil Sermons." *Concordia Theological Monthly* 20 (1949): 241–67.

Creel, Richard E. *Divine Impassibility: An Essay in Philosophical Theology*. Cambridge: Cambridge University Press, 1986.

Cross, Richard. *The Metaphysics of the Incarnation: Thomas Aquinas to Duns Scotus*. New York: Oxford University Press, 2002.

_________. "Perichoresis, Deification and Christological Predication in John of Damascus." *Mediaeval Studies* 62 (2000): 361–84.

Cyril of Alexandria. *On the Unity of Christ*, ed. John Anthony McGuckin. Crestwood, NY: St. Vladimir's Seminary Press, 2000.

Dalferth, Ingolf U. *Der auferweckte Gekreuzigte: zur Grammatik der Christologie*. Tübingen: J. C. B. Mohr, 1994.

Dillenberger, John. *Protestant Thought and Natural Science: A Historical Interpretation*. London: Collins, 1961.

Dingel, Irene. *Concordia controversa: die öffentlichen Diskussionen um das lutherische Konkordienwerk am Ende des 16. Jahrhunderts*. Quellen und Forschungen zur Reformationsgeschichte, Bd. 63. Gütersloh: Gütersloher Verlagshaus, 1996.

Dorner, I. A. *History of the Development of the Doctrine of the Person of Christ.* Edinburgh: Clark, 1891.

Dunn, Geoffrey D. "Divine Impassibility and Christology in the Christmas Homilies of Leo the Great." *Theological Studies* 62 (2001): 71–85.

Ebeling, Gerhard. *Luther: An Introduction to His Thought.* Philadelphia: Fortress Press, 1970.

Edwards, Mark U. *Luther's Last Battles: Politics and Polemics, 1531–46.* Ithaca: Cornell University Press, 1983.

Elze, Martin. "Das Verständnis der Passion Jesu im ausgehenden Mittelalter und bei Luther." In *Geist und Geschichte der Reformation*, 127–51. Berlin: Walter de Gruyter, 1966.

Faulkner, John Alfred. "Luther and the Divinity of Christ." *Methodist Review* 95 (May 1, 1913): 373–88.

Fiddes, Paul S. *The Creative Suffering of God.* Oxford: Clarendon, 1988.

Gavrilyuk, Paul L. *The Suffering of the Impassible God: The Dialectics of Patristic Thought.* Oxford Early Christian Studies. New York: Oxford University Press, 2004.

Gawrisch, Wilbert R. "On Christology, Brenz and the Question of Ubiquity." In *No Other Gospel*, 229–53. Milwaukee: Northwestern Publishing House, 1980.

Gennrich, Paul Wilhelm. *Die christologie Luthers im Abendmahlsstreit, 1524–1529.* Königsberg i. Pr: Buch- und Steindruckerei von O. Kümmel, 1929.

Gorman, Michael. "Christ as Composite according to Aquinas" *Traditio* 55 (2000): 143–57.

Grane, Leif. *Modus loquendi theologicus: Luthers Kampf um die Erneuerung der Theologie (1515–1518).* Leiden: Brill, 1975.

Grass, Hans, and Werner Georg Kümmel. *Jesus Christus: das Christusverständnis im Wandel der Zeiten, eine Ringvorlesung.* Marburger theologische Studien, 1. Marburg: N. G. Elwert, 1963.

Haanes, Vidar L. "Christological Themes in Luther's Theology." *Studia Theologica* 61 (2007): 21–46.

Hägglund, Bengt. "Majestas hominis Christi: Wie hat Martin Chemnitz die Christologie Luthers gedeutet?" *Luther Jahrbuch* 47 (1980): 71–88.

_________. *Theologie und Philosophie bei Luther und in der Occamistischen Tradition; Luthers Stellung zur Theorie von der doppelten Wahrheit.* Lund: C. W. K. Gleerup, 1955.

Harnack, Adolf von. *History of Dogma.* New York: Dover, 1961.

Harnack, Theodore. *Luthers Theologie mit besonderer Beziehung auf seine Versöhnungs- und Erlösungslehre.* Amsterdam: Editions Rodopi, 1969.

Hauber, Reinhard. "Christologie und metaphysischer Gottesbegriff bei Werner Elert." *Kerygma Und Dogma* 35 (1989): 128–63.

Hart, David Bentley. *The Beauty of the Infinite: The Aesthetics of Christian Truth.* Grand Rapids: Eerdmans, 2003.

_________. "No Shadow of Turning: On Divine Impassibility." *Pro Ecclesia* 11, no. 2 (March 1, 2002): 184–206.

Hayes, Zachary. *The Hidden Center: Spirituality and Speculative Christology in St. Bonaventure.* New York: Paulist, 1981.

Helmer, Christine. "Luther's Theology of Glory." *Neue Zeitschrift für systematische Theologie und Religionsphilosophie* 42 (2000): 237–45.

_________. *The Trinity and Martin Luther: A Study on the Relationship between Genre, Language and the Trinity in Luther's Works, 1523–1546.* Mainz: P. von Zabern, 1999.

Heron, Alasdair I. C. "*Communicatio Idiomatum* and *Deificatio* of Human Nature: A Reformed Perspective." *Greek Orthodox Theological Review* 43 (1998): 367–76.

Hillerbrand, Hans Joachim. *The Division of Christendom: Christianity in the Sixteenth Century.* Louisville: Westminster John Knox, 2007.

Hinlicky, Paul R. "Luther's Anti-Docetism in the Disputatio de divinitate et humanitate Christi (1540)." In *Creator est Creatura: Luthers Christologie als Lehre von der Idiomenkommunikation*. Theologische Bibliothek Töpelmann, 138. Ed. O. Bayer and W. Härle, 139–85. New York: Walter de Gruyter, 2007.

_________. *Luther and the Beloved Community: A Path for Christian Theology after Christendom*. Grand Rapids: Eerdmans, 2010.

Hofmann, Frank. *Albrecht Ritschls Lutherrezeption*. Gütersloh: Gütersloher Verlagshaus, 1998.

Holl, Karl. *Gesammelte Aufsätze zur Kirchengeschichte*. Tübingen: J. C. B. Mohr (Paul Siebeck), 1928.

_________. *What Did Luther Understand by Religion?* Philadelphia: Fortress Press, 1977.

Hünermann, Peter. "Geschichte der Christologie: Geschichte Jesu Christi mit den Menschen?" *Theologische Quartalschrift* 164 (1984): 102–120.

Hund, Johannes. *Das Wort ward Fleisch: eine systematisch-theologische Untersuchung zur Debatte um die Wittenberger Christologie und Abendmahlslehre in den Jahren 1567 und 1574*. Forschungen zur systematischen und ökumenischen Theologie, Bd. 114. Göttingen: Vandenhoeck & Ruprecht, 2006.

Iserloh, Erwin. "Der fröhliche Wechsel und Streit: zu Theobald Beers Werk über Grundzüge der Theologie Martin Luthers." *Catholica* 36 (1982): 101–114.

_________. "Luther's Christ-Mysticism." In *Catholic Scholars Dialogue with Luther*, 37–58. Chicago: Loyola University Press, 1970.

Iwand, Hans Joachim. *Rechtfertigungslehre und Christusglaube: eine Untersuchung zur Systematik der Rechfertigungslehre Luthers in ihren Anfängen*. München: Chr. Kaiser, 1961.

Janz, Denis. *Luther and Late Medieval Thomism: A Study in Theological Anthropology*. Waterloo: Wilfred Laurier University Press, 1983.

_________. *Luther on Thomas Aquinas: The Angelic Doctor in the Thought of the Reformer*. Stuttgart: Franz Steiner Verlag Wiesbaden, 1989.

Jenson, Robert W. "Christ in the Trinity: Communicatio Idiomatum." In *The Person of Christ*, ed. Stephen R. Holmes and Murray Rae,61–69. New York: T&T Clark, 2005.

_________. *Systematic Theology*. New York: Oxford University Press, 1997.

_________. *Unbaptized God: The Basic Flaw in Ecumenical Theology*. Minneapolis: Fortress Press, 1992.

Joest, Wilfried. *Ontologie der Person bei Luther*. Göttingen: Vandenhoeck & Ruprecht, 1967.

Jürgens, Heiko. "Christus non est spiritus: Luthers Aussagen über den Menschen Jesus von Nazareth." In *Lutheriana*, 271–79. Köln: Böhlau Verlag, 1984.

Jüngel, Eberhard. *The Freedom of a Christian: Luther's Significance for Contemporary Theology*, trans. Roy A. Harrisville. Minneapolis: Augsburg, 1988.

_________. *God As the Mystery of the World: On the Foundation of the Theology of the Crucified One in the Dispute between Theism and Atheism*. Grand Rapids: Eerdmans, 1983.

_________. *Unterwegs Zur Sache; Theologische Bemerkungen*. München: Chr. Kaiser, 1972.

_________. "Vom Tod des lebendigen Gottes: ein Plakat." *Zeitschrift Für Theologie Und Kirche* 65, no. 1 (January 1, 1968): 93–116.

Juntunen, Sammeli. "The Christological Background of Luther's Understanding of Justification," *Seminary Ridge Review* 5, no. 2 (2003): 6–36.

Keating, James, and Thomas Joseph White. *Divine Impassibility and the Mystery of Human Suffering*. Grand Rapids: Eerdmans, 2009.

Keller, Rudolf, and Michael Roth. *Mit dem Menschen verhandeln über den Sachgehalt des Evangeliums: die Bedeutung der Theologie Werner Elerts für die Gegenwart*. Erlangen: Martin-Luther-Verlag, 2004.

Kirjavainen, Heikki. *Faith, Will, and Grammar: Some Themes of Intentional Logic and Semantics in Medieval and Reformation Thought.* Publications of Luther-Agricola Society 15. Helsinki: Luther-Agricola Society, 1986.

Kišš, Igor. "Die Analogie zwischen Christus und dem Christen bei Luther." *Luther* 68 (1997): 82–89.

Kolb, Robert. "Altering the Agenda, Shifting the Strategy: The Grundfest of 1571 as Philippist Program for Lutheran Concord." *Sixteenth Century Journal* 30, no. 3 (September 1, 1999): 705–726.

_________. "Luther on the Theology of the Cross." *Lutheran Quarterly* 16 (2002): 443–66.

_________. *Martin Luther: Confessor of the Faith.* New York: Oxford University Press, 2009.

Lexutt, Athina. "Christologie als Soteriologie: ein Blick in die späten Disputationen Martin Luthers." In *Relationen*, 201–216. Münster: LIT, 2000.

Lienhard, Marc. *Luther: Witness to Jesus Christ: Stages and Themes of the Reformer's Christology*. Minneapolis: Augsburg, 1982.

Loewenich, Walther von. *Luther's Theology of the Cross.* Minneapolis: Augsburg, 1976.

Lohse, Bernard. *Luther's Theology: Its Historical and Systematic Development*, trans. Roy A. Harrisville. Minneapolis: Fortress Press, 1999.

Long, D. Stephen. *Speaking of God: Theology, Language, and Truth.* Grand Rapids: Eerdmans, 2009.

Lotz, David W. *Ritschl and Luther: A Fresh Perspective on Albrecht Ritschl's Theology in the Light of His Luther Study*. Nashville: Abingdon, 1974.

Mahlmann, Theodor. *Das neue Dogma der lutherischen Christologie; Problem und Geschichte seiner Begründung*. Gütersloh: Gütersloher, 1969.

Maier, Paul L. *Caspar Schwenckfeld on the Person and Work of Christ; A Study of Schwenckfeldian Theology at Its Core.* Assen: Van Gorcum, 1959.

Mannermaa, Tuomo, and Kirsi Irmeli Stjerna. *Christ Present in Faith: Luther's View of Justification.* Minneapolis: Fortress Press, 2005.

McLaughlin, R. Emmet. *Caspar Schwenckfeld, Reluctant Radical: His Life to 1540.* Yale Historical Publications 134. New Haven: Yale University Press, 1986.

McGuckin, John Anthony. *St. Cyril of Alexandria: The Christological Controversy: Its History, Theology, and Texts.* Crestwood, NY: St. Vladimir's Seminary Press, 2004.

McKim, Donald K. *The Cambridge Companion to Martin Luther.* Cambridge Companions to Religion. Cambridge: Cambridge University Press, 2003.

Meijering, E. P. *Der "ganze" und der "wahre" Luther: Hintergrund und Bedeutung der Lutherinterpretation A. von Harnacks.* Amsterdam: Noord-Hollandsche Uitgevers Maatschappij, 1983.

_________. *Theologische Urteile über die Dogmengeschichte: Ritschls Einfluss auf von Harnack.* Leiden: Brill, 1978.

_________. *Die Hellenisierung des Christentums im Urteil Adolf von Harnacks.* Amsterdam: North-Holland, 1985.

Moltmann, Jürgen. *The Crucified God: The Cross of Christ as the Foundation and Criticism of Christian Theology*, trans. R. A. Wilson and John Bowden. Minneapolis: Fortress Press, 1993 (1974/German ed. 1973).

Mosheim, Johann Lorenz, and Johann Anselm Steiger. *Die Macht der Lehre Jesu über die Macht des Todes.* Doctrina et Pietas, Bd. 1. Stuttgart-Bad Cannstatt: Frommann-Holzboog, 1998.

Mühlen, Heribert. *Die Veränderlichkeit Gottes als Horizont einer zukünftigen Christologie.* Münster: Aschendorff, 1969.

Nagel, Norman E. "Heresy, Doctor Luther, Heresy: The Person and Work of Christ." In *Seven-headed Luther*, 25–49. New York: Oxford University Press, 1983.

Ngien, Dennis. "Reaping the Right Fruits: Luther's Meditation in the 'Earnest Mirror, Christ.'" *International Journal of Systematic Theology* 8, no. 4 (October 1, 2006): 382–410.

_________. "Chalcedonian Christology and Beyond: Luther's Understanding of the Communicatio Idiomatum." *Heythrop Journal* 45 (2004): 54–68.

_________. *The Suffering of God According to Martin Luther's 'Theologia Crucis'*. Vancouver: Regent College Publishing, 2005.

_________. "Ultimate Reality and Meaning in Luther's Theology of the Cross: No Other God, but the Incarnate Human God." *Andrews University Seminary Studies* 42 (2004): 383–405.

Nilsson, Kjell Ove. *Simul das Miteinander von Göttlichem und Menschlichem in Luthers Theologie*. Forschungen zur Kirchen- und Dogmengeschichte, Bd. 17. Göttingen: Vandenhoeck & Ruprecht, 1966.

Nüssel, Friederike. "Ich lebe, doch nun nicht ich, sondern Christus lebt in mir" (Gal 2,20a): dogmatische Überlegungen zur Rede vom 'Sein in Christus.'" *Zeitschrift für Theologie und Kirche* 99, no. 4 (December 1, 2002): 480–502.

Oberman, Heiko Augustinus. *Forerunners of the Reformation; The Shape of Late Medieval Thought*. New York: Holt, Rinehart and Winston, 1966.

_________. *Luther: Man between God and the Devil*. New Haven: Yale University Press, 1989.

_________. *Masters of the Reformation: The Emergence of a New Intellectual Climate in Europe*. Cambridge: Cambridge University Press, 1981.

_________. *The Dawn of the Reformation: Essays in Late Medieval and Early Reformation Thought*. Edinburgh: T&T Clark, 1986.

_________. *The Harvest of Medieval Theology: Gabriel Biel and Late Medieval Nominalism*. The Robert Troup Paine Prize-Treatise, 1962. Cambridge: Harvard University Press, 1963.

_________. *The Reformation: Roots and Ramifications.* Grand Rapids: Eerdmans, 1994.

_________, and Kenneth Hagen. *Augustine, The Harvest, and Theology (1300–1650): Essays Dedicated to Heiko Augustinus Oberman in Honor of His Sixtieth Birthday*. Leiden: Brill, 1990.

O'Keefe, John J. "Impassible Suffering? Divine Passion and Fifth-Century Christology." *Theological Studies* 58 (1997): 39–60.

O'Regan, Cyril. *The Heterodox Hegel.* Suny Series in Hegelian Studies. Albany: State University of New York Press, 1994.

Ozment, Steven E. *Homo Spiritualis: A Comparative Study of the Anthropology of Johannes Tauler, Jean Gerson and Martin Luther (1509–16) in the Context of Their Theological Thought.* Studies in Medieval and Reformation Thought 6. Leiden: Brill, 1969.

Pannenberg, Wolfhart. "Die Aufnahme des philosophischen Gottesbegriffs als dogmatisches Problem der frühchristlichen Theologie." *Zeitschrift Für Kirchengeschichte* 70, nos. 1–2 (January 1, 1959): 1–45.

_________. "Christologie und Theologie." *Kerygma Und Dogma* 21, no. 3 (July 1, 1975): 159–75.

Pelikan, Jaroslav, ed. *Interpreters of Luther: Essays in Honor of Wilhelm Pauck.* Philadelphia: Fortress Press, 1968.

Peters, Ted. *God—The World's Future: Systematic Theology for a Postmodern Era.* Minneapolis: Fortress Press, 1992.

Peura, Simo. "Die Teilhabe an Christus bei Luther." In *Luther und Theosis*, 121–61. Helsinki: Luther-Agricola-Gesellschaft, 1990.

Piepkorn, Arthur Carl, Philip J. Secker, and Robert Kolb. *The Sacred Scriptures and the Lutheran Confessions*. Mansfield, CT: CEC Press, 2007.

Posset, Franz. *Luther's Catholic Christology: According to His Johannine Lectures of 1527*. Milwaukee: Northwestern Publishing House, 1988.

_________. *Pater Bernhardus: Martin Luther and Bernard of Clairvaux.* Cistercian Studies Series168. Kalamazoo: Cistercian, 1999.

Price, Richard, and Mary Whitby. *Chalcedon in Context: Church Councils 400–700*. Liverpool: Liverpool University Press, 2009.

Principe, Walter H. *The Theology of the Hypostatic Union in the Early Thirteenth Century*. Toronto: Pontifical Institute of Mediaeval Studies, 1963.

Ratschow, Carl Heinz. "Christologie und Rechtfertigung: Luthers Christologie nach seinen Disputationen." In *Iustificatio impii*, 204–226. Helsinki: Suomalaisen Teologisen Kirjallisuusseura, 1977.

Rieske-Braun, Uwe. *Duellum mirabile: Studien zum Kampfmotiv in Martin Luthers Theologie*. Forschungen zur Kirchen- und Dogmengeschichte, Bd. 73. Göttingen: Vandenhoeck & Ruprecht, 1999.

Ringleben, Joachim. "Luther zur Metapher." *Zeitschrift für Theologie und Kirche* 94 (1997): 336–69.

Rolf, Sibylle. "'Christum und nichts anders': die Kommunikation von Gott und Mensch und die Predigt des Evangeliums." *Luther* 80, no. 3 (January 1, 2009): 150–69.

Rorem, Paul. "Martin Luther's Christocentric Critique of Pseudo-Dionysian Spirituality." *Lutheran Quarterly* 11 (1997): 291–307.

Saarinen, Risto. "In Sinu Patris: Die Barmherzige Trinität in Luthers Gebrauch Von Joh 1,8." *Neue Zeitschrift für Systematische Theologie und Religionsphilosopie* 46 (2004): 431–47.

__________. "Gottes Sein—Gottes Wirken: Die Grunddifferenz von Substanzdenken und Wirkungsdenken in der evangelischen Lutherdeutung." In *Luther und Theosis*, 103–19. Helsinki: Luther-Agricola-Gesellschaft, 1990.

__________. *Gottes Wirken auf uns: die transzendentale Deutung des Gegenwart-Christi-Motivs in der Lutherforschung*. Stuttgart: Steiner Vlg Wiesbaden, 1989.

Sauter, Gerhard, and Austra Reinis. "Luther on the Resurrection: The Proclamation of the Risen One as the Promise of Our Everlasting Life with God." *Lutheran Quarterly* 15 (2001): 195–216.

Schlink, Edmund. *Theology of the Lutheran Confessions.* Philadelphia: Fortress Press, 1975.

Schmidt, Axel. *Die Christologie in Martin Luthers späten Disputationen.* St. Ottilien: EOS Verlag, 1990.

Schneider, Florian. *Christus praedicatus et creditus: die reformatorische Christologie Luthers in den "Operationes in Psalmos" (1519–1521), dargestellt mit beständigem Bezug zu seiner Frühzeitchristologie.* Neukirchen-Vluyn: Neukirchener, 2004.

Schwager, Raymund. *Der wunderbare Tausch: zur Geschichte und Deutung der Erlösungslehre.* München: Kösel, 1986.

Schwarz, Reinhard. "Gott ist Mensch: zur Lehre von der Person Christi bei den Ockhamisten und bei Luther." *Zeitschrift für Theologie und Kirche* 63 (1966): 289–351.

Seebass, Gottfried. "Zum Hintergrund der christologischen Disputation Luthers von 1540/43." In *Creator est creatura*, 125–38. Berlin: Walter de Gruyter, 2007.

Seeberg, Erich. *Luthers Theologie 2, Christus-Wirklichkeit und Urbild.* Darmstadt: Wiss. Buchges, 1969.

Siggins, Ian D. Kingston. *Martin Luther's Doctrine of Christ.* Yale Publications in Religion 14. New Haven: Yale University Press, 1970.

Stayer, James M. *Martin Luther, German Saviour: German Evangelical Theological Factions and the Interpretation of Luther, 1917–1933.* Montreal: McGill-Queen's University Press, 2000.

Steiger, Johann Anselm. "Die communicatio idiomatum als Achse und Motor der Theologie Luthers: Der "fröhliche Wechsel" als hermeneutischer Schlüssel zu Abendmahlslehre, Anthropologie, Seelsorge, Naturtheologie,

Rhetorik und Humor." *Neue Zeitschrift für systematische Theologie und Religionsphilosophie* 38, no. 1 (January 1, 1996): 1–28.

_________. *Fünf Zentralthemen der Theologie Luthers und seiner Erben: Communicatio, Figura, Imago, Maria, Exempla*. Leiden: Brill, 2002.

Streiff, Stefan, and Martin Luther. *"Novis linguis loqui": Martin Luthers Disputation über Joh 1,14 "verbum caro factum est" aus dem Jahr 1539.* Göttingen: Vandenhoeck and Ruprecht, 1993.

Stump, Eleanore. "Aquinas' Metaphysics of the Incarnation." In *The Incarnation: An Interdisciplinary Symposium on the Incarnation of the Son of God*, ed. Stephen T. Davis, Daniel Kendall, SJ, and Gerald O'Collins, SJ, 197–218. New York: Oxford University Press, 2002.

Tolpingrud, Mitchell. "Luther's Disputation Concerning the Divinity and the Humanity of Christ." *Lutheran Quarterly* 10 (1996): 151–78.

Työrinoja, Reijo. "Nova vocabula et nova lingua: Luther's Conception of Doctrinal Formulas." In *Thesaurus Lutheri*, 221–36. Helsinki: Suomalainen Teologinen Kirjallisuusseura, 1987.

_________. "Propiertas Verbi: Luther's Conception of Philosophical and Theological Language in the Disputation: Verbum caro factum est (Joh. 1:14), 1539." In *Faith, Will, and Grammar: Some Themes of Intensional Logic and Semantics in Medieval and Reformation Thought*, 143–78. Schriften der Luther-Agricola-Society, no B 15. Helsinki: Vammalan Kirjapaino Oy, 1986.

Vanhoozer, Kevin J. *Remythologizing Theology: Divine Action, Passion, and Authorship*. Cambridge: Cambridge University Press, 2010.

Vercruysse, Jos E. "Luther's Theology of the Cross at the Time of the Heidelberg Disputation." *Gregorianum* 57 (1976): 523–48.

Vogelsang, Erich. *Die anfänge von Luthers Christologie; nach der ersten Psalmenvorlesung, insbesondere in ihren exegetischen und systematischen zusammenhängen mit Augustin und der scholastik dargestellt*. Arbeiten zur Kirchengeschichte 15. Berlin/Leipzig: Walter de Gruyter, 1929.

Vorländer, Dorothea. *Deus incarnatus: die Zweinaturenchristologie Luthers bis 1521*. Untersuchungen zur Kirchengeschichte, Bd. 9. Witten: Luther-Verlag, 1974.

Watson, J. Francis. "Martin Chemnitz and the Eastern Church: A Christology of the Catholic Consensus of the Fathers." *St. Vladimir's Theological Quarterly* 38 (1994): 73–86.

Weinandy, Thomas G. *Does God Suffer?* Notre Dame, IN: University of Notre Dame, 2000.

White, Graham. *Luther as Nominalist: A Study of the Logical Methods Used in Martin Luther's Disputations in the Light of Their Medieval Background*. Helsinki: Luther-Agricola Society, 1994.

Wolff, Jens. *Metapher und Kreuz: Studien zu Luthers Christusbild*. Tübingen: Mohr Siebeck, 2005.

Zur Mühlen, Karl-Heinz. *Nos extra nos: Luthers Theologie zwischen Mystik und Scholastik*. Beiträge zur historischen Theologie 46. Tübingen: Mohr, 1972.

Zwanepol, Klaas. "A Human God: Some Remarks on Luther's Christology." *Concordia Journal* 30 (2004): 40–53.

Index of Names

Index of Subjects